The World Has Forgotten Us

'A comprehensive, indispensable work.'

—*Sudwing*

'The discrimination, exclusion and persecution of the Yezidis did not just begin in 2014 with the so-called Islamic State. Thomas Schmidinger shows with great dedication the anatomy of a subtle genocide against the Yezidis in the last two hundred years.'

—Professor Jan Ilhan Kizilhan, Director of the Institute for Genocide and Peace Studies, Stuttgart

'An important book delving into the history and recent memory of the community, a vivid reminder of how the past and present of the Yezidis continue to be painfully intertwined.'

—Nelida Fuccaro, Professor of Modern Middle Eastern History at the New York University Abu Dhabi

'Thomas Schmidinger is one of the best experts on the region. This book is a must read.'

—Josef Weidenholzer, former MEP and Professor Emeritus, University of Linz

The World Has Forgotten Us

Sinjar and the Islamic State's Genocide of the Yezidis

Thomas Schmidinger

Translated by Michael Schiffmann

PLUTO PRESS

First published as 'Die Welt Hat Uns Vergessen': Der Genozid des 'Islamischen Staates' an den JesidInnen und die Folgen by Mandelbaum Verlag, Vienna, www.mandelbaum.at

English-language edition first published 2022 by Pluto Press
New Wing, Somerset House, Strand, London WC2R 1LA

www.plutobooks.com

British Library Cataloguing in Publication Data
A catalogue record for this book is available from the British Library

ISBN   978 0 7453 4606 9   Hardback
ISBN   978 0 7453 4605 2   Paperback
ISBN   978 0 7453 4607 6   EPUB
ISBN   978 0 7453 4609 0   PDF

This book is printed on paper suitable for recycling and made from fully managed and sustained forest sources. Logging, pulping and manufacturing processes are expected to conform to the environmental standards of the country of origin.

Typeset by Stanford DTP Services, Northampton, England

Simultaneously printed in the United Kingdom and United States of America

Contents

Acknowledgements

This book would have been impossible without the many interviews and conversations I was able to carry out with a very broad range of Êzîdî, Christian and Shiite survivors of the IS genocide. It would go beyond the scope of these acknowledgements to thank them all by name. However, I want to thank in particular those who – like Şerihan Rajo and Ali Saleh Qasim – shared with me stories that were extremely painful to them. And of all those who have supported me in this project, I want to thank a few additional people by name. My special thanks go to Mirza Dinnay, who I have known as a friend for one and a half decades. As far back as 2010, he enabled me and my wife, Mary Kreutzer, to visit Lališ and have a long conversation with the Baba Sheikh, and he has often lent a helping hand in arranging important contacts. Without him, this book could not have been written. I want to thank Pir Dayan for not hesitating to take me in his office car to the mountain in September 2017, when it was completely impossible to get permission from the Kurdish authorities to travel to Sinjar. I also thank Muhammad Hassan from Rojava for accompanying me from Syria to Sinjar in January 2019 and for organising important interviews that I felt were still necessary for the book. And finally, I want to thank the many Êzîdî friends in Xanke, in Rojava, and at the Sinjar Mountains who opened their houses for me and offered me their hospitality during my field research. In a region where there are neither hotels nor hostels, the hospitality of the people is a basic precondition for any extended stay at all. I thank you all for these wonderful encounters, for your stories, for the meals together and for the nights under the clear star-spattered sky in the mountains of Şingal. I will forget none of this for the rest of my life.

Preface to the English edition

When I wrote the first version of this book in 2019, I deliberately wrote it in German, not only because German, as my first language, is still more familiar to me than English, but also because I wanted as many Êzîdî as possible to be able to read this book themselves. After Iraq, Germany is now the country where more members of this religious community live than anywhere else. The conflicts in Turkey and Syria, the poverty in the Caucasus, but also the persecution in Iraq have led to a situation where a locally anchored religion with its local sanctuaries has in part become a diaspora religion.

This is one of the reasons why interest in the Êzîdî and the genocide of 2014 is often more pronounced in German-speaking countries than in Britain, the USA, Canada or Australia. German was thus the obvious first language for this book. However, from the beginning I was also keen to make English, Arabic and Kurdish editions possible. The English edition is now appearing more than a year later than planned due to the consequences of the COVID-19 crisis for the English-language book market.

However, this also made it possible to update the book even more and to include the results of further research visits in spring 2021 and following developments in autumn 2021. The English edition is thus more up to date and complete than the German version. It also contains significantly more photos from the region.

The text of the German edition was translated by Michael Schiffmann, but the entire edition was reviewed. I inserted the additions and updates in English. The book is thus not just a translation of the German edition but updated to the summer of 2021. However, no further interviews have been inserted in the interview section. The original voices of various actors in the region still speak for themselves today, just as they did in 2019 when the first German-language version of this book was published.

I hope that on the basis of this version there will soon be Arabic and Kurdish editions of this book, and in the meantime I hope this

English edition will meet with international interest, and also that this book, like my earlier books on Rojava and Afrin, can be discussed at events in the English-speaking world.

Vienna, 3 July 2021

A note on spelling: readers will notice that the transliteration of *Êzîdî* is inconsistent with the book's subtitle. The most common English spelling was used for the subtitle to ensure that the book will be more easily found by readers searching for information on this subject. For the main text I have used a spelling consistent with the system of transliteration used throughout the rest of the book.

Timeline

1832	Attack by Muhammed Pasha from Rawanduz
1837	Attack by the Ottoman governor of Diyarbakır Hafiz Pasha
1849	First permanent representative of the Ottoman Empire in Sinjar
1892	Attack by Omar Wahbi Pasha from Mosul
1915	Christians and Êzîdî from other parts of the Ottoman Empire flee the Genocide of the Young Turks and are protected by Hemoyê Şero
1918	British occupation of Sinjar
1932	Sinjar becomes part of the new Kingdom of Iraq
1957	First villages in the mountain destroyed and resettlement projects
1960	Land used by Êzîdî in the south of Sinjar transferred to Arab farmers
1970s	Destruction of 400 villages in the mountain and resettlement of the Êzîdî in 'collective towns' (*mujama'at*); Êzîdî counted as Arabs
1991	Sinjar stays under control of the regime of Saddam Hussein, while parts of the Şêxan region, including Lališ, become part of the Kurdistan Region controlled by Kurdish Peshmerga
12 April 2003	US troops occupy Sinjar, local resistance in Sinunê against US-troops
2005	Sunni Islamist uprising in Tal Afar
14 August 2007	Terrorist attacks in Tel Ezêr and Sîba Şêx Xidir
29 June 2014	'Islamic State' (IS) declared in Mosul

3 August 2014	IS attacks Sinjar and the Êzîdî villages around Sinjar, about 50,000 people flee to Mount Sinjar
3–5 August 2014	About 500 Êzîdî men executed in and around Sinjar City
8 August 2014	US starts air strikes on IS units and convoys
9–11 August 2014	PKK, YPG and YPJ open corridor between mount Sinjar and Syria
15 August 2014	Massacre of Koço
21 October 2014	IS takes over additional territories in the north of Sinjar and cuts the escape routes
17 December 2014	First Kurdish offensive against IS starts; north of Sinjar Mountains liberated
12 November 2015	Second Kurdish offensive to liberate Sinjar City starts
13 November 2015	Sinjar City liberated
3 March 2017	Armed conflict between Roj Peshmerga and YBŞ near Xanasor
12–29 May 2017	Liberation of southern Sinjar by People's Mobilisation Units (PMU) and Iraqi army
25 September 2017	Referendum on Kurdish independence, also held in the PDK-controlled parts of Sinjar
17 October 2017	Withdrawal of PDK Peshmerga from Sinjar
15 August 2018	YBŞ-commander Zekî Şengalî killed by a Turkish attack
17 March 2019	Clashes between YBŞ and the Iraqi army near Xanasor
15 January 2020	Zerdaşt Şengali, another local commander of YBŞ and its press spokesman, killed together with other fighters of YBŞ
June 2020	Hundreds of families return to Sinjar due to the harsh conditions in the camps during the COVID-19 crisis
14 June 2020	Turkish air force bombing of several places in the Sinjar region
9 October 2020	Security and administrative agreement on Sinjar district between Baghdad and Erbil

31 October 2020	The International Organization for Migration (IOM) Displacement Tracking Matrix records around 6,394 households returning to non-camp locations in Sinjar between 31 August and 31 October 2020
22 January 2021	Turkish president Erdoğan announces that his military might launch a joint operation with the Iraqi government against the PKK in the Region of Sinjar
6 February 2021	In a solemn ceremony, the remains of the victims of the Koço massacre are buried in Koço after being transferred from Baghdad
24 April 2021	Protests by local activists and supporters of the PKK prevent the implementation of the agreement between Baghdad and Erbil
18 August 2021	A Turkish air strike kills eight people in a hospital in the village of Sikeniye in the southwest of the Sinjar region
10 October 2021	In the Iraqi parliamentary elections, the PDK wins all three mandates in Sinjar with two Êzîdî and one Muslim Kurd; the mandate reserved for the minority is won by Naif Khalaf Seydou of the Êzîdî Progress Party (PPÊ); the PKK-affiliated PADÊ does not win a mandate
November 2021	More and more Êzîdî from Sinjar appear at the Polish–Belarusian border and try to flee to the EU via Belarus
7 December 2021	Politician and YBŞ-commander Merwan Bedel Xwedêda (Dijwar) is killed by a Turkish drone in Xanasor
11 December 2021	Turkish airstrike against the People's Council (Meclîsa Gel) in Xanasor.

Abbreviations

ENKS Encûmena Niştimanî ya Kurdî li Sûriyeyê, Kurdish National Council in Syria: a Kurdish alliance of parties in Syria that is allied with the PDK in Iraq and is opposed to the autonomy project in Northeast Syria which was organised by a sister party of the PKK.

HDP Halkların Demokratik Partisi, Democratic Party of the Peoples: leftist party which was founded by activists of the PKK-oriented part of the Kurdish movement in Turkey. It is represented in the Turkish parliament and is in charge of a number of municipal administrations in the Turkish part of Kurdistan.

HPÊ Hêza Parastina Êzîdxanê, Protection Force of Êzîdxan: name used for the HPŞ since November 2015.

HPŞ Hêza Parastina Şingal, Protection Force of Sinjar: Êzîdî militia in in Sinjar founded by and under the command of Haydar Shesho. Renamed HPÊ in 2015.

HTY Hizb al-taqadam al-yezīdī, Êzîdî Progress Party: Êzîdî party, led by the Arab-speaking Êzîdî Saib Khidir from Bashiqa, who won the minority mandate of the Êzîdî in the Iraqi parliament in 2018. Because the party is dominated by Arabic-speaking Êzîdî, it only uses an Arabic name, but not a Kurdish one.

IS ad-daula al-islāmiyya, Islamic State: name used by ISIS after the proclamation of the caliphate at the end of July 2014.

ISI Dawlat al-'Irāq al-'Islāmiyyah, Islamic State in Iraq: jihadist successor organisation of al-Qaida in Mesopotamia and predecessor organisation of the Islamic State in Iraq and Greater Syria (ISIS).

ISIS ad-daula al-islāmiyya fī l-'Irāq wa-š-Šām, Islamic State in Iraq and Greater Syria: jihadist successor organisation of the Islamic State in Iraq (ISI), which emerged from a fusion of ISI with parts of the Syrian al-Qaida organisa-

	tion Jabhat al-Nusra, a process that led to the split from al-Qaida and to a rivalry of the new organisation with the remaining part of Jabhat al-Nusra.
ITC	Irak Türkmen Cephesi, Turkmen Front of Iraq: Turkish nationalist Turkmen party supported by the Turkish state.
PADÊ	Partiya Azadî û Demokrasiyê ya Êzidiyan, Êzîdî Party for Freedom and Democracy: Êzîdî party close to the PKK whose stronghold is in in Sinjar.
PDK	Partiya Demokrata Kurdistanê, Kurdistan Democratic Party: a party that is conservative in social politics, economic-liberal and tribalist, under the leadership of the Barzani family.
PÊD	Partiya Êzidiyên Demokrat, Democratic Êzîdî Party: Êzîdî party founded by Haydar Shesho and functioning as the political arm of the HPÊ.
PKK	Partiya Karkerên Kurdistanê, Kurdistan Workers' Party: leftist party, party founded in the Turkish part of Kurdistan and guerrilla movement led by Abdullah Öcalan with an originally Marxist-Leninist orientation. After 2000, its ideology changed into a communalist-libertarian direction.
PPÊ	Partiya Pêşverû ya Êzidiyan, Êzîdî Progressive Party: independent party partly supported by former PUK members.
PUK	Yekêtiy Nîştimaniy Kurdistan, YNK, Patriotic Union of Kurdistan: party front originally to the left under the leadership of the later Iraqi president Jalal Talabani. Today, it is officially a social-democratic party, and indeed a largely economic-liberal and clientelist party.
SCIRI	al-Madschlis al-a'lā lith-thaura l-islāmiyya fī l-'Irāq, Supreme Council for the Islamic Revolution in Iraq: Shiite resistance organisation against the regime of Saddam Hussein in Iraq founded in1982 which after 2003 became an important Shiite party and which renamed itself into Supreme Islamic Council in Iraq (al-Madschlis al-a'lā l-islāmī l-'Irāqī, SIIC) in 2007.
SDF	Arabic: Quwwāt Sūriyā al-Dīmuqrāṭīya, Kurdish: Hêzên Sûriya Demokratîk, Syrian Democratic Forces: US-supported Syrian military alliance built up by the YPG since

2015, which also includes secular Arab and Christian militias as well as a small Turkmen one.

TAJÊ   Tevgera Azadiya Jinên Êzidxanê, Êzîdxan Women's Freedom Movement: civil women's movement close to the YBŞ and the YJŞ. A synonym for the group is the name Tevgera Azadiya Jinên Êzîdî, that is, the Free Women's Movement of the Êzîdî.

YBŞ   Yekîneyên Berxwedana Şengalê, Sinjar Resistance Units: Êzîdî militia in Sinjar which is politically close to the PKK.

YJŞ   Yekinêyen Jinên Şengalê, Women's Units of Sinjar: women's units of the YBŞ, close to the PKK.

YPG   Yekîneyên Parastina Gel, People's Protection Units: Syrian-Kurdish army built up by the sister party of the PKK in Syria, which came to the rescue of the Êzîdî from Syria in 2014.

YPJ   Yekîneyên Parastina Jin, Women's Protection Units: women's units of the YPG in Syria, close to the PKK.

YPJŞ   Yekîneyên Parastina Jin ê Şengalê, Women's Protection Units of Sinjar: predecessor organisation of the YJŞ until April 2016.

Maps

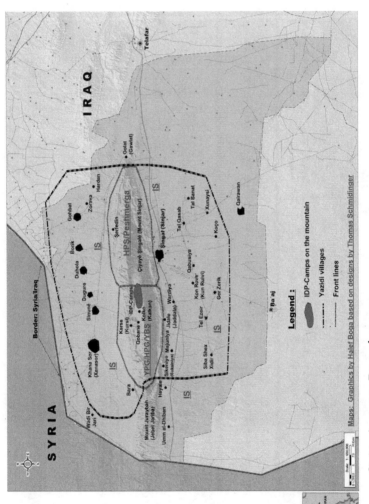

1   Sinjar: August to December 2014

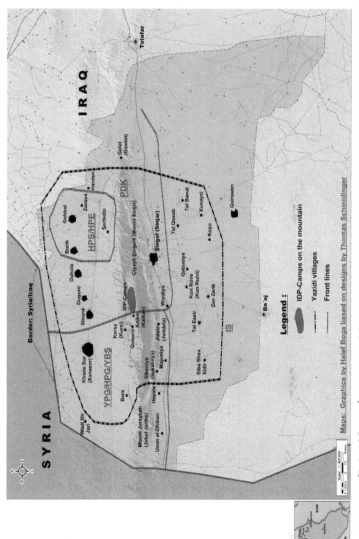

Maps: Graphics by Halef Boga based on designs by Thomas Schmidinger

2   Sinjar: November 2015 to May 2017

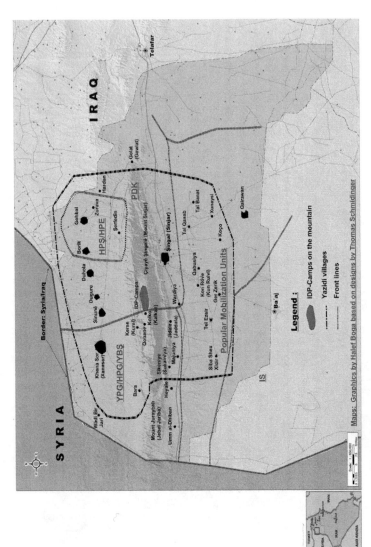

Maps: Graphics by Halef Boga based on designs by Thomas Schmidinger

Legend :

IDP-Camps on the mountain

Yazidi villages

Front lines

3   Sinjar: May 2017

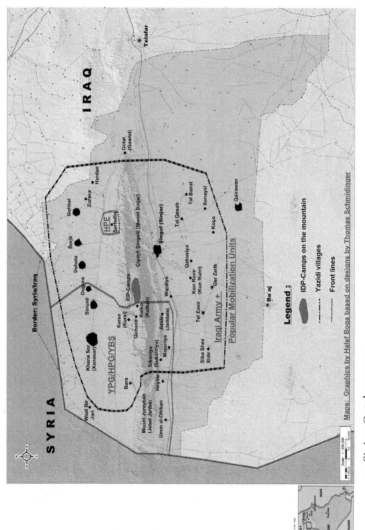

4   Sinjar: October 2017

Maps. Graphics by Halef Boga based on designs by Thomas Schmidinger

Legend:

IDP-Camps on the mountain

Yazidi villages

Front lines

Introduction

When the fighters of the so-called Islamic State (IS) attacked the region of Sinjar ('Şingal' in Kurdish) on 3 August 2014, for most Europeans and Americans this was the first time they had ever heard of the Êzîdî – often refered as 'Yazidis' or 'Yezidis' in English – a religious group in Kurdistan which had endured a long history of persecution as alleged 'devil's worshippers' even before IS's reign of terror. The genocide perpetrated against the Êzîdî showed the global public with unprecedented clarity how brutally the jihadis enforced their delusionary ideology and their strategic goals.

But the attacks by IS have a long history, and despite the military victory over IS, the suffering of the survivors has not yet come to an end. This book, which appears seven years after the events of August 2014, is more than just a book on the genocide. It also recounts the historical background and gives an account of the long history of the region, the various religious and ethnic groups that have lived together in it and of the religion and the society of the Êzîdî. And finally, it also describes what happened with the survivors after August 2014 as well as the development of the political and military situation in Sinjar after 2014.

For the survivors, the consequences of the genocide are still palpable; it is far from clear whether the region can ever be rebuilt in a way that allows it to become a centre of Êzîdî culture again.

Since Germany has now become the most important part of the diaspora for the Êzîdî, I wrote this book in German first. However, I am very happy that an English version is available now that enables even more people to read about this region, the genocide of and its consequences. As the survivors of the Genocide not only migrated to Germany, but to Australia and North America as well, I also hope to give the second generation of English-speaking Êzîdî a tool for dealing with an important aspect of their history.

This book is based not just on working through the literature, but also on extensive field research in the region. For the German version of this book, I visited the Sinjar Mountains four times, in addition to several visits to the camps of the displaced and refugees in Iraq, Syria and Turkey. For the English version additional fieldwork was conducted in spring 2021. The book is based on conversations with survivors, a collection of qualitative interviews in the Xanke refugee camp, and a number of interviews with personalities from different political and military movements in the region. These conversations and interviews are reproduced in chronological order in Part III of the book. They should enable the reader to get a glimpse into the quite contradictory original voices of actors who are frequently in rivalry with each other.

PART I

History of Sinjar and the genocide

1
The Sinjar Mountains as a natural space

The Sinjar Mountains – 'Jebel Sinjar' in Arabic, and 'Çiyayê Şingalê' in Kurdish – is a massif approximately 60 kilometres in length that protrudes from the Mesopotamian lowlands. In a certain sense, it is the southernmost prolongation of the Kurdish mountainous region into the Mesopotamian plains and stands alone between the alluvial lands of the Tigris in the east and the Euphrates in the west. The highest peak of this mountain range, the Çêl Mêra, is 1,453 metres above sea level.

In geographic terms, this range is the visible part of the 150 kilometres of the Sinjar elevated area whose rock strata in part go back to the Palaeozoic. Like other mountain ranges further to the north and east, the Sinjar Mountains emerged through a complex geological process during which the Arabian Plate broke away from the African Plate and was pushed in the direction of the Eurasian Plate. Today, the resulting mountain crest is characterised by deeply incised valleys and ravines on the southern slope, relatively flatly layered cuestas at the crown of the mountain range, and steeply descending mountains with deep, somewhat broader valleys at the northern slope. In the west, the range finds its continuation in the Jariba Mountains, whose northwestern flank borders the lake Khatuniyya, which is called Bahra by the local Êzîdî. Up until the colonial demarcation of boundaries between Syria and Iraq by the United Kingdom and France after the First World War, the region around the lake and the Jariba Mountains formed a natural continuation of the Sinjar Mountains and was in part also inhabited and used by Êzîdî. It was only with the establishment of the Syrian and the Iraqi national states that a border was created which split the western continuation of the Sinjar from the rest, leading to a migration of the Êzîdî to what had now become the Iraqi side. Since then, the area on the Syrian side has only been used by Arab nomads mostly belonging to the Shammar tribe.

Surrounded by dry steppeland, the Sinjar Mountains in a way forms an oasis that provides water all year long and allows for the growing of vegetables, tobacco and fruit. In winter, the mountains are covered with snow. Apart from that, the climate is largely subtropical with hot, dry summers and cold, moist winters. Many of the rivers dry up in the course of the summer. But in contrast with the surrounding steppe, in the mountains there were always water reserves, which enabled the mountain villages to practise terrace cultivation.

At heights of over 800 metres, in the past the mountains were in part covered with holly oak forests which were later sharply reduced by lumbering and grazing. But even today, there are still older and younger trees here and there which have the potential to form a real forest again in the future. In the ravines with larger water resources, a fig (*Ficus carica*) grows for which this region is famous in all of Northern Iraq. These small and very sweet Sinjar figs are grown by the farmers of the region.

The centuries-old local mountain farmer culture used to practise a relatively solicitous handling of the resources of the region, particularly of the soil and of water. The destruction of this culture during the Ba'thist rule over Iraq has also left a permanent stamp on the natural space of the region. The uncultivated, exposed soils were subjected to strong erosion. The diversion of water to the farms in the plains led to a drying up of many mountain brooks. Today's traveller in Sinjar will find a much dryer and rockier massif than the one of a hundred years ago.

However, since 2014, it has become apparent that the interior of the mountains still has the potential for agriculture as well. Since some of the displaced people have settled back in the mountains and partly repopulate the old mountain villages, even long abandoned gardens have been restored. Lonely mountain valleys and slopes have been increasingly cultivated again, especially since 2019, and greenery is slowly returning to the region. The years 2018 to 2020 in particular saw above-average rainfall. This again allowed the cultivation of tobacco around the village of Kerse and made it possible to plant fig and olive trees. In 2021, however, as in all of Iraq, there is an extreme drought that could undo these successes. The first effects of climate change have also been felt here in recent years. It is getting significantly hotter. If the rise in temperature, especially during the summer months, is accompanied by periods of extreme drought in the coming years, the tentative attempts to replant the mountains could prove to be a failure.

2
Sinjar in ancient times

On the one hand, the history of Sinjar is one of a peripheral mountain region which has for centuries served as a retreat area for minorities, but on the other, it is also the history of an urban settlement, Sinjar City (Arabic: Balad Sinjar), which is located at the southern foot of this mountain chain. This city itself was also never the centre of an empire or any other important regional administrative structure, but its history reaches far back into antiquity. It has always been characterised by a very diverse population.

Already early on, the southern edge of the mountains was important as a migration area between Syria and Assyria. Even the Bible (Gen. 10.10 and Jos. 7.21) already mentions a region called Shinar, which is often considered the same as today's Sinjar, though this attribution cannot be regarded as verified. Ancient Egyptian and Assyrian sources also mention a region with a similar name. In the museum of Dohuk,[1] there are a number of ancient objects from Sinjar on display which prove that the city was settled in the Hellenistic period and that in the Roman period, it had become a permanent urban settlement by the name of Singara (Greek τὰ Σίγγαρα), in which a Roman legion was garrisoned. But because of the lack of systematic archaeological excavations in this politically sensitive border region, the documentation of the early history of Sinjar remains very fragmentary.

In any case, the fact is that even today Greek, Roman and Sassanian coins are still being found in the region, although they are often sold on by the local population without ever being submitted to research. However, such finds at various places on the mountain and at its foot testify to the fact that the region was already heavily populated in ancient times and was integrated into the trade routes of the region. The geography and climate also suggest that one of the most important connections between Syria and Mesopotamia was already to be found here in antiquity. On the one hand, traders did not have to pass through the

Kurdish mountains, but on the other hand, they did not have to pass through the much hotter and drier steppe and desert areas to the south. The city of Sinjar was certainly never a political metropolis, but it probably represented an important intermediate station between the Levant and the Tigris Valley with its centres of upper Mesopotamia.

The city must have had a substantial Christian population already early on. During the seventh century, the Christian scholar Gabriel of Sinjar is mentioned, who came from the Assyrian Church (which was called Nestorian by its enemies) and who later converted to Syrian Orthodox Monophysitism. He played an important role in the intra-Christian power struggles under the Sassanid ruler Chosrau II.[2] The Apocalypse of Pseudo-Methodius, which was previously attributed to Bishop Methodius of the fourth century but which today tends to be regarded as a work of the seventh century, also mentions in its preamble that its author received his revelations in Sinjar.[3]

Not much is known about the population on the mountain and away from the urban settlement at that time. For a reasonably consistent local history of the region, many more archaeological digs would be necessary. The only thing that can be said with certainty is that the city of Sinjar has been permanently settled from the Roman time until today, and that the mountain areas were also populated already in antiquity.

Due to a lack of documentation, it is impossible to say which languages were predominantly spoken in the mountain area. As for the city itself, it is quite certain that until the Arab conquest certain forms of Aramaic dominated and were used by Christians and Jews (in the latter case, together with Hebrew as a liturgical language) both in everyday life and in liturgy. Even though there is no proof of the continuous presence of Christians and Jews, their later presence in the city suggests that it was predominantly populated by Christians and Jews even before the Arab, or Islamic, conquest. Given the current state of knowledge, it is impossible to say whether, and if so, in which form the region was then home to proto-forms of western Iranian religious traditions which later became part of the religion of the Êzîdî. The region was certainly not among the most important settlement areas of today's Kurds; it was part of the section of the Middle East which, under the rule of the Achaemenids and Seleucids, developed into a place where Aramaic was the lingua franca and in which Greek, Persian, Mesopotamian influences had coalesced into the Hellenistic culture since the time of Alexander the Great.

In contrast with most other areas of today's Iraq, before the Arab-Islamic expansion Sinjar had not been a permanent part of the Iranian Sassanid Empire but had long represented one of the eastern outposts of the Roman Empire. As a part of the defence against the Sassanids, it played an important military role in the defence of the empire. The whole region was dotted with Roman forts and military roads whose function was to prevent Parthian and Sassanid incursions into Roman Syria.[4] For that reason, Sinjar is also the only region of today's Iraq in which there have been archaeological findings from the Roman era. It was only in the year 360 that the Sassanids finally conquered Sinjar; from that time on, the region formed a part of the territory of this dynasty, whose home was in today's Iraq and Iran and which extended to Nisbis, today's Nusaybin.

Thereafter, the border region frequently was the scene of wars between the Sassanid Empire and the East Roman/Byzantine Empire, wars which in the end contributed to weakening both sides. The last great Sassanid–Byzantine war (602 to 628 CE), which devastated large parts of the Middle East and led to a period of civil war and internal instability in the Sassanid Empire, finally enabled the Arabs to conquer the region by invading it from the south.

3
From the Islamic conquest to the periphery of the Ottoman Empire

The conquest of the Middle East by the Islamic Empire took place after the death of the prophet Muhammad and under the first two caliphs Abū Bakr and 'Umar ibn al-Khattāb. Sinjar was subdued by the Arab military leader 'Iyād ibn Ghanm shortly before the latter's death in 641 as part of his conquest of Northern Mesopotamia and was integrated into the province Diyār Rabī'a, which comprised the eastern part of Upper Mesopotamia.

Just as the northern Diyār Bakr[1] and the western Diyār Mudar, the province got its name from the Arab tribes which were settled there under the Umayyad caliph Mu'āwiyah in the seventh century. The eponym was the tribe of the Rabī'a, which originally came from the Tihamah, the coastal region of the Arab peninsula bordering the Red Sea. In Iraq, the designation of these early Arab settlers lives on to this day in the name of the border town of Rabī'a between Sinjar and the autonomous Kurdistan Region, which is, however, not mainly populated by the descendants of the Rabī'a, but by the Shammar, an Arab tribe which came to Upper Mesopotamia from the north of the Arab peninsula.[2]

In 750, the Umayyads were replaced by the Abbasids, whose centre was in Baghdad. Just as under the Umayyads, the Sinjar Mountains now constituted a rather peripheral area that had much less strategic importance than during the Sassanid period. The new rulers brought Islam to the region. Thus, Islam too became represented in the city of Sinjar in addition to Christianity and Judaism.

The oldest evidence of Êzîdî existence in the region dates back to the thirteenth century, when the sanctuary of Şerfedîn[3] was built. At the end of the fourteenth century, Upper Mesopotamia came under the rule of the Turkmen Aq Qoyunlu ('white sheep') who, however, mostly focused on the most important cities and trade routes. Their rule extended only minimally into inaccessible mountain regions. It was probably around this time that the totally autonomous tribal society and mountain farmer culture of the Êzîdî became dominant in the mountainous areas of Sinjar, a society and culture that existed largely unchanged until the 1960s.

In 1508, Mesopotamia, and Sinjar City with it, were conquered by the Safavids. It is very likely that Shiite Islam was also brought to the region of the Sinjar Mountains by the new rulers, who at first belonged to a heterodox group of the Shiites,[4] but then proceeded to convert Iran to the Twelver Shia. The Kurdish–Shiite tribe of the Babawat continues to live in the region to this day; in the city of Sinjar, there are a number of Shiite mosques.

The conquest of Mesopotamia by the Safavids initiated a series of armed conflicts between the emerging Ottoman Empire and Iran, then under the rule of the Safavids, which basically took place in Mesopotamia and Armenia. In the Ottoman–Safavid war (1552–1555), Upper Mesopotamia was conquered by the Ottomans. In 1534, the Ottomans captured Baghdad. In the Ottoman–Safavid war (1623–1639), the Safavids first reconquered Iraq, only to lose it to the Ottomans for good shortly thereafter. The peace of Qasr-e Shirin led to an agreement on the Persian–Ottoman border and turned today's Iraq – including Sinjar – into a part of the Ottoman Empire. Apart from a few small changes, this border is still the same today and separates Turkey from Iran and Iraq.

But the Ottoman Empire of the seventeenth century was not a centrally governed modern nation state, but rather, in many respects, a premodern empire with differing sovereignties overlapping each other and with the central government not exercising any direct control in many regions. Just as the Kurdish principalities, which were nominally under Ottoman control but were actually ruled by local aristocracies, the Sinjar Mountains was actually a totally autonomous area to which the empire didn't have any direct access. Since the beginning of the eighteenth century, Sinjar was located at the edge of Iraq, which was then ruled by Mamelukes[5] under Ottoman suzerainty, as well as at the periphery of the Paşalık[6] of Mosul, which was governed by the local dynasty of the al-Jalili.[7] Politically, the Ottoman Empire was almost completely absent from the region. Securing the safety of the caravan routes from Mosul to the west, particularly to Nusaybin, was a task that the Mamelukes and the al-Jalili delegated to the Shammar, an Arab tribal federation living in the plains around the Sinjar Mountains.[8] But because of attacks from the mountains, these routes always remained precarious. Even though in later periods, there was a certain presence of the Ottoman Empire in the city of Sinjar, this never extended the mountain ranges themselves. This was the place where the mountain farmers of the Êzîdî lived. The Ottoman rule didn't have any clout there and their society worked according to its own tribal rules.

4

The religion of the Êzîdî

Scientifically speaking, the question of when this population (which finally ended up being the majority in the region and which, in 2014, was to became the victim of the genocide perpetrated by the so-called Islamic State) started to settle on the Sinjar Mountains cannot be answered unequivocally. According to local tradition, the settlement was founded by Sheikh Sharaf ad-Din (Kurdish: Şêx Şerfedîn), who lived from 1215 to 1257 or 1258 and who spent his life fighting the Mongol invaders with a force of Kurds and Turks.[1] To this day, his grave is one of the most important religious sites of the Êzîdî in Sinjar.

This myth is actually impossible to prove. As a predominantly rural population which was totally illiterate until well into the twentieth century, the Êzîdî barely left any written record or archaeological traces. It can be safely assumed that, while the central mountain area of the Sinjar massif had been settled by Êzîdî already for centuries, many Êzîdî had found their way to Sinjar only later on. Until the twentieth century, the inaccessible mountain lands offered a refuge for persecuted minorities from other regions of Kurdistan. Many of today's Êzîdî families of the Sinjar region still know that their ancestors had come from other parts of Kurdistan in the seventeenth, eighteenth or nineteenth centuries, hailing from regions where bigger Êzîdî tribes once used to live until they were driven out by Muslim attacks and forced to find a new home in Sinjar.

But what is the specific mark of this religion of the Êzîdî, and why have its members so frequently been subjected to persecution? The Êzîdî merged influences of the most diverse Middle-eastern religious orientations into a unique religion which cannot be assigned to any of the world religions. Even though it has similarities with the Old Iranian religion, unlike Zoroastrianism Yazidism never underwent the development to dualism.[2] While Judaism, Christianity and Islam all adopted from Zoroastrian dualism the idea of an evil counter-god, the Êzîdî know neither the concept of the devil nor that of hell. Nevertheless – or perhaps for that very reason – Muslims, and in part also Christians, have over and over accused them of being devil worshippers.

In rational terms, the background of this denunciation must probably be sought in the psyche of those who, of all people, single out for their hatred those who have not adopted their own fear of the devil and thus actually practise a purer form of monotheism than Christians and Muslims, who have imported the Zoroastrian Angra Mainyu into their respective belief systems as the 'devil'. The hatred of the supposed 'devil worshippers' might thus be viewed as internalised self-hatred, punishing all believers who have rejected the introduction of the evil counter-god and who have thus refused to succumb to the fear of hell that the Christian and Muslim dualists subject themselves to. On the other hand, the accusation of devil worship is based on a misunderstanding resulting from the ignorance of the differences between Zoroastrianism and Yazidism. Superficial similarities between Angra Mainyu, or the devil, and the Êzîdî angel Tawûsê Melek can result in the fallacious conclusion that the two figures are one and the same and that veneration for Tawûsê Melek thus equals worship of the devil.

But who is Tawûsê Melek? Apart from God (Xwedê), the Êzîdî also venerate the Peacock Angel (Tawûsê Melek), who is regarded as the first and most faithful angel of God. God himself is a very abstract and remote god. In the view of the Êzîdî, getting into contact with him requires a mediator, and that mediator is the Peacock Angel.

While Tawûsê Melek is thus not identical with Angra Mainyu, he does have certain similarities with him; both figures probably go back to the same figure from the Old Iranian religion. The Iranologist Philip Kreyenbroek, who has studied Yazidism and Zoroastrianism for decades, assumes that, as a consequence of the far-reaching reforms by Zarathustra around 1000 BCE, in the east of Iran Zoroastrianism separated itself from the West Iranian religion, and that the latter later on led to Mithraism, the Ahl-e Haqq (Yarsan) still present in today's Kurdish Hawraman, and the Êzîdî. While the Old Iranian religion assumed one God and one mediator between God and humans, in Zoroastrianism this mediator turned into the 'evil' god Angra Mainyu (who, in German, is often called Ahriman). But in Mithraism (a religion which competed with Christianity during the Roman Empire and which venerated the sun) and among the Êzîdî and the Ahl-e Haqq the mediator remained 'good': Mithras in Mithraism and Tawûsê Melek among the Êzîdî. Kreyenbroek summarises:

> After the dominant religion of Iran, Zoroastrianism, had come into contact with this old west Iranian tradition at some time in the pre-Islamic period, the 'good' mediator was identified with the evil Ahriman. This also explains why the good 'mediator' in Yazidism is incorrectly associated with the Satan of other religions.[3]

Tawûsê Melek is thus *not* the evil counter-god, but a mediator between God and the humans in the world; he executes God's plan and is 'the manifestation of the creator, but not the creator himself, he is God's alter ego and inseparably connected with him'.[4]

Within Yazidism, there are different narratives with regard to the emergence of Tawûsê Melek and his role. In a religious tradition basically passed on orally, there are naturally many narratives, which do not necessarily have to agree with each other. One of these narratives has similarities with the Islamic story of the devil, even though its essence is totally different. This similarity could, however, have contributed to the accusation of devil worship. In this narrative, Tawûsê Melek is regarded as one of the most important angels of God, similar to Satan or the Christian Lucifer before his fall:

> Because the Peacock Angel was particularly reverent in his faith in God, he also kept God's first commandment, namely, to venerate *nobody* but God. Therefore, after God made Adam, Tawûsê Melek refused the order to prostrate himself before the newly created human being. He was thus tested by God and passed, a narrative that starkly contradicts the Christian and Islamic idea of hell, in which this angel was punished and then transformed into the devil. Unlike these two religions, the Êzîdî have no concept of hell as a place of eternal condemnation. For

the Êzîdî, God is almighty to such an extent that there can be no second force that represents personified evil.[5]

The superficial similarity of this story to the one of the Islamic and the Christian devil, who refused to throw himself down before the humans out of arrogance, was used for centuries to accuse the Êzîdî of being devil worshippers.

A further reproach Muslims frequently direct at Yazidism is that, as opposed to Judaism, Christianity and Zoroastrianism, it is no religion of the book,[6] which is why Islam does not accord it the protection and respect given to those religions by classical Islamic law. And indeed, the Qewel, the religious contents and chants of Yazidism, are exclusively transmitted orally. Therefore, the Êzîdî do have a problem with Muslims, as the latter's tolerance is limited to the religions of the book. Because of this, there is a myth among many Êzîdî according to which there *is* a holy book Meshaf-i Reş (the Black Book) that is said to have disappeared some time ago. I was even asked about that book by Êzîdî Sheikhs during my field research in Syria. Rumour had it that this book had been stolen by Austrians and was now located in a museum in Vienna. I was therefore asked to advocate for sending this supposed book back to the Êzîdî. But in truth, this alleged holy book of the Êzîdî is to be found neither in the Austrian National Library nor in any Austrian museum.

The background to this myth is that in 1913, the Austrian orientalist Maximilian Bittner published a book with the title *The Holy Books of the Êzîdî or Devil Worshippers*,[7] which was based on writings that were bought at the time by local Christians and whose authenticity is controversial to this day. Among the Êzîdî of the Middle East, they certainly didn't have the importance that the Quran has for Muslims or the significance that the Bible has for Jews and Christians. This is also indicated by the fact that no original copies of this Holy Scripture have been preserved.

Both reproaches – devil worship and the lack of authoritative texts – have been used since the fifteenth century to justify the persecution of the Êzîdî. This persecution has left strong marks in the Êzîdî perspective on their own history. Until the end of the twentieth century, the Êzîdî were believed to have been the victims of 72 firmans. The Ottoman term firman (writ, decree) was used by the Êzîdî to describe persecution, massacre and genocide. Here, the number 72 was simply a symbol for 'very much'. It was only in the twenty-first century, when the mythical dimension of that number was no longer clear for most of the Êzîdî, that they began to count further and called the attack on two villages in the Sinjar region the 73rd, and the genocide by IS of August 2014 the 74th firman.

Just as controversial as the origin of the Êzîdî religion is its age. In an environment in which seniority is an important badge of legitimacy, many Êzîdî tend to describe their religion as a community which is thousands of years old, or even as the oldest religion in history. Thus, phantasy numbers are circulating among certain Êzîdî authors. A video published by German-language Êzîdî calls Yazidism 'the oldest religion of the world' and claims that it is '7,650 years old'.[8] In the description of the video, it is asserted that archaeological findings prove that the Êzîdî are a 'religious community up to 15,000 years old'.[9]

Actually, in its present form the religion goes back to the Sufi Sheikh 'Adī ibn Musāfir, who hailed from today's Lebanon and who died in Lališ, the holiest place of the Êzîdî in today's northern Iraq, in 1162 or 1163. Sheikh 'Adī (Kurdish: Şêx Adî) brought together several different religious traditions that already existed before, and depending on the exact point in time at which one wants to fix the beginning of Yazidism, one can calculate very different ages for this religion. As already noted above, many parts of the teachings of the Êzîdî are undoubtedly based on pre-Islamic, west Iranian religious traditions that were already available to 'Adī ibn Musāfir when he retreated to Lališ with the followers of his Sufi community. But the influence of a Sufi variety of Islam on today's Yazidism is also impossible to deny. Thus, in the Êzîdî year there are both holidays following the solar calendar and holidays that follow the Islamic moon calendar. In Lališ itself, one finds geographical names – such as the Zamzam Spring and the 'Arafât Mountain – which remind one of the Islamic Holy City of Mecca. According to the Êzîdî tradition, the Zamzam Spring (Kanîya Zemzem) is even supposed to have a direct connection to the Zamzam Spring in Mecca.

In addition to the grave of Sheikh 'Adī, there are also other holy sites in Lališ, such as the 'White Spring' (Kanîya Sipî), which is used to baptise Êzîdî children: Only a few metres from Sheikh 'Adī's grave, there is a subterranean building which is probably the oldest part of the whole compound and which is regarded as so sacred that only the Êzîdî themselves are allowed to enter it. This is the place where the Zamzam Spring originates. Whether this sanctuary is a pre-Islamic mithraeum (i.e. a place of prayer of the Mithra cult) or another Old Iranian cult site is impossible to ascertain because this area is inaccessible to any archaeological research. A local legend circulating among both Christians and Êzîdî reports that the sanctuary of Lališ was originally an Assyrian (Nestorian) church.[10] It is in any case certain that a holy site had existed here even before Sheikh 'Adī and that it was then taken over and continued to be used.

Êzîdî from all over the world make the pilgrimage to Lališ. On particular holidays such as the 'Festival of Coming Together', which is also called 'Feast of God' (Îda Êzî), or on the Êzîdî New Year's festival (Carşema Sor/Îda Serê sal), the small place is literally swamped by tens of thousands of believers.

But Lališ is not the only holy site of the Êzîdî. There are local sanctuaries in all regions with an Êzîdî population. These are often (but not always) located at the graves of saints. Especially in the Sinjar Mountains, we know of important mountain sanctuaries at topographically significant points, such as the mausoleum of Şerfedîn at the bottom of the northern side of the mountains as well as the mausoleum of Sheikh Mand and the Çêl-Mêra temple (temple of the 40 men) on the highest elevation of the mountains.

Like all religious communities of the world, the Êzîdî religion also has a number of transition rites that its members are obliged to pass through in the course of their lives. Among these are the rite of the first haircut (*bisk*), a rite similar to the Christian baptism (*mor kirin*), and the rite of circumcision (*sinet*), which was probably adopted from Islam. Just as with circumcision, the rite of the first haircut is reserved for boys: 'After a prayer, the Sheikh responsible for the family removes hair locks from three different locations. The hair is collected in a white cloth and then kept hidden, together with the hair that may have fallen to the ground during the cutting.'[11] During youth, a so-called brother (*birayê axiretê*) or sister (*xuşka axiretê*) for the afterlife is selected, and finally, the wedding (*dawet*) is also part of the important transition rites in the life of the Êzîdî.

Apart from the belief in God (Xwedê), the Peacock Angel (Tawûsê Melek), and various, often local, saints, the Êzîdî tradition also knows guardian spirits such as Xatûna Ferxa, the patroness of the women. But in part, the local traditions are quite different from each other in this regard.

5
Social order and religious office-holders of the Êzîdî

As an isolated minority persecuted for centuries, the Êzîdî have developed their own social order, which strongly insists on separating itself from the rest of the world. This mechanism has reduced potential frictions with the Muslim environment and, at the same time, served to shore up the Êzîdî's own community. Today, however, the strict adherence to the marriage rules connected with this tradition and the hierarchical structure of society both lead to big problems, particularly in the European diaspora.

The society of the Êzîdî is basically divided into three status groups, which the literature mostly describes as castes similar to the Hinduist model. But this designation is not entirely correct because it adopts a much more hierarchical model of society to analyse the social structure of the Êzîdî. While it is true that these three groups among the Êzîdî are each assigned clear functions and that marriages can take place only within each group, they are not separated in everyday life in the same way as are the castes of Hinduism. What one finds instead is that the different status groups have clear mutual responsibilities and do entertain social relation with each other. The two groups of the Sheikhs (Şêx) and Pîr are regarded as being above the ordinary believers, the Murîd (also Mirîd), but between the group of the Şêx and the group of the Pîr, no clear hierarchy can be determined, only different functions. Members of the Murîd can also occupy important social and political functions, particularly in the diaspora, even though they are excluded from certain religious responsibilities. A caste of 'untouchables' such as in India does not exist among the Êzîdî. Moreover, the Êzîdî do not have any ban on joint meals including members of different 'castes'. There is also no obligatory assignment to certain professions as in the Indian lower castes, the Jatis. Apart from the distinction between the Şêx and the Pîr on the one hand and the Murîd on the other hand, the Êzîdî society is much more egalitarian than the Indian caste system and is characterised more by its tribes than by social hierarchies.

Nevertheless, this division of society still plays an important religious and social role, which, even today, is more pronounced in Iraq than in other settlement areas. Thus, in Iraq the marriage rules are still respected very strictly. In Sinjar, neither a marriage outside of the Êzîdî as a group nor a marriage outside of the respective status group is even thinkable. Romantic relationships between young Êzîdî and Muslims all too often result in the Êzîdî family murdering its own child in order to prevent a marriage with a Muslim or a conversion to Islam. But in most cases, the prevalent massive social pressure is sufficient to prevent such relations developing outside people's own group.

In the Caucasus and in Syria, these strict rules are slowly beginning to lose their force. In Syria, there *are* marriages between Muslims and Êzîdî. Particularly in the socially quite liberal Efrîn, which until the Turkish invasion at the beginning of 2018 had been the home of the largest Êzîdî minority of the country, the relationships between the Muslim and the Êzîdî Kurds were so close that there were fairly frequent marriages between them; even though these were frowned upon, they were at least possible. This may in part be due to the fact that many of the Muslims in Efrîn have Êzîdî ancestors, which explains why the Êzîdî there can somehow be regarded as 'relatives'.

To some Êzîdî families, members of other religious minorities are less problematic than Muslims. Thus, relationships between Êzîdî and Alevi or members of the Ahl-e Haqq are more readily tolerated than relationships to Muslims, a fact that has to do with the specific history of the persecution of Êzîdî by Muslims.

Eighty to eight-five per cent of the Êzîdî belong to the status group of ordinary believers, that is, the Murîd/Mirîd.[1] In comparison, the groups of the Şêx (ten to fifteen per cent) and the Pîr (at most five per cent) are much smaller. The Pîr are again divided into four groups which fulfil different functions, whereas the Şêx are divided into three subgroups.

Each Murîd family has a personal relation to a Şêx and a Pîr, who are responsible for the religious supervision of that family. But these Şêx and Pîr are not theologians in the Christian or Muslim sense, but rather, are religious dignitaries who have inherited this function and haven't acquired their knowledge in any educational institution, but through transmission within their own family.

From the Şêx subgroup of the Qatanî, the so-called Mîr is chosen, the 'prince' of the Êzîdî. He once used to be the political chieftain and still fulfils a traditional function as a political leader. Even though historically, it was often one of the sons of the previous Mîr who was appointed to that office, there is no clear rule of succession in the sense of a monarchical devolution of the office, but rather, an election within the religious council, something that has often led to controversies between the various branches of the Qatanî Sheikhs.

The traditional religious head of the Êzîdî, the Baba Sheikh (Kurdish: Bavê Şêx) has to come from the Şêx subgroup of the Şemsani. He must live an ascetic life, fasts much more than the other Êzîdî, and is tasked with regularly travelling through the villages of the Êzîdî in order to disseminate religious knowledge. In addition, his presence is obligatory for certain religious celebrations. He is exclusively chosen from the Fakhreddîn branch of the Şemsani. Even though he must formally be confirmed by the Mîr, his position is normally passed on from father to son.[2]

Apart from these important representatives, there are further religious dignitaries from the Şêx and Pîr group such as the Peşîmam, the Feqîr, or the Koçek. These functions are exercised in various parts of the settlement area of the Êzîdî. But just as with the Mîr and the Bavê Şêx, there is only one Bavê Çawîş. He is responsible for the administration of the sanctuary in Lališ and is obliged to lead a pious and chaste life there.

Lališ is also the residence of the religious council, which functions as a collective organ. This council is authorised to decide religious questions, and, when a Mîr dies, elects the successor from the group of the Qatanî Sheikhs. Among the members of the council are the Mîr, the Bavê Şêx, the Bavê Çawîş, and other religious dignitaries – and they are all men. Even though there is also a women's order in Lališ, it is mainly responsible for the housekeeping, for taking care of guests, and the cleanliness of the sanctuary, and it has no influence on the religious council.

Both the Bavê Şêx and the Mîr, the traditional heads of the Êzîdî, have their seat and their residence in the direct neighbourhood of

Lališ. The Bavê Şêx lives in the small town of Şêxan (Arabic: 'Ayn Sifni), the Mîr in Ba'adra. Both places are located at the bottom of the mountains one has to cross to get to Lališ. In contrast to his politically compromised predecessor, Khurto Haci Ismail (also called Keto or in Kurdish, Xeto), the last Bavê Şêx, who has been in office since 1995, enjoys great prestige and has played an important role in the social rehabilitation of kidnapped Êzîdî women after 2014. The last Mîr, Tehsîn Seîd Beg, who held this function for almost 75 years from 1944 until his death in January 2019, had been a much more controversial figure; he was frequently criticised for his compromises with political power (e.g. the regime of Saddam Hussein or the Democratic Party of Kurdistan of Masoud Barzani). During the last years of his life, Tehsîn Seîd Beg, who was then already ill and weak, resided in Germany most of the time. Even though he officially never went into exile and was buried in Iraq after his death, his de facto emigration to Germany was symbolic for the shift of the gravitational centre of Êzîdî life to the diaspora.

With the death of Mîr Tehsîn Seîd Beg on 28 January 2019, a whole era came to a end. Tehsîn Seîd Beg was the last Mîr who had grown up in a traditional religious rural society; he had represented the Êzîdî politically for many decades. This political function was concentrated on the region of Şêxan, while he didn't play much of a role in Sinjar. But in Şêxan, in the 1940s and 1950s he still functioned as the head of the traditional Êzîdî emirate, a role which he lost only after the revolution of 1958. That revolution and the ensuing reconstruction of Iraq into a centralised national state deprived the traditional feudal lords such as the Êzîdî Mîr or the Kurdish tribal leaders of their basis of existence. During the incumbency of Mîr Tehsîn Seîd Beg, the centre of the lives of very many believers shifted from the Kurdish mountains to the cities of Europe, but the lives of most Êzîdî also underwent enormous changes in many other respects. In 1944, only a handful of Êzîdî could read and write, but today, Êzîdî academics teach at European universities, and in Germany, there are Êzîdî judges, lawyers, businesspeople, politicians and filmmakers who are often much more educated than the traditional religious elites. They are now increasingly calling the social order of the Êzîdî – particularly the marriage rules and the oppression of the women – into question.

After the death of Mîr Tehsîn Seîd, women were for the first time considered as potential successors. Even though at the time of this writing in 2019, Mîr Tehsîn Seîd Beg's son Hazîm was considered to be his most likely successor, two women were mentioned over and over in the course of the conflict-laden internal debates on the succession. Women had already held important informal positions of power in the past. Thus, Mayan Khatun (1873–1956), the grandmother and mentor of Mîr Tehsîn Seîd Beg, who himself was appointed to his position at the age of eleven, is still vividly remembered by many Êzîdî. All the same, a Mîra instead of a Mîr would represent a total break with the tradition – but a break that would be quite popular among many Êzîdî in the European diaspora. Under normal circumstances, the successor of a deceased Mîr is elected by the religious council 40 days after the Mîr's death. The fact that this took much longer after the death of Mîr Tehsîn Seîd Beg is a clear indication of the conflicts within the council and the family of the Mîr. This conflict is, however, not primarily about religion, but rather, about politics. In the end the Democratic Party of Kurdistan (Partiya Demokrata Kurdistanê, PDK), which, apart from Dohuk and Erbil, also controls the Êzîdî region of Şêxan, was able to push through its preferred candidate, the previous Mîr's son Hazîm. However, political influence in the decision meant that the new Mîr remains controversial to this day and has so far been unable to match the influence of his father.

Some voices in the diaspora have even demanded to leave the position of the deceased Mîr vacant. After all, the principality of Şêxan which had been ruled by the Qatanî Sheikhs since the fourteenth century no longer exists as a political entity today. During the last decades of his tenure, Mîr Tehsîn Seîd Beg had been no more than the symbolic leader of a princedom that was initially a completelely integral part of the Iraqi state and was later divided between Iraq and the Kurdistan Region of Iraq, that is, a leader who had barely any real function to fulfil. Many Êzîdî from the diaspora openly demanded a politically independent reformer, who then might even be a woman.

Even more conflicts arose after the death of Bavê Şêx in October 2020, again over the political influence of the PDK and ultimately over political rather than religious conflicts. The new Bavê Şêx, Ali Elias Nasir, who was 41 years old when he took office, and so strongly opposed among opponents of the PDK that even counter-Bavê Şêx were appointed, although they also have no real influence. It is unmistakable that the generational change of the two most important offices created a leadership crisis in the religious structure and that there are currently no undisputed leaders in the religious community. Today, the Bavê Çawîş is considered the most likely neutral integration figure.

Just as other religious groups in the region, the life of the Iraqi Êzîdî is generally characterised by a patriarchal social order, and nowhere has this order survived more rigidly than in Sinjar, which has to do with the fact that this region had in a certain sense been the periphery of a periphery. It has been politically and economically neglected for many decades. On the one hand, this state of affairs created a haven for a religious minority, but on the other, it has conserved forms of a patriarchal order which is by now for many Êzîdî a thing of the past.

As with the Êzîdî in Syria, in Turkey and in the Caucasus, the Êzîdî living in Sinjar speak Kurdish; in fact, they speak the most widespread variety of that language, Kurmancî. Kurmancî itself, however, is fragmented into many local dialects. One part of the Êzîdî, particularly in the areas of the former Soviet Union, regard their own idiom as an autonomous language of its own which they call Êzdîkî. Though they do not deny that Kurmancî and Êzdîkî are one and the same language, they regard the glossonym Êzdîkî as an equally proper name for their language, similar to the cases of Catalan and Valencian or Dutch and Flemish. Be that as it may, for the Kurds in Iraq the variety of Kurmancî spoken in Sinjar is identifiable as an autonomous dialect which is different from the Êzîdî dialect in Şêxan and includes a fair number of Arabic words.

However, this dialect is spoken not only by the Êzîdî in Sinjar, but essentially also by Sunni and Shiite Kurds in the region, thus representing a regional rather than a religiously defined phenomenon. Ultimately, the Kurdish spoken in the Sinjar region is a linguistic island surrounded by Arabic speakers, which is significantly closer to Kurdish as spoken in northeastern Syria than to the various forms of Kurdish spoken in the Kurdistan Region of Iraq.

6
The tribal society in Sinjar

In contrast to the emirate of Şêxan, in Sinjar a number of tribes continue to play an enormous role to this day. For 'tribe', the Êzîdî groups use the originally Arabic term 'Eşîret', which is widespread in all of Kurdistan. It can refer both to larger units and smaller subunits. Most tribes in Sinjar exclusively consist of Êzîdî, but there are also mixed tribes that consist of Êzîdî as well as Sunni and/or Shiite Muslims. Thus, in some Eşîret the tribal organisation runs counter to the ethno-religious self-description of the group or its description by others. These mixed tribes emerged via the conversion of part of the tribe or by the inclusion of families with a different religious heritage. Even if a tribe is, in its own ideological understanding, rooted in a common kinship or ancestry, in historical reality new tribes continued to emerge through political alliances which were turned into alleged 'kinship relations' only later by construed genealogies.

The Êzîdî or Êzîdî-dominated tribes of Sinjar formed two big tribal federations, the Jawanah and Khurkan. These were characterised by different ways of life. While the Jawanah used to live in permanent villages and based their economy on growing fruit, vegetables and tobacco as well as on beekeeping, the Khurkan were semi-nomads who primarily raised sheep but also grew corn and vegetables on a seasonal basis. The Jawanah tended to live in the east of the mountains while the Khurkan mostly lived in the west. In winter, the Khurkan used to descend to the plain. But this geographical division offers a rather crude picture because various tribes or subgroups invaded the area of the respective other federation, leading to various territorial shifts. The biggest tribes among the Khurkan were the Haskan, the Samuqah and the Qiran, while the Mandikan, the Chalkan, the Chilkan, the Kurkurkan, the Rashakan and the Haywiriyyah represented somewhat smaller groups. The Mandikan traditionally lived in the east of the Sinjar Mountains and were one of the religiously mixed tribes that included Sunni Muslims, but they were still considered as part of the Khurkan.[1]

The Jawanah consisted of only three big tribes, the Habbabat, the Mihirkan and the Musqurah. Around ten per cent of the Mihirkan were Sunni Muslims.[2] As for the Musqurah, apart from a majority of Êzîdî families and a minority of Sunni Muslims, they also included a number of Shiite families.[3]

Apart from the tribes belonging to the big federations of the Khurkan and the Jawanah, there are many smaller tribes whose ancestors migrated from today's Turkey to Sinjar only over the last 200 years. The reasons for this were both expulsions from the more easily accessible regions of the Ottoman Empire and persecutions by Kurdish princes, for example by Bedirxan Beg in the middle of the nineteenth century. These groups, the Dinna, Khalta (Xalta), Sharqiyan and Çêlka, can still remember the areas of origin of their families and maintain connections to relatives in Turkey and Syria.

Until well into the twentieth century, membership in a tribe was an important organisational feature of social life which was pushed back by the centralisation of the state only slowly, a form which could augment the religious identity of the member, but could sometimes also run counter to it. Just as is the case among the Muslim Kurds, in Sinjar the tribes also play a political role, even though this role is often not immediately visible. For the most part, whole extended families are members of particular parties. But at the same time, there are tribes which attempt to place their contact persons strategically in *all* political and military groups. The tribal system of the region is thus *one* political factor, but it is far from the only one.

It is important to point out that some tribes do not consist of members of only a single religion, but are, in a certain sense, interdenominational, which adds an additional layer to the complex social order of the region. It was only the confessionalised violence of the so-called Islamic State in the twenty-first century that has brought about a clear dividing line between the Êzîdî and the Muslims of the region.

Tribal society was thus to a certain extent interreligious. The rules and norms of customary law in Sinjar also differed little between the Êzîdî and the Muslim tribes. In addition to the already religiously mixed tribes, many Êzîdî also had the habit of consciously entering into kinship relations with Arab or Muslim tribes until 2014. Since marriages between the religions were not possible, other ways were sought to establish such binding relationships. Particularly in northern Sinjar, many Êzîdî had their children circumcised on the lap of a Muslim, creating a quasi-kinship sponsor relationship. The Muslim on whose knees the boy was circumcised became the *kriv*, the boy's godfather. Some of these sponsorship relationships continued in 2014 and resulted in Êzîdî being rescued by their Muslim *kriv*. Conversely, Êzîdî interpreted it as even worse betrayal when this did not happen and they were also betrayed by their godparents.

In the twentieth century, these relations also supported smuggling with Syria, which was an important source of income for both the Arab tribes and the Êzîdî tribes.

7
Sinjar in the late Ottoman Empire

As described in the previous chapters, the access of the central state to the periphery of the Ottoman Empire was quite limited. Until the midst of the nineteenth century, the Kurdish areas in particular were not administered directly from Istanbul, but rather, by local Kurdish princes and tribes. For a long time, this arrangement accorded the Êzîdî in Sinjar a fairly far-reaching political autonomy. On the other hand, Sinjar was over and over again the victim of Kurdish and Muslim attacks.

As for the first half of the nineteenth century, we know only of two military expeditions to Sinjar. A fairly extensive attack by the Mameluke ruler Ali Pasha from Baghdad in 1803 led to the destruction of three or four villages and to the enslavement of several families. His successor Suleiman Pasha attacked Sinjar again six years later.[1]

After Baghdad had, in 1831, again come under the direct rule of the Ottoman Empire in the course of centralisation measures, its ruler, Ali Ridha Pasha, again ruled as a proconsul directly appointed by the High Porte. At that time, the Ottomans also tried to bring Sinjar under the control of the empire. This was caused less by religious motives or resentment against the Êzîdî but had serious political and economic reasons. The goal of the 1837 military expedition against Sinjar by Hafiz Pasha, the governor of Diyabarkır, who was counselled by the German baron Helmuth von Moltke,[2] consisted in becoming able to collect taxes from the Êzîdî in Sinjar and in putting an end to a lucrative economic enterprise practised by some tribes: A number of the Êzîdî in the Sinjar mountains had specialised in attacking travellers and caravans between Mosul and Mardin and felt protected from any criminal prosecution by the isolation of the mountains, a situation that put important trade routes in danger. It was only Hafiz Pasha's military expedition that put a brake on those attacks and led to the establishment of an Ottoman presence in the form of tax collectors in two villages in the north of Sinjar.[3]

For the villages in the mountains, this newly established presence of the state represented a serious blow. A British voyager who travelled the Sinjar Mountains in 1838 described a totally impoverished village on the northern flank of the mountain. When he asked his guide why the inhabitants of the village were not working, the guide is quoted as having answered that until the expedition of Hafiz Pasha, the villagers had occupied themselves all day by being on the lookout for travellers or caravans which they could rob. Since this had now come to an end, there was nothing left to do for the villagers.[4]

But the consolidation of the state at the margins of the Ottoman Empire was not an easy business since it provoked counterreactions. In the course of the Tanzimat reforms of the nineteenth century, Kurdish princes frequently broke with the empire and attempted to expand their own principalities and sovereignty vis-à-vis the High Porte by force. Some of these princes, who many Muslim Kurds today regard as predecessors of the Kurdish national movement, also targeted the regional Christian and Êzîdî minorities in the process.

One of the worst massacres against the Êzîdî in Sinjar was the 1832 'revenge campaign' by Muhammed Pasha from Rawanduz (1783–1838).[5] In retaliation for the killing of a tribal leader of the Muslim Mzuri by an Êzîdî, Pasha had several thousand Êzîdî in Sinjar massacred,[6] and in addition, he also had Christian churches and monasteries looted and destroyed as part of his extermination campaign. No less terrible were the massacres of the Kurdish emir of Cizîra Botan, Bedirxan Beg, who exterminated and expelled parts of the Êzîdî population of the Tur Abdin region[7] between 1836 and 1844. Many of the survivors of this massacre found their way to Sinjar, where they could feel safe because of the Êzîdî majority there. But Bedirxan Beg did not only devastate the Êzîdî settlements on the Tur Abdin, but also attacked Şêxan, destroyed Lališ and had the Mîr sentenced to death. Some of the survivors also fled to Sinjar.[8]

In 1892, the Ottoman general Wahbi Pasha was sent from Mosul to Şêxan and Sinjar with the order to collect unpaid taxes from the Êzîdî. Apparently, he was also tasked with violently converting as many Êzîdî as possible to Islam.⁹ Many of them were only able to escape a certain death by doing Pasha's bidding and converting. The sanctuary in Lališ was transformed into an Islamic religious school and remained in Ottoman hands for a number of years. But from Sinjar, Omar Wahbi Pasha's troops retreated much faster than from the more easily accessible Şêxan. Once more, Sinjar functioned as a retreat area for the Êzîdî.

Thus, even though the Êzîdî in Sinjar were also again and again hit by persecution, the massacres and expulsions in other regions of Kurdistan had the effect that the Êzîdî character of Sinjar became more pronounced and that the region turned into one of the last strongholds of Êzîdxans – the land of the Êzîdî.

The First World War was the last time that Sinjar became a haven for the persecuted, and this time not just for the Êzîdî, but also for the Christians who fled from the genocide perpetrated by the government of the Young Turks and managed to make it to Sinjar, where they were protected by Êzîdî Sheikhs. The Armenian community of Sinjar began with the Christian inhabitants of Mardin who found a refuge in the Sinjar Mountains in 1915 and were able to connect to the region through the Êzîdî tribes that had fled from the Tur Abdin region east of Mardin a couple of decades before because of the persecution by Bedirxan Beg.¹⁰ During the genocide of 1915, the Êzîdî tribal leader Hemoyê Şero, who was the leader of the Dinna tribe which originally came from the Tur Abdin region, saved the lives of almost 20,000 Christians, many whom then chose to stay in the Sinjar region even after the demise of the Ottoman Empire. According to the Êzîdî narrative, during a meeting of Êzîdî tribal leaders in Sinjar which discussed the extradition of the Christian refugees that was then demanded by the Ottomans, Hemoyê Şero refused the demand by saying:

> How can I accept extradite the Armenians, who have come to us for help, to the Ottomans? I promised and swore on my honour to defend them and not to hand them over to the Ottomans as long as I have still a tear to shed. If my sons and I have to die for this, so be it!¹¹

Even though we can't be sure whether the words just quoted are an exact rendition of what was said at the time, they still reflect the concept of honour of the Êzîdî tribes of Sinjar, which includes both hospitality and complying with the promises one has made. His honour would never have permitted to Hemoyê Şero to extradite his guests and thus the Armenian Christians were able to survive in the Sinjar Mountains – until the genocide by IS in 2014.

1849 was the first time that a permanent representative of the Ottoman central power was stationed in Sinjar City, soon to be followed by a military garrison. Though the introduction of the draft in 1854 in theory also applied to the Êzîdî in Sinjar, it could not really be enforced because of the massive resistance of the population. In the 1870s, the Ottoman Qaim Maqam[12] tried to bring the mountain area under control by integrating Êzîdî tribal leaders into the political system, a project that never entirely succeeded. The region thus largely remained autonomous throughout the late phase of the Ottoman Empire.

In February 1918, the shelter that the Êzîdî had been providing for the Armenian and Assyrian Christians[13] during the First World War led to yet another Ottoman attack on Sinjar. The refusal of Hemoyê Şero and the other tribal leaders to extradite the Christians led to heavy losses among the Êzîdî. Finally, the Êzîdî saw themselves forced to send Îsmaîl Çol Beg – who lived in Sinjar and was both a relative and rival of the incumbent Mîr of the Êzîdî – as well as two Armenian refugees and a bodyguard to the British army at the latter's front line near Samarra. Once there, the delegation from Sinjar asked for arms and support to enable it to work out a plan for an attack on Mosul. In Baghdad, Îsmaîl Çol Beg met the British supreme commander General William Raine Marshall and the British archaeologist, explorer and secret service agent Gertrude Bell, who would later draw the borders of Iraq. In July 1918, Îsmaîl Çol Beg returned to Sinjar accompanied by a British officer and an Indian army doctor.[14]

8
The British occupation and protectorate

On 10 September 1918, the Ottoman army, equipped with machine guns and with the support of the air force, undertook its last attempt to bring the Sinjar Mountains under its control. The invasion led to the destruction of many villages. Hemoyê Şero and the other tribal leaders had to hide in caves in the mountains. A few weeks later, the British army achieved a breakthrough at the Palestinian front and was then able to advance up to Syria. But when the ceasefire of Moudros between the United Kingdom and the Ottoman Empire was concluded on 30 October 1918, Musul was still in the hands of the Ottomans. The British army invaded Mosul only on 10 November 1918 after it was evacuated by the commander of the 6th Ottoman army, Ali Ishan Pasha, but after this it secured the whole former Ottoman province of Mosul for itself.

Later on, this became a problem of international law. According to the initially secret Sykes-Picot Agreement, Mosul was meant to end up under French sovereignty. Turkey and the United Kingdom were thus not the only parties to compete for the former Ottoman Wilayat Mosul, but yet another party was France, which had been given the protectorate over Syria. In this book, it would lead us too far afield to discuss the solution of the so-called Mosul question, a question that was only solved by a border treaty concluded in 1926 and which has been over and over again called into question ever since by Turkish nationalists including Turkey's current president, Recep Tayyip Erdoğan.[1]

For Sinjar, this meant to be again in the midst of a controversial border area. Whereas the local Sheikhs wanted to avoid an annexation by Turkey come what might and even though Hemoyê Şero, who was strongly anti-Turkish, entertained close relations with the British, the actual contest for the region was primarily between France and Britain. Initially, in 1919, Hemoyê Şero ruled over an independent region with the support of the British. It was only in 1920 that Sinjar became an administrative unit of British Iraq with two subdistricts called Nahiyya. These subdistricts were Sinjar and Shimal (north). The first had its seat in Sinjar City, the second in the northern settlement of Kerse, one of the few villages in the mountains that are still inhabited today.

The first Iraqi to be appointed as the Qaim Maqam was a Chaldean Christian from Mosul, Yusuf Rassam, in 1920.[2] To the British, Christians with their traditionally good relationships with the local elites seemed better suited for this office than Muslims, even though the Qaim Maqam normally had Arab personnel at his disposal. Êzîdî were not qualified because at that time, there were no schools in the region and there was not a single Êzîdî to be found in the whole Sinjar region who could even read or write. Even though Hemoyê Şero remained an important contact person for the British and was awarded the title of a Hākim[3] of Sinjar, he did not hold any formal office within the new administration.

At the beginning of the twentieth century, school education was offered only in the big cities, but not in mountain regions as far away as the Sinjar Mountains. Hemoyê Şero, who remained the Hākim of Sinjar until his death in 1932, was politically progressive and advocated for the creation of a school for Êzîdî children in Sinjar City. But the school project that was then established with British support did not have a good start because two of the first five students drowned on their way to school in a creek that had swollen from the rain.[4]

On the Sinjar Mountains, the tribes continued to function as important organisational systems. In the 1920s, Hemoyê Şero was faced with increasing challenges from the Sheikh of the Mihirkan, Daud al-Daud. In 1925, the controversies between the Dinna leader Hemoyê Şero, whose tribes had fled from Mardin to Sinjar only in the middle of the nineteenth century and who had adopted a strictly anti-Ottoman and anti-Muslim course, and the Sheikh of the religiously mixed Mihirkan, who had already worked with the Ottomans in previous years, developed into a civil war-like conflict which led to the intervention of the British. In April 1925, the Royal Air Force bombed several villages of the Mihirkan and their allies, and at the beginning of May, all tribal leaders with the exception of Daud al-Daud capitulated. The latter gave up only in July 1925 and was exiled in Nasiriyya in South Iraq, where he stayed until 1928.[5]

The conflict between two factions of the family of the Êzîdî Mîr, which had already been simmering for quite a time and manifested itself in a schism between Mîr Said Beg in Şêxan and Îsmaîl Çol Beg in Sinjar, was solved under the British protectorate by an arrangement in which one third of the revenues of the Mîr family was used for general expenses and various members of the family, and each of the remaining thirds was allocated to Mîr Said Beg in Şêxan and Îsmaîl Çol Beg in Sinjar, respectively.[6]

The border between the French protectorate of Syria and the British protectorate of Iraq was fixed only at the beginning of the 1930s. In the meantime, there had repeatedly been tentative plans for a division of the Sinjar Mountains. But with the final demarcation of the border, only the region of the Khatuniyya Lake and the western continuation of the Sinjar Mountains, the Jariba Mountains, became part of Syria, while the whole proper part of the Sinjar Mountains became a part of Iraq.

But the demarcation of the border divided the areas of the nomadic subtribes of the Arab Shammar who lived around the Sinjar Mountains and entertained mutually advantageous economic relations with the Êzîdî in the mountains. Many of the Shammar on the Syrian side of the border are nomads to this day. The only significant settlement in the border strip that was assigned to Syria is the small town of al-Hawl (also spelled al-Hol) with its 3,000 inhabitants, which has grown very much in recent years because of a large refugee camp that includes a prison camp for women of IS members.

The interception of the large traffic flows along the Sinjar Mountains and its geographical marginality contributed to a much slower development of the region than in other regions of Iraq. The border impeded the connections to the Kurds now on the Syrian side, and in addition, Sinjar was separated from other Kurdish areas in Iraq by the Arabic-speaking regions around Rabiʾa and Mosul as well as by the Turkmen-dominated Tal Afar. The Kurdish areas of the Cizîrê and Sinjar were now separated from each other by the Syrian-Iraqi national border.

At the time when King Faisal I, who was appointed in 1921, led Iraq into the League of Nations in 1932, Sinjar found itself once more at the outer periphery of a state. While that state was one of the first nominally independent Arab states, it continued to be under strong British influence until the fall of the Iraqi monarchy in 1958.

One of the problems in the further history of the Êzîdî – and also in that of other religious and ethnic minorities of Iraq – turned out to be that the British rulers of the protectorate with their system of *indirect rule* used the protection they allegedly gave to the Iraqi minorities increasingly to justify their continued presence in Iraq. In the end, Iraq was heavily pressurised by the British to sign a declaration on minorities as a precondition for the end of the British mandate.[7] The minority question was one of the biggest political obstacles for the release of Iraq into independence and was used by the British to continue to exert its influence on Iraq, even though in Europe itself questions of this sort were often solved in a manner very much to the disadvantage of minorities.[8] This development decisively contributed to a configuration in which Arab-nationalist and anti-colonial circles increasingly tended to identify the protection of minorities with British imperialism,[9] a development that was soon to become a heavy burden for the future of these minorities.

9
The Êzîdî in Iraq

In the new state, the Êzîdî represented a small minority which was geographically limited to a few peripheral areas and whose importance came neither politically nor economically close to that of the Sunni or Shiite Muslims, the Christians, or the Jews. Even though the Êzîdî did not, as the Assyrian Christians,[1] become the victims of persecutions immediately after the founding of the state, they played a role neither in Iraqi politics nor in the cultural life of the Iraqi cities. It was only in 1957, when, towards the end of the monarchy, the first modern university of the country was founded that the small minority of Êzîdî started to be alphabetised.

But compared to their Soviet, Turkish and Syrian counterparts, the Iraqi Êzîdî enjoyed the advantage of not being cut off from their traditional religious sites. Iraq is the home of the religious centre of the Êzîdî religion and has also traditionally been the largest settlement region of that group. The region Şêxan contains the most important religious sanctuary (Lališ) of the Êzîdî as well as the office seats of the Bavê Şêx and the Mîr. Until a few decades ago, the Êzîdî even represented the majority of the population of the region. But the expulsion policy of the Saddam Hussein regime and the settlement of Sunni Kurds by the government of the Kurdistan Region of Iraq after 2003 had turned the Êzîdî into a minority already by 2014.

Apart from Şêxan, the mountain massif of Sinjar (Kurdish: Şingal) and the plains bordering it are also core parts of the Êzîdî settlement area in Iraq. Until the construction of the Mosul dam in 1984/85, there were also a number of Êzîdî villages between Sinjar and Şêxan which included important sanctuaries such as the mausoleum of Sheikh Sebatis.[2] By 2014, Sinjar was the only place where the Êzîdî were in the majority. But all these complexities notwithstanding, more than 500,000 Êzîdî lived in Iraq until the 2014 genocide.[3]

As mentioned above, most Êzîdî in Iraq speak Kurmancî. In the Nineveh Governorate east of Mosul, in Bashiqa and Bahzani, there is an enclave of Êzîdî whose native language is Arabic. Whether that group stopped speaking Kurdish in the course of its history or whether it spoke Arabic right from the beginning is controversial even among the Êzîdî in Bashiqa and Bahzani themselves. The enclave is mostly surrounded by an Arabic- and Aramaic-speaking Christian population and does not directly border on the Kurdish settlement area.

Similar to many other minorities, the Êzîdî of the mountains also came under the pressure of the Iraqi central government and the various Arab-nationalist currents which dominated politics in Baghdad. Already in 1957, that is, still under the Iraqi monarchy, the government had 61 villages on the mountains destroyed for no detectable reason, and their inhabitants were expelled from the mountains.[4] In 1960, after the 1958 overthrow of the monarchy by Abd al-Karim Qasim, in the south of Sinjar 40,000 hectares of land that had hitherto been used by Êzîdî were confiscated and handed over to Arab peasants.

During the rule of the Arab-nationalist Ba'th Party, the Êzîdî were subjected to harsh repression. Under Saddam Hussein, the Arabisation pressure increased enormously. In the 1970s, the regime forced the Êzîdî in Sinjar to leave their mountain villages and resettled them in easily monitored state-organised 'collective towns' (*mujama'at*) in the plains. Only a few mountain settlements were able to survive the rule of Saddam Hussein. Once again, the regime confiscated land and gave it to Arab settlers, which inevitably led to massive conflicts between the Êzîdî and those settlers after the overthrow of Saddam Hussein.[5]

However, the Arabs settled on the border with Syria were mostly from the region. They, too, represented partly forcibly settled former Bedouins. A more detailed analysis of the land reform, in which some landless Êzîdî also profited while large landowners lost land, has yet to be conducted. However, the connection with the regime's Arabisation policy caused a conflictual situation that continues to this day.

10
Resentments against the Êzîdî

There are widespread prejudices against the Êzîdî among both the Arab and the Kurdish Muslims. Apart from the remonstrances of devil worship and the lack of a written narrative already discussed above, many Muslims and Christians accuse the Êzîdî of being dirty and unclean.[1]

In the course of many conversations I had with Muslims and Christians in the region, I was told that the religion of the Êzîdî doesn't allow them to wash themselves. For that reason, it was supposedly unhealthy to eat with them. Apart from the few towns in which the Êzîdî are in the majority, they could never successfully run a restaurant or bakery because they simply would not have any customers.

The accusation of uncleanliness does not have any basis in reality at all, of course. In fact, accusations of this sort have over and over again been levelled against marginalised groups and minorities in both Europe and the Middle East. Of course, 100 years ago the hygienic conditions in the rural villages of an arid region were not optimal. But this had nothing to do with religion and was just as true for Muslim villages as it was for Êzîdî ones.

Even today, almost all Muslims of the region regard Êzîdî food as bad and inedible. Though my own experiences in this realm are rather anecdotal and not really based on any systematic research, they still indicate how deep-seated the cultural and religious resentments are. I have repeatedly noted how Muslim Kurds looked at me in astonishment when I told them that I had eaten with Êzîdî. Many of my friends, including those who are neither particularly religious nor politically reactionary, discouraged me from eating with Êzîdî families. Just for the sake of completeness, I'd like to say that my Êzîdî hosts always treated me with delicious meals and that I have never seen the slightest indication that 'Êzîdî food' is worse or less clean than 'Muslim food'. Nevertheless, the culturally and religiously transmitted prejudice against Êzîdî is so strong that even many progressive, non-religious Kurds or Arabs from Muslim families have great reservations against dining with Êzîdî families. Of course, with very religious and/or conservative people things are even worse.

The relation between the anti-Êzîdî resentments in the Muslim and Christian population of Iraq and the crimes of IS is similar to the relation between anti-Semitic prejudices in Europe in the nineteenth century and the crimes of Nazism. Even under the latter, not everyone was an anti-Semite, but most non-Jews had adopted at least one of the socially dominant anti-Semitic resentments. Just as Nazism only had to systematise, ideologise and radicalise the existing anti-Semitism, IS was able to build on widespread stereotypes and prejudices about the Êzîdî when it attacked the largest settlement area of the Êzîdî in Iraq in 2014.

11
Ethno-confessional groups in the Sinjar region
Êzîdî, Christians, Jews and Muslims

Different from the two other Êzîdî settlement areas in Şêxan and in Bashiqa and Bahzani, the Êzîdî in Sinjar for a long time used to live a predominantly Êzîdî daily life in relatively remote mountain villages. However, this does not mean that Sinjar was exclusively inhabited by Êzîdî and that they did not entertain any relations with non-Êzîdî.

Until the end of the rule of the Ba'th Party under Saddam Hussein, Sinjar City was even predominantly inhabited by non-Êzîdî. The city had always had a mixed population: Thus, in the 1930s the population of Sinjar City consisted of 1,950 Sunni and 476 Shiite Muslims as well as 660 Christians, 485 Êzîdî and 15 Jews.[1]

In contrast to the villages in the mountains, Sinjar City always had a Muslim majority. Moreover, the Saddam regime didn't trust the Êzîdî and only rarely permitted them to settle in the city itself. But as mentioned above, some of the predominantly Êzîdî tribes on the mountain also had a Muslim minority.

In Sinjar City, four languages are spoken: Kurdish, Arabic, Aramaic and Armenian. The city is thus in many respects a microcosm of Iraq in terms of diversity.

The group whose history is perhaps the worst documented one of the many minorities in Sinjar is the small Jewish community. So far, only a handful of persons is historically known, such as Asher Ben Levi from the fourth century, a Jewish shepherd who, after his conversion to Christianity and his alleged martyr's death, became a Christian legendary figure under the name of Abd al-Masih. It is, however, not clear whether there is any historical continuity between the Jewish population of that time and the Jewish community of the twentieth century. But in the first half of the twentieth century, Sinjar City was home to a small Jewish community with a synagogue, a fact that is still visible today in the form of a number of Jewish graves in the Christian cemetery of the city. The synagogue itself has no longer been in use after the emigration of most Iraqi Jews in 1950/51; like a large part of the town in general, the building itself was destroyed in the battles with the so-called Islamic State. Only a few of the older inhabitants of the city still remember the location of the synagogue.

As already discussed, the city Sinjar looks back to a long Christian history. In 1915, the Aramaic-speaking Christian population, which was divided into a Syriac-Orthodox and a Syriac-Catholic community, was joined by Armenian refugees mostly from Mardin, who enjoyed the protection of Hemoyê Şero, the tribal head of the time. The Armenians who had fled from Mardin[2] to Sinjar mostly belonged to the Armenian-Catholic Church, a form of Armenian Christianity which had been unified with the Roman Catholic church in 1742. There was, however, not a single priest among the surviving Armenians. During the visit of the Armenian priest Melkon Dasbazian in 1920, approximately 70 Armenian families used the church building of the Syriac-Catholic community. When another Armenian Catholic priest, Jacob Nessimian, visited in December 1929, the Armenian families expressed their wish for their own church, which was built a short time thereafter and was dedicated to St. George the Martyr on 30 November 1930.[3] In 1936, a congregation of Armenian-Catholic nuns even opened a girls' school in the city. Even though the wish articulated by the community after 1947 to be allowed to emigrate to the Armenian Socialist Soviet Republic was not granted, in 2014 the number of Armenians still living in Sinjar had fallen dramatically.[4]

But even so, in 2014 there were an Armenian-Catholic, a Syriac-Catholic and a Syriac-Orthodox Church in Sinjar City. Almost all Christians lived right in the city of Sinjar; the few Christian families on the north side of the mountains in Sinunê and Xanasor did not have their own church building but were visited on important holidays by priests from Sinjar City.[5]

The religious diversity of the Sinjar region also included various Muslim groups. Both among the Kurdish and the Arabic-speaking inhabitants of the region, a number of Sunni Muslims cooperated with the Islamic State in 2014. Almost the whole Arab population in the environment of Sinjar City is Sunni; in the city itself and in some villages, there are Sunni Kurds as well. The Sunni-Kurdish tribe of the Kêçela is regarded as particularly orthodox and had the reputation of being 'Wahhabite'[6] even before the attack of IS. The Kêçela traditionally used to live in the village Qapûsi, but in the twentieth century, some of them also migrated to the city of Sinjar. Sunni Kurds also lived in the north of the Sinjar Mountains, where they were usually referred to as Tatan and where there is a *ziyaret*,[7] Sheikh Gureish's Ziyaret, visited by both Êzîdî and Muslims and located in a Sunni cemetery.

The Kurdish-speaking tribe of the Babawat is a special group which has often been described in the literature as the group of the Ali Ilahi, a current of the heterodox Shiite 'exaggerators' or Ghulāt sects.[8] One of those who has done so is Nelida Fuccaro, the most important historian of the Êzîdî during the British colonial period in Iraq.[9] The extent to which this characterisation is correct for the beginning of the twentieth century is difficult to determine. The relatively sparse literature and my own conversations with members of the tribe rather tend to yield the picture of a relatively fluid, permanently changing Shiite heterodoxy whose followers entertained close social and religious relations with the Êzîdî and were situated in between Shiite Islam and non-Islamic, particularly Êzîdî influences. Fuccaro reports offerings by members of the Babawat to religious dignitaries of the Êzîdî as well as pictorial representations of the Peacock Angel (Tawûsê Melek).[10] It is said that both groups were almost indistinguishable in their everyday life until well into the twentieth century. Babawat took part in Êzîdî religious ceremonies and conversely, and Êzîdî accompanied the Babawat on their pilgrimages to Pîr Zekr.[11] There was a particularly close relationship between the Babawat and the Êzîdî tribe of the Habbabat.

But in the last fifteen years, the specific form of the pro-Êzîdî Shiite heterodoxy of the Babawat has increasingly made room for an orthodox Shia. The confessionalisation of the political system of Iraq after the overthrow of Saddam Hussein has led to a situation in which small heterodox groups such as the Shabak, the Bajalan, the Sarli, or the Babawat were forced to join larger and more influential groups. Both the influence of parties of the Twelver Shia

and access to education – and therefore, to 'official' Shiite literature – have been leading to a replacement of heterodox practices
by a Twelver Shia orthodoxy. A rural heterodox popular Islam was
thus driven out by the orthodox Islam of the urban scripturalists
who, moreover, enjoyed the support of the Shiite parties and Iran
and whose ideology was regarded as 'urban and progressive' in
comparison to popular Islam.

12
Sinjar under the rule of the Ba'th Party

For the Êzîdî of the Sinjar Mountains, the period of the Ba'thist rule over Iraq represented a massive caesura in their traditional lifestyle. Only a few years after the overthrow of the Iraqi monarchy by the free officers under Abd al-Karim Qasim in 1958, the Arab-nationalist Party of the Socialist Arab Reawakening (hizb al-ba'th al-'arabī al-ischtirākī) took power in a bloody coup in February 1963, even though it lost that power in a series of power struggles in Baghdad, which the inhabitants of Sinjar often only learned about when the tide in Baghdad had already turned again.

All the same, one can detect a certain continuity in the policy of the Iraqi state vis-à-vis the Êzîdî. The destruction of villages and the traditional economy of the mountain farmers on the Sinjar Mountains began already in 1957, continued in 1965, and also went on under the rule of the Ba'th Party. These measures were not always specifically directed against the Êzîdî as a religious minority, but guided by an ideology of progress that regarded isolated mountain villages as backward and was aimed at the complete penetration of the whole Iraqi national territory. Regions that had existed autonomously for centuries, that were largely independent economically, and whose miniscule settlements resisted the grip of state control represented a barrier for the modernisation that was an important goal of the centralist national state. The creation of a modern infrastructure with schools, roads and electricity in the course of the various phases of the authoritarian modernisation of Iraq was only feasible if the citizens of remote mountain areas could be forced to assemble in larger and more easily accessible settlements.

The second coup of the Ba'th Party in July 1968 proved more durable than the previous regime changes. Now, the party started to build an increasingly authoritarian system which finally resulted in the 1979 takeover of Saddam Hussein. First between 1973 and

1975 and then between 1986 and 1987, almost 400 villages on the Sinjar Mountains were destroyed and their inhabitants were resettled in so-called collective towns (*mujama'at*). The original villages 'were rendered uninhabitable by flattening their houses with bulldozers and similar methods'.[1]

The collective towns, which were also built for Sunni Kurds and other rebellious parts of the population, were big guarded settlements with an infrastructure much more modern than that of many of the villages their new inhabitants came from; this was the basis on which the Iraqi government presented them internationally as 'development projects'. All *mujama'at* consisted of uniform town house complexes with small vegetable gardens and easily controllable asphalted streets in a chess board pattern, and all of them had a school, a police station and a health centre. The houses had electricity and running water, which were provided for free by the state. On the other hand, these settlements also served the purpose of a systematic supervision of the population in which the schools and the infrastructure of the state were used for propaganda and the totalitarian penetration of the whole society. It is thus not by accident that most model villages were established during the two big Kurdish uprisings in Iraq between 1970 and 1975 (the uprising under Mulla Mustafa Barzani) and in the 1980s (the uprising under the leadership of the Patriotic Union of Kurdistan, PUK). During its so-called Anfal campaign against Iraqi Kurdistan between February and August 1988, the Iraqi regime once again built model villages to resettle the survivors of this genocidal counterinsurgency campaign there.[2]

Even though the Anfal operations didn't take place in Sinjar, but in the provinces Dohuk, Kirkuk, Silêmanî and, in particular, the Germiyan region around today's city of Kalar, the construction of model villages in Sinjar had a similar function as in the core of Kurdistan. While the model villages in Dohuk, Kirkuk and Silêmanî openly served the goal of counterinsurgency, the goal of those in Sinjar was to prevent an expansion of the uprising. This tactic was known from Latin America: It was designed to prevent the guerrilla from getting support from the population and from being able to hide within it. In the calculations of the military, in the absence of lonely mountain villages and hamlets difficult to control by the government, the Kurdish guerrilla fighters, the

Peshmerga, would have a hard time procuring food and creating a durable infrastructure.

In contrast to the region of Silêmanî, which bordered Iran with which Iraq was at war at the time, Sinjar was not a centre of the uprisings against the regime of Saddam Hussein, but here, too, there had been a number of smaller incidents in the 1970s. Furthermore, Sinjar was in a potentially dangerous proximity to a hostile neighbouring state: During the Iran–Iraq war, Syria supported Iran, harboured Iraqi oppositionists, and promoted a faction of the Ba'th Party hostile to Saddam Hussein. Moreover, oppositionists from Sinjar went into exile in Syria, among them, in 1982, the Shesho (Kurdish: Şeşo) family, which has by now become very important. Qasim Shesho owes his reputation as an unbending oppositionist and greatly feared fighter primarily to the fact that he simply shot the members of the Iraqi secret service who secretly met with him to persuade him to return to Iraq.

According to an official investigation, in 1976 there were 11,544 houses in the *mujama'at* of the Sinjar Mountains. All newly built settlements were given Arabic names. In the north of the mountains, there were al-Yarmūk with 1,120, at-Ta'mīm with 1,195 houses, a-'Urūba with 510, al-Andalus with 771, Huttīn with 1,531 and al-Qādisīya with 858 houses, and in the south, al-Walīd with 907, al-Ba'th with 1,300, al-'Adnānīya with 838, al-Qahtanīya with 1,334 and al-Jazīra with 1,180 houses.[3]

The Êzîdî in Sinjar were not the only ones affected by these forced resettlements as they were also carried out in Şêxan, and between 1985 and 1986, the Êzîdî villages along the Tigris north of Mosul, which had been a kind of connecting link between Sinjar and Şêxan, were drowned in the floods of the Mosul dam. Moreover, the Iraqi regime tried to split the Êzîdî from any kind of Kurdish identity and to Arabise them. To that effect, it used both the newly created Arab-language schools in the *mujama'at* and a plan to utilise certain personalities in the Arabic-speaking minority among the Êzîdî in Bashiqa and Bahzani to promote the claim that the Êzîdî were actually a part of Arabhood. After the census of 1977, the Êzîdî were officially registered as Arabs.[4]

Part of the Arabisation efforts were projects for the political instrumentalisation of Mîr Tehsîn Se'îd Beg, who had been in office since 1944, and to ram through a new Baba Sheikh (Kurdish:

Bavê Şêx) agreeable to the regime. And indeed, at the end of the 1970s the regime succeeded in installing a Baba Sheikh, Sheikh Ilyas (Şêx Îlyas), who was loyal to the regime; he governed until 1995 and publicly described the Êzîdî as Arabs.[5]

In its secular phase, that is, before 1991, the Ba'th regime tried to present itself to the Êzîdî as a guarantor against encroachments by political Islam. To this day, Êzîdî who served in the army report that the Ba'thist officers had always protected them against religiously motivated hostilities. In 1991, the regime resorted to the classical policy of 'divide and rule' and pointedly employed Êzîdî soldiers to fight the Shiite rebels in southern Iraq. Moreover, both Êzîdî fighters and Muslim Kurds were deployed as so-called Fursān, that is, paramilitary auxiliary troops, against Kurdish insurgents. Dismissively described as 'Cahş' (donkey foals) by the Kurds, the Fursān played an important role in crushing the insurgencies in the region. Just as the Kurdish Muslims, the Êzîdî found themselves, for various reasons, on both sides of the conflict. During the Ba'th period, Sinjar itself was mostly under the rule of Fursān loyal to the regime. Even though many Fursān were massively pressurised to participate in the counterinsurgency campaign and even though the Êzîdî as a group became a victim of the forced Arabisation policy of the Ba'th regime, in this period there was no persecution of the Êzîdî that could be said to have been specifically motivated by religion.

The destruction of the villages in the 1970s and 1980s led to an end of the traditional mountain farmer culture of the Sinjar Mountains. Only very few villages survived; one of them was Kerse, the former seat of the northern subdistrict. At the end of the Ba'th regime, the overwhelming majority of the mountain peasants found themselves as farmers in the model villages the regime had established for them, most of which were located at the bottom of the mountains or even, as Koço, quite far away from them. In Sinjar City itself, only very few privileged Êzîdî families with good connections to the regime where allowed to settle, while many Sunni Arabs from hitherto nomadic tribes or the small city of al-B'aj now flocked to the city.

When uprisings against the Ba'th regime broke out in many Kurdish areas and South Iraq after the second Gulf war of 1991, the situation in Sinjar remained relatively quiet. Even though Sinjar is

north of the 36th parallel and was therefore covered by UN Resolution 688 of 5 April 1991, which established the northern no-fly
zone for the protection of the Kurdish civil population, Sinjar
never fell into the hands of the insurgents. The Kurdish Peshmerga
never crossed the Tigris in a western direction but rather focused
their activities on the Kurdish core areas east of the Tigris. Different from some Kurdish and south Iraqi cities, Sinjar also did not
witness any spontaneous popular uprising. Just as the provincial
capital, Mosul, Sinjar remained under the control of the regime.

The ceasefire line between the forces of the Iraqi regime and
the new, de facto autonomous Kurdistan Region ran through the
Şêxan region, right through Êzîdî settlement areas. While Şêxan
itself and the Arab-speaking Êzîdî strongholds in Bashiqa and
Bahzani remained under the administration of the regime, Ba'adra,
the seat of the Mîr, and Lališ, as well as a few villages further to the
east ended up under Kurdish control. With this development, the
Êzîdî population of Iraq was split into two parts. For most Êzîdî,
the ceasefire line was now an insurmountable barrier. The Êzîdî
from Sinjar were cut off from the religious celebrations in Lališ.
Only the Baba Sheikh got a special permit to make his traditional
religious visits on both sides of the ceasefire line.

For Sinjar, the period between 1991 and 2003 was a phase of
intensified alienation from the Kurds, who were building their
own para-state in Erbil (Kurdish: Hewlêr), Silêmanî and Dohuk
(Kurdish: Duhok), fought out a war from 1994 and 1997 between
their two big parties, the Democratic Party of Kurdistan (Partiya
Demokrata Kurdistanê, PDK) and the Patriotic Union of Kurdistan (Yekêtiy Nîştimaniy Kurdistan, YNK, PUK),[6] and, in 2003,
joined the United States in its bid to overthrow Saddam Hussein
and the ruling Ba'th Party after all. In the parts of the Êzîdî settlement area ruled by the PDK, so-called 'Lališ Cultural Centres'
were established which were supposed to represent the Êzîdî community but were under the exclusive control of partisans of the
PDK and were regarded with a lot of scepticism by most Êzîdî
outside of the PDK.

Meanwhile, Sinjar remained under the control of the regime
in Baghdad, which was no less totalitarian than in 1991 but was
weakened by the UN embargo established in August 1990 by the
UN Security Council Resolutions 660 adopted after the Iraqi

occupation of Kuwait. For Sinjar, this meant further economic marginalisation. In this period, many people could survive only by smuggling. People who did not participate in one or another form in smuggling networks, which were in turn closely connected to the regime, barely had a chance to survive. Moreover, and in contrast to the rest of Kurdistan, independent aid organisations had no access to Sinjar. The infrastructure and the conditions of life in the region could only be described as disastrous when, during the night from 19 March to 20 March 2003, President George W. Bush gave the order to begin 'Operation Iraqi Freedom', which ended the Ba'th regime after 35 years in power.

13

After the fall of Saddam Hussein

Between Baghdad and Erbil

Sinjar was conquered only right at the end of the third Gulf war. The Kurdish Peshmerga who participated in the liberation of Iraq as allies of the US also remained east of the Tigris and were for the moment satisfied with conquering the Kurdish areas around Kirkuk and participating in the conquest of Mosul. While Baghdad was captured already between 7 April and 9 April 2003, the US troops reached Sinjar only on 12 April. After the collapse of the regime in Baghdad, the mountain fell into the hands of the US army with barely a struggle.

But not everyone in the Sinjar region welcomed the new rulers as liberators. In Sinunê, after 12 April parts of the local population even rose to fight against the approaching US and Kurdish units. The continuing armed resistance of some groups of young men resulted in a street in Sinunê being temporarily nicknamed 'Falluja', alluding to the city in central Iraq which was the site of heavy fighting between armed Sunni rebels and the US army between the end of 2003 and November 2004.

With the US army, the Kurdish Peshmerga and the Lališ cultural centres came to Sinjar as well. The Sinjar Mountains came under the influence of the PDK, whereas the PUK secured Kirkuk for itself. However, like the Nineveh Governorate or Xaneqîn, both regions remained 'Contested Areas' which were claimed by the newly recognised autonomous Kurdistan Region of Iraq while the new Iraqi central government saw things quite differently. Even though article 140 of the new Iraqi constitution provides for referendums in Kirkuk and all other 'Contested Areas' which are to decide whether or not they shall belong to the Kurdistan Region, up until now, these votes have never been held despite the fact that this article of the constitution envisioned both a 'normalisation process' for Kirkuk and a deadline for the referendums on 31

December 2007.[1] Though this contest focused primarily on the oil-rich province of Kirkuk, for Sinjar this permanent delay of a settlement of the status of the 'Contested Areas' also meant permanent insecurity with regard to the future of the region and the creation of parallel structures on the political, and even more so, on the security level. In Sinjar, the Peshmerga of both the PDK and (to a far lesser extent) the PUK were present, but in accord with the Iraqi curriculum, the teaching in the schools was done in Arabic. Parallel structures of this sort did not enhance the security of the region but undermined the possibility to establish a state's monopoly on the legitimate use of force.

But the biggest problem for the region was the emergence of a military underground network which increasingly underwent a development from Arab nationalism to Sunni jihadism and was able to gain a foothold among the Sunni neighbours of the Êzîdî. The confessionalised violence which swept Iraq since the end of 2003 complicated the relationships between the Sunni Arabs (and, in part, the Sunni Kurds) on the one hand and the Êzîdî, the Christians, the Babawat, and the other Shiites on the other hand.

In Sinjar, the confessionalised conflict in Iraq interlocked with a number of conflicts which must be regarded in part as legacies of the old regime. With the regime change, the (Sunni) Arabs lost their privileged positions. After the arrival of Kurdish Peshmerga, some Arabs loyal to Saddam Hussein who had settled in Sinjar during the Ba'th regime returned to their original region around al-B'aj, where they felt more and more marginalised because of the new political situation. For many followers of the Ba'th regime who regarded the occupation of the country by the United States and the presence of Kurdish military troops as humiliating and who drew a connection between this experience and their own status loss, armed underground groups became increasingly attractive, and among these, confessional Sunni groups more and more got the edge on secular nationalist groups.

The armed underground was to a mounting degree dominated by jihadist formations. Immediately after the overthrow of Saddam Hussein, the Jordanian jihadist Abu Musab al-Zarqawi first rallied dispersed groups around a so-called 'Community for Monotheism and Jihad' (Jamā'at al-Tauhīd wa al-Jihād) and then, on 14 October 2004, swore an oath of allegiance to Osama bin

Laden, thus turning his organisation into a part of the globally active network of al-Qaida. The organisation worked under the name 'Organisation of the Base of the Jihad in Mesopotamia' (Tanzim Qā'idat al-Jihād fī Bilād ar-Rāfidain) before rechristening itself 'Islamic State in Iraq' (dawlat al-'Irāq al-'Islāmiyyah, ISI).[2] It used targeted attacks on Shiites to foster confessional violence and became the most important Sunni terror organisation in Iraq.

The confessionalisation of all conflicts was accompanied by a revitalisation of old resentments against the Êzîdî. In a similar way, the Shiites were accused of heresy, and the Christians were suspected to be part of the invasion of 'crusaders'.

For the heterodox Babawat, these developments had consequences that were possibly even more far-reaching than the ones for the Êzîdî. The increasing confessionalisation led to a clearly visible drift of this group towards the orthodox Shia, which by now had also gained a lot of political strength. This group of heterodox followers of a Ghulāt cult, which used to share many of its practices with the Êzîdî, was now increasingly morphing into a Twelver Shiite tribe. The retrospective justification for this development is the claim that the group had gained the knowledge that was necessary to acquire the 'correct Islam' only after 2003. A Babawat I talked to put it this way:

We didn't know anything about our religion and did things that were contrary to it. After the exit of the Saddam regime, we were finally able to practise it freely and to learn more about our true religion. Now, the Shiites are no longer oppressed. Now, we can learn more about our religion and practise it just as other Shiites in Najaf or Kerbala do.[3]

Though there are Babawat who regret the loss of their traditions, according to the narrative dominant today the turn towards the orthodox Twelver Shiite Islam represents a 'return' to 'true Islam' and is a result of freedom and education. Many Êzîdî see this switch in religious affiliation differently. An Êzîdî friend explained his own view of this development of the Babawat as follows:

In the past, [the Babawat] were with us. They had a close relationship to us and were not particularly religious. But in the past years, they have become religious. Now, they don't want to participate in our ceremonies and celebrations anymore. Now, they are with the Shiites.[4]

A number of Êzîdî also felt forced to take refuge with a bigger group by the ethnicised and confessionalised conflict situation. A substantial part of the Êzîdî tried to find a haven in Kurdishness, or rather, in the Democratic Party of Kurdistan (PDK), which dominated the north of the autonomous Kurdistan Region and supplied most of the Peshmerga present in the region. Here, we can mention the accession of Qasim Shesho and Mahma Khalil, who later became the mayor of Sinjar City, to the PDK. Since 2003, the PDK, which expanded its primarily oil-rent-based patronage system[5] to Sinjar after that date, gained more and more influence on the Êzîdî in the region, whereas the Êzîdî associated with the PUK did not have much to offer to anyone. Though the PUK had important Êzîdî representatives such as Haydar Shesho, who was elected as a member of the Iraqi transitional parliament in January 2005, or the doctor and intellectual Mirza Dinnayi, who became counsellor for religious minorities of the new Iraqi president Jalal Talabani, in Sinjar the PUK fell victim to the intra-Kurdish division of territory between the PUK and the PDK. Moreover, the PUK-ruled areas around Silêmanî and Kirkuk were far from Sinjar; the revenues of the PUK were much lower than the ones of the PDK and because of its focus on the central government in Baghdad it lost much of its influence in Kurdistan. Even more ineffectual in gaining a foothold in Sinjar was a splinter group of the PUK, the List for Change (Lîstî Gorran) founded in 2009 by Newşîr-wan Mistefa Emîn. Throughout his life, Newşîrwan Mistefa Emîn remained focused on Silêmanî, a place where Gorran managed to develop into a regional party which, even though it claimed to represent all of Kurdistan, was never present in the Kurdish north. The Iraqi Communist Party or the Communist Party of Kurdistan (Partiya Komunîstî Kurdistan) proved to be just as incapable of gaining a foothold in Sinjar. Immediately after 2003, the Kurdish Workers' Party (Partiya Karkerên Kurdistanê, PKK) was also totally absent from the region. The first contacts with the PKK developed only after the attacks of 2007, when some members of the Khalta (Xalta) who had immigrated to Sinjar from a region of today's Turkey only in the nineteenth century and were related to other Êzîdî in Turkey, drew closer to the group.

The economic and infrastructural development in Sinjar lagged miles behind the one in Erbil or Dohuk. Apart from the LALiş cultural centres, which many people regarded more as parts of a spying apparatus of the PDK than as meaningful cultural institutions, the Kurdistan Regional Government did very little in this area. It almost seems as if neither Baghdad nor Erbil felt any real responsibility for the population of this politically contested religion.

14
The massacre of 14 August 2007
The 73rd firman?

Many Êzîdî regard the attack on two Êzîdî villages in Sinjar on 14 August 2007 as the 73rd firman. The original meaning of this Ottoman concept was 'edict' or 'decree', but because of the experience of the Êzîdî with persecution, it became a symbol for massacre or genocide. The Êzîdî had talked for a long time about the 72 firmans they had had to suffer, but this number was actually a euphemism for 'very many'. There are many other examples for this in the Middle East: Hacıbektaş Veli, who is revered by the Alevi, is reported to have said that 'all 72 peoples' must be regarded as equal, and even in the Christian New Testament, in Luke 10.1 we find a story about the 72 disciples of Jesus. In the Êzîdî context, the 72 languages or peoples,[1] the 72 feathers of a bird[2] or the 72 bones of a fish[3] are mentioned over and over again. The 72 firmans thus refer to a large number of massacres perpetrated against the Êzîdî. With the secularisation and modernisation of the region, most Êzîdî lost their knowledge about the mythical significance of the number, which has led them, both in the diaspora and in Iraq, to actually count the massacres. For this reason, for many Êzîdî the attacks on 14 August 2007 became the 73rd ferman.

These attacks were preceded by an intensified anti-Êzîdî propaganda, which was first and foremost sparked by the murder of a young woman. On 7 April, the seventeen-year-old Êzîdî girl Du'a Khalil Aswad had been stoned to death by her own relatives in the Arab-Êzîdî enclave of Bashiqa in the Nineveh Governorate. After the Baba Sheikh himself had given shelter to the young woman who had fallen in love with a Muslim, she later trusted the assurances of her family and returned to Bashiqa, where she was stoned in broad daylight and in the presence of police officers. Since the murder was filmed with a mobile phone and the video was put on the internet, for many Muslims it became a symbol of Êzîdî cruelty. While the killing of young women who engage in partnerships with persons deemed as illegitimate by their society is unfortunately widespread in Iraq, including its Muslim population, in this case various Muslim groups portrayed the crime as an anti-Islamic murder, claiming that Du'a Khalil Aswad had converted to Islam, which meant in turn that the Êzîdî had actually murdered a Muslim. Neither the clear condemnation of the murder by the highest Êzîdî clerics nor the fact that four of the murderers were sentenced to death in 2010 were able to change this narrative.[4] Though the brutality of the murder, the non-interference of the police, the participation of an enraged mob and the fact that, after the murder, the victim was buried together with the remains of a dog as a further sign of humiliation did not fail to trigger indignation within the Êzîdî community as well, these factors combined to serve as the ideal background for a jihadist propaganda offensive against the Êzîdî.

On 22 April 2007, 23 Êzîdî workers from Bashiqa were dragged from a bus by jihadists who then proceeded to execute them in the open street. The perpetrators explicitly justified the massacre as revenge for the death of Du'a Khalil Aswad.

Many observers also relate the later attacks of 14 August 2007 to the murder of the seventeen-year-old woman, but the evidence for this is very unclear. The anti-Êzîdî propaganda in the months after 7 April may have played a role in them, but no group or organisation has ever claimed responsibility for the attacks or provided any public explanation. Because the perpetrators were Muslims and the victims Êzîdî, it is generally assumed that the assault was an attack by the Islamic State in Iraq (ISI), but in contrast to other, similar attacks, the organisation never published a letter claiming responsibility. That cells of ISI were present in the surroundings of Sinjar is proven by a document found by the US army in the course of a house search near Sinjar in October 2007. It was a list of international fighters who had come to Iraq from Syria.[5] But nevertheless, it remains unclear who was responsible for the attacks of 14 August 2007.

What *is* clear is that on 14 August 2007, two lorries loaded with explosives arrived almost simultaneously – at 7:30 and 8:00 a.m. respectively – in the Êzîdî villages of Til Êzêr and Siba Şêx

Xidir, and were designed in such a way that the local population believed they were carrying aid, inducing them to rush towards them. The two suicide attacks killed more than 500 people and wounded another 1,500. The background remains unclear to this day. Some observers assume jihadist perpetrators, while others claim that one of the perpetrators was a Muslim who had fallen in love with a young Êzîdî woman who was then also killed by her own family.[6] But this version is denied by other local Êzîdî, though a combination might also be possible in which this particular perpetrator coordinated his actions with ISI. Some Êzîdî think that the attack was the work of an extremist nationalist Turkish organisation; others suspect a cabal by the secret service, while still others even accuse the Democratic Party of Kurdistan (PDK) to have been behind the attacks to construct a pretext to subject the region to the control of the Kurdistan Regional Government. The majority of these theories are likely to be conspiracy theories; on the other hand, none of them can definitely be excluded. The fact that these theories circulate to this day is not just a result of the lacking solution of this case, but also shows how upset and unsure the local population is. The only unequivocal conclusion is that this was not the work of individual perpetrators.

For the Êzîdî population of the region, the attacks of August 2007 were a continuation of previous violent acts 'by Muslims' (a continuum which is reflected in the description as the '73rd firman'), but also showed that the Êzîdî could not expect sufficient protection from the state in the new Iraq. The attacks helped to strengthen the dominance of the PDK Peshmerga, but the region remained a 'Contested Area' which was controlled by Kurdish security forces, but whose school education was still provided in Arabic and by Iraqi schools run by the central state, and which did not profit from the economic boom of the Kurdistan Region of Iraq.

After the attacks, many local Êzîdî began to look for allies, but not all of them turned to the PDK and its Peshmerga. Thus, the Khalta (Xalta) started to gravitate towards the PKK and made their first contacts with a political and military movement which would later, in 2014, gain decisive importance in the struggle against the so-called Islamic State.

15
Encircled by jihadists

After 2006, the jihadist Islamic State in Iraq (ISI) began to gain the upper hand as the strongest terrorist group among the initially very diverse underground organisations in Iraq.

One of the strongholds of the jihadist underground network was in Mosul, which is not far from Sinjar. Already since 2007, many Êzîdî and Christians regarded the city as extremely dangerous territory which had to be avoided if possible. Êzîdî students went to universities in Baghdad, Dohuk, or Erbil and avoided the much closer and quite prestigious university of Mosul. For the Christians in the Nineveh Governorate, an offshoot of the University of Mosul was founded in the Christian-Aramaic town Bakhdida,[1] which became a university of its own in 2014. Sinjar remained cut off from these projects and didn't get any institutions of higher education.

With the beginning of the Syrian civil war, ISI began to build jihadist groups in Syria and in the process, it used the networks which had supported the jihadist underground in Iraq from Syrian bases before 2006. The stretch south of Sinjar became one of the central supply routes for Jabhat al Nusra, which was founded in Syria at the end of January 2012. Jabhat al-Nusra functioned as the Syrian branch organisation of the global al-Qaida network and brought, in part in collaboration with other oppositional militias, large parts of eastern Syria under its control. In April 2013, the leader of the Islamic State in Iraq (ISI), Ibrāhīm 'Awād Ibrāhīm al-Badrī, who became known under the name Abū Bakr al-Baġdādī, declared the Syrian group to be a part of his own organisation which would hence be called Islamic State in Iraq and Greater Syria (Šām) (ad-dawla al-islāmiyya fī al-'Irāq wa'š-Šām, ISIS). But this fusion was rejected by the leadership of Jabhat al-Nusra, which was by now largely acting autonomously, and thus sparked the beginning of the split between al-Qaida and ISIS.[2] Months of uncertainty between the two jihadist currents followed. Finally, ISIS succeeded in getting the upper hand in eastern Syria and pushing what was left of Jabhat al-Nusra to northwestern Syria.

Even before ISIS captured larger territories in Iraq, a substantial part of its supply was smuggled to Syria via routes south of the Sinjar Mountains through Tal Afar or south of Sinjar via al-B'aj. In the small town of al-B'aj, there were many Arab Sunni who had once profited from the Ba'thist Arabisation policy and who now felt expelled from Sinjar. Quite probably, some Sunni from Sinjar were also involved in the smuggling of arms and other resources. The main thoroughfare from Mosul to eastern Syria went through Rabi'a in the northeast of Sinjar, but until August 2014, one had to pass Arabic-speaking areas under the control of Kurdish Peshmerga on this route.

The city Tal Afar to the east of Sinjar was also a stronghold of ISIS, which had many followers and a strong underground structure in the town. This relatively big city with a population of more than 200,000 before 2014 is almost completely inhabited by Shiite and Sunni Turkmens.[3] After 2003, the Sunni Turkmens turned towards Turkish nationalism; their parties, particularly the Turkmen Front of Iraq (Irak Türkmen Cephesi, ITC), were lavishly supported by Ankara. But a part of them cooperated with jihadist underground groups already in 2004. The Shiite Turkmens on their part enjoyed the support of various parties in Iraq. Here, too, the legacy of Saddam Hussein contributed to the social division of the city. The B'ath regime had built generous new neighbourhoods such as Hay al-S'ad, Qadisiyah and Hay al-Bouri for its Sunni supporters which, in contrast to the Shiite residential areas, had a well-functioning infrastructure with running water and permanent power supply.

But after 2003, the Shiites gained the upper hand while the Sunni Turkmens felt betrayed because they had lost their dominance. Both the fact that the Shiites who had been despised until 2003 were now able to do business and became the new upper class while the formerly privileged Sunni had to face social degradation and the fact that the Badr Brigades, the military wing of the Supreme Council of the Islamic Revolution in Iraq (SCIRI), invaded the city and increasingly dominated politics and the economy led to massive dissatisfaction on the part of the former favourites of the regime. Mutual acts of revenge led to a permanent and massive increase in confessional tensions. Already in 2004, there were uprisings by Sunni Turkmens. The bombardment of Sunni neighbourhoods by the US army was ended by the intervention of Turkey. In May 2005, the city fell almost completely into the hands of Sunni rebels under the leadership of al-Qaida, causing thousands of Shiites to flee. In September 2005, Tal Afar was recaptured by Iraqi and US units and the Shiite dominance was re-established. On 27 March 2007, there were two bomb attacks using lorries loaded with explosives, killing 152 people.[4] In the following unrest, more than 100 people were reportedly killed.

In the succeeding years, the city remained insecure territory and was regularly haunted by smaller attacks and shootings. Sunni Turkmens from Tal Afar rose to important posts within ISIS even before 2014. Many Turkmen ISIS commanders in Iraq were known to hold strategic positions in the organisation and to harbour a particular hatred against Shiites, but also against other religious minorities.

Only a week after Mosul had fallen into the hands of ISIS almost without a battle, on 16 June 2014 the jihadists also succeeded in capturing Tal Afar after two days of fighting. Tens of thousands of Shiite Turkmens fled to Kurdistan, to southern Iraq, and to Sinjar, which at that time was still under the control of Kurdish Peshmerga of the PDK. The refugees were warmly received by the local Êzîdî, Christians and Shiites. They told of rapes and murders by the ISIS fighters and reported that many of their Sunni neighbours had turned against them. The Shiite Turkmens from Tal Afar did not only identify ISIS with Iraqi or international jihadist fighters, but also with their Sunni neighbours whose names they knew and with which they had often been in conflict, but with whom they had also entertained normal social relations which had now been violently cut off.

Spurred by their success in Mosul and Tal Afar, on 29 June 2014 the jihadis proclaimed a caliphate and renamed their organisation into 'Islamic State' (ad-daula al-islāmiyya, IS), a step with which they also asserted their claim to be the *only* Islamic State and to be establishing a worldwide caliphate which was supposed to include all Muslims.

The reaction of the Kurdistan Regional Government was muted. Even though it formally condemned IS, initially – in June and July 2014 – IS was not perceived as a particular threat to the Kurds. With the almost complete dissolution of the Iraqi army in the northern provinces of Iraq, many Kurds now saw an alternative way to solve the question of the 'Contested Areas' and of article 140 of the Iraqi constitution, which had never been put into practise. Already on 10 June 2014, the Peshmerga declared that they had taken over all areas with a Kurdish population falling under article 140. This included large parts of Kirkuk and several south Kurdish regions, but also the Nineveh Governorate and Sinjar. At that time, the Peshmerga were the only military force that could have stopped IS.

But many functionaries of the governing PDK actually regarded IS as an opportunity to finally smash the unloved state of Iraq and to proclaim an independent Kurdish state on its ruins. The private reaction of quite a few followers and office-holders of the PDK to the IS campaigns of conquest was literally euphoric. On 1 July 2014, Masoud Barzani, the president of the autonomous Kurdistan Region of Iraq, told the BBC that Iraq was already 'effectively divided' and that the Kurds would carry out a referendum on their independence from Iraq within the next few months.[5]

Horror of a new neighbour certainly sounds different. At the beginning of July 2014, IS was perceived as a problem of the Arabs. Almost all Kurdish actors were sure that IS would be satisfied with capturing the Sunni-Arab areas of Iraq. What exactly went on behind the scenes we will probably never know, even though to this day there are rumours in Kurdistan that until the beginning of July 2014 there were arrangements between IS and the Kurdistan Regional Government that the leadership in Erbil expected IS to keep. In any case, there certainly were communication channels between IS and Erbil which initially nourished the latter's hope that IS could be a good neighbour for an independent Kurdistan. But for the religious minorities such as the Christians and Êzîdî whose settlement areas now bordered on the areas under IS rule, the situation looked much more ominous.

16
The IS genocide in August 2014

After the conquest of Mosul and Tal Afar, the Êzîdî knew that they were in enormous danger, even though the Peshmerga of the PDK were still in the city and assured them that they felt responsible for the protection of the population, and would act differently from the Iraqi army in Mosul, which had largely run away without a fight.

The partial dissolution of the Iraqi army was accompanied by the return of young Êzîdî recruits to Sinjar. Many of them had taken their weapons with them and were willing to defend their homeland. Haydar Shesho, the ex-member of parliament of the PDK, rallied the young men around himself and tried to build a self-defence militia supposed to support the Peshmerga in the defence of the region. Some 3,500 men registered. But the Peshmerga and the leadership of the PDK under the Sunni Muslim Sarbast Baiperi from Dohuk prohibited Haydar Shesho and the Êzîdî men from arming and organising themselves. In addition to that, the security forces of the PDK collected most of the weapons that the Êzîdî had brought with them from the army. According to Haydar Shesho, the Êzîdî lost about 80 per cent of their weapons in this way.

But Haydar Shesho was not the only one who tried to prepare for the defence of the region. The followers of the PKK had gained a foothold in the region since 2007, and since the withdrawal of the Syrian army from the Kurdish areas of Syria in 2012,[1] they entertained close relationships both to the sister party of the PKK, the Democratic Union Party (Partiya Yekîtiya Demokrat, PYD) ruling there and to the People's Defence Units (Yekîneyên Parastina Gel, YPG) founded by the PYD. Now, they also began to arm themselves. In July 2014, the YPG trained a first group of fighters who would later, in August 2014, form the Resistance Units of Şingal (Yekîneyên Berxwedana Şingal, YBŞ).

The fact that even despite the threat represented by IS, there was no wave of refugees in the region in July 2014 and that Sinjar even became a sanctuary for Shiite Turkmens from Tal Afar demonstrated that the majority of the population trusted the assurances of the Peshmerga. But this trust was severely shattered in the early morning hours of 3 August 2014, when IS fighters attacked Ger Zerik (also Gir Zerik), a small village southwest of Sinjar City midway to Ba'j. Even though the men of the village were able to keep the IS fighters at bay for several hours, thus enabling the flight of women and children in the direction of the mountains, the promised help from the Peshmerga who were stationed only 15 kilometres away did not materialise. After a little more than three hours, the men from Ger Zerik had to give in to the superior force of the IS fighters and retreated in the direction of Sinjar. But even so, the Êzîdî fighters from Ger Zerik also succeeded in retarding IS long enough to enable messengers to alert the population in the other places in the area. Without this delay, probably even fewer civilians would have been able to make it to the mountains.

As the leaders of the Êzîdî would soon realise, the Peshmerga were not willing to defend the population; instead, they organised their own retreat. On 3 August 2014, all 8,000 Kurdish Peshmerga stationed in the Êzîdî villages and towns in Sinjar retreated without a fight.[2] Sinjar City was handed over without a struggle in the morning hours of the same day. Perplexed Êzîdî observers later reported that offices and official buildings were orderly transferred and that sometimes even the official records in those places were relinquished to the new power holders.

While many Êzîdî civilians from Sinjar City and the surrounding areas succeeded in fleeing to the mountains and many of the residents of the cities and towns on the northern side of the mountains were able to flee into the direction of Kurdistan, in the early morning hours of 3 August 2014 around 1,700 inhabitants of the former 'model village' Koço were cut off from all getaway routes. On that day, an Arab Sheikh from al-Ba'j gave Ahmad Jaso Mato, the mayor of Koço, a call and invited him to a meal in a private home. Once there, the mayor was confronted with the demand that the citizens of Koço and the nearby village Hatimiya raise the white flag. If they did, they would be treated well and would be able to continue to lead their normal lives.[3] Most inhabitants acceded to the demand and the village fell into the hands of IS without a fight. At first, the situation remained quiet, a fact which nourished the hope of normalisation in the residents who were still there. The IS fighters forced the villagers to hand over their weapons, but otherwise the Êzîdî of Koço could freely move around in their village. Mayor Ahmad Jaso Mato was in phone contact with his brother Naif Jaso Mato. The latter tried to convince the Kurdish authorities and international opinion of the necessity of a rescue operation for the trapped villagers but met with deaf ears on all sides. Only a few media outlets reported on the situation in Koço which increasingly receded into the background in the face of the suffering of the refugees on the mountain.

More than 50,000 Êzîdî, Christians and Shiites had fled there because they had not been able in time to take their cars and flee in the direction of the Kurdistan Region of Iraq. More than a quarter of the roughly 200,000 refugees from the Sinjar region were travelling by foot. Among the expelled, there were many old people, sick persons and children, all of whom now had to hold out somehow in the scorching August heat of the largely shadowless mountain slopes of the Sinjar Mountains. During the first hours and days of this siege, numerous people died from sunstroke and thirst. The Sinjar Mountains has too few waterholes for such a large number of people, and for many of them, the supply brought by helicopters of the Iraqi army began too late. In the beginning, medical treatment was also lacking. In August 2014, the temperatures on the Sinjar Mountains reached 41 degrees in the shade. Anyone who has ever been on the mountain in August knows what that means.

On 3 August 2014, the IS fighters perpetrated a massacre among those who did not manage to flee to the mountain. On that day, more than 500 Êzîdî and Shiites were shot in Sinjar City alone. The inhabitants of the small village of Hardan, northeast of the Sinjar Mountains, left their village too late and were mostly murdered by their Muslim neighbours, who belonged to the Arab Juhayish tribe. Next to the massacre of Koço, this massacre was probably the worst single massacre of the Êzîdî. Altogether, on 3 and 4 August, about 2,000 civilians in the region were murdered and unceremoniously dumped into mass graves. Many graves were filled in with earth only superficially. In the following weeks, dogs dug out many of the bodies and fed on the flesh of the dead. Even in the summer of 2016, one could still see bleached bones and skulls lying about between the clothes and car keys of those who had been murdered. It was only on 15 March 2019 that experts of the United Nations Investigative Team for Accountability of Da'esh/ISIL (UNITAD) and the Iraqi government began with an orderly exhumation of the mass graves[4] in order to match the human remains with the persons they had once belonged to, to bury them in dignity, and to collect evidence for the pending trials of the war criminals. Altogether, 82 mass graves of victims of IS were found in the region until the beginning of April 2019.[5]

For those on the mountain, it turned out to be critical to survive the first few days. Helicopters of the Iraqi army brought water, food, tents and blankets, and took some of the refugees with them on their way back, flying them into safety in the Kurdistan Region.

The IS forces pointedly destroyed religious sites of the Êzîdî and did the same to the Shiite Sîti Zayinab Mosque on a hill at the edge of Sinjar City, to the (also Shiite) Pîr Zekr shrine, the Ahl ul-Bayt mosque, and to all the churches of the city. Alarmed by the news from their relatives and by the media reports, the Êzîdî in the diaspora tried to organise help. In Europe, this turned out to be very difficult. I know from personal experience that innumerable emails to politicians went unanswered almost all the time. In Europe, the beginning of August was holiday season. Like everyone else, the politicians were either on the beach or hiking in the mountains. The office staff of the ministerial bureaus were reduced to a minimum, the parliaments closed.[6] Against the odds of this initially difficult situation, the diaspora of the Êzîdî and their few friends played an important role in focusing public attention on this topic and in finally bringing about a US military intervention against IS. In this enterprise, the mostly young Êzîdî activists profited a lot from the modern social media.

On 5 August, the Iraqi parliament convened in Baghdad. The Êzîdî Vian Dakhil Sheikh Said, an MP for the Democratic Party of Kurdistan (PDK) since 2010, made an interpellation to the president of the parliament which she used for a flaming appeal in support of her fellow believers in Sinjar. With a tearful voice, she cried out:

I do not stand here to give a speech to the Iraqi people but to tell you about the bitter reality the Êzîdî are experiencing on Mount Sinjar right now. Mr President, under the banner of the call 'There is no god but God', 500 men and boys have been slaughtered up to now!

Despite the request from the presidium to return to the topic of her interpellation, Vian Dakhil unwaveringly continued her emotional speech: 'Mr President, our women are turned into slaves and sold on slave markets. There is a genocidal campaign under way against the Êzîdî.' After yet another unsuccessful attempt by the presidium to interrupt her, the MP ended her speech with the words:

Please, Mr Speaker, my people are being slaughtered! Just as all Iraqis are being slaughtered, Shiites, Sunnites, Christians, Turkmens and Shabak. Today, it's the Êzîdî who are being slaughtered. Brothers, despite our political differences, we demand human solidarity. I am speaking in the name of humanity! Save us! Save us! For 42 hours, 30,000 families on the Mount Sinjar have been under siege, without water and food. They are dying! So far, 70 babies have died from thirst and dehydration. Fifty old people have died because of these terrible conditions. Our women are taken as slaves and sold on slave markets. Mr President, we demand that the Iraqi parliament intervenes to immediately stop this massacre. The Êzîdî have suffered 72 genocides and this is now repeated in the twenty-first century. They are slaughtering and destroying us! A whole religion is obliterated from the face of the earth. Brothers, I am appealing to your human solidarity: Save us!

Immediately after this, Vian Dakhil broke down in tears. Her speech went around the world. Vian Dakhil gave a face to the desperation of the Êzîdî, the face of an educated woman in a parliament, a face that even US politicians could not so easily shove aside.

In these August days in 2014, it was certain individuals who made all the difference. The MEP Michel Reimon flew to the Mount Sinjar and reported about the horror; in Washington DC a handful of Êzîdî personalities succeeded in getting President Barack Obama to intervene militarily. The US public hardly even knew about the existence of the Êzîdî. So urgent was the search for scholars somewhat competent in the topic that the *National Geographic* gave me a call during a mountain hike in the Alps because they wanted to understand why IS proceeded with such particular ferocity against the Êzîdî. Fortunately, there was another expert, Khanna Omarkhali, an Êzîdî colleague from Armenia who teaches at a German university, who I could also refer to the very interested journalist of the *National Geographic* as a contact.

Even though it appears unimaginable from an Iraqi perspective, the political establishment in Washington DC was completely surprised by the events in Sinjar. In this situation, a very significant role fell to the small Êzîdî diaspora in the United States. Already on 6 August, a handful of Êzîdî protested in front of the White House to call attention to the events in Sinjar. Of particular importance in these days was Dakhil Shammo, a young Êzîdî journalist who worked for the Kurdish service of the US government channel *Voice of America*.[7] Together with Hadi Pir, a former army interpreter from the small Êzîdî community in Lincoln, Nebraska,[8] Hussein Khalaf and a few other US Êzîdî, he contributed significantly to convincing the Obama administration that it had to rush to the help of the Êzîdî fighters on Mount Sinjar.

From 8 August on, these men also helped to establish the communication with the local fighters in a very practical way. On that day, the US began with its air strikes against IS. In order to identify the right targets, part of the communication with the local fighters was arranged through the mobile phones of the group around Dakhil Shammo, Hadi Pir and Hussein Khalaf in the US, who had suggested a meeting at the White House to coordinate with the Kurdish People's Defence Units (Yekîneyên Parastina Gel, YPG) in Syria and not with the Iraqi Peshmerga who had run away from IS only shortly before.[9] Already on the following day, the Syrian YPG and the fighters of the People's Defence Forces (Hêzên Parastina Gel, HPG), that is, the fighting units of the PKK, managed to open a corridor from the Syrian border to the Sinjar Mountains that enabled around 35,000 of the 50,000 civilians encircled on the mountain to flee into the YPG-controlled areas in Syria. Most of those who were saved in this way were immediately brought back to Iraq via the border crossing near Semalka/Faysh Khabur (Kurdish: Pêşabûr) and found refuge in the camps for expelled people in the province Dohuk in the Kurdistan Region of Iraq. There, they were able to meet relatives who had managed to flee IS through the north of the region. But about 5,000 Êzîdî from Sinjar remained in Rojava, which is how the Kurdish-controlled area in Syria was called at the time, and settled in the Newroz camp that was established especially for them near the town of Dêrik.

After the corridor to Syria had been closed, around 15,000 people remained on the mountain under the siege of IS and had to be supplied by air. They were defended by two Êzîdî militia, which had only light weapons and almost no military training but were highly motivated and knew their home region inside out. Since the opening of the corridor, the Resistance Units of Şingal (Yekîneyên Berxwedana Şengalê, YBŞ), who were supported by the YPG and the PKK, were reinforced by fighters of the YPG and the YPJ, the Syrian People's and Women's Defence Units, as well as by the HPG. The Resistance Group of Şingal (Hêza Parastina Şingal, HPŞ) founded by Haydar Shesho at first largely fought on its own.

In the meantime, the residents of Koço were still encircled by IS and found themselves in a trap. The mayor and the other notables tried to find a modus vivendi with IS. But guarantees by a local IS emir by the name of Abu Hamza Salem Yunus Hamza Al-Ahmadi[10] to the contrary, it became clearer and clearer that the condition for the continued existence of the village was the conversion of the population to Islam and participation in the activities of IS. The mayor, Ahmad Jaso Mato, then contacted the mayor of the much smaller village of Hatimiyah, which was also cut off, to work out a joint strategy. The two agreed to join their efforts to organise an escape to the mountain.[11] But the mayor of Hatimiyah did not stick to the agreement and apparently thought he was able to sneak his population to the mountain more or less unnoticed if he tried to do this without the much more numerous residents of Koço. And indeed, on 12 August the villagers of Hatimiyah fled to the mountain without IS noticing.

For the population of Koço, this meant a massive aggravation of the situation. At first, the IS fighters put on an ostensibly generous air and spread the rumour that Abu Bakr al-Baghdadi himself had decided that it was no longer obligatory for them to convert to Islam. Another group of fighters asked whether the population wanted to convert to Islam or whether it wanted to go to the mountain. The mayor explained that the inhabitants preferred the road to the mountain, after which the IS fighters offered to escort the villagers there. On 15 August at 11 a.m., around 100 lorries and military vehicles arrived and took the whole population including the mayor to the fairly spacious village school. The men were brought to the ground floor, the women to the floor above. The IS fighters then asked everyone to hand over all their possessions. At that point, many villagers still believed they would be taken to the mountain to join the other Êzîdî. Ahmad Jaso Mato, the only male taken to the first floor along with the women, told them to hand over their property so as not to anger the fighters.[12] While the women did so, the males were taken outside of the village, forced to dig pits, and then shot right at the edge of the holes they had dug. Only a very few managed to survive because the perpetrators had erroneously left them for dead. Altogether, on 15 August about 600 men and boys from Koço became victims of IS. Ahmad Jaso Mato's increasingly desperate attempts to move the Iraqi or US army to undertake a rescue mission had failed. In the end, when the mayor and the women became aware of what had happened to the men, and when it was no longer possible for them to doubt their own fate, the women held captive in the school even asked, via the brother of the mayor, to have the building bombed by the air force in order to be spared the fate of being dragged away and raped by IS. But this wish also fell on deaf ears. The captive women were neither released nor bombed.[13] Ahmad Jaso Mato was shot in the schoolyard, and the women and children were distributed among the IS fighters and marched into slavery.

Some of the women from Koço, such as the later Sakharov Prize winner Lamiya Aji Bashar, and Nadia Murad, the 2018 Nobel Peace Prize winner, later reported about the torture the kidnapped women from Koço had to go through. By now, almost all of the survivors have left Iraq and emigrated to Germany, Australia or other places. The village itself, which was liberated only in 2017, is now completely empty. In the school, the US-Êzîdî NGO Yazda has established a small provisional memorial site. In March 2019, the Iraqi government proclaimed its intention to establish an official memorial for the victims of the genocide of the Êzîdî in Koço.[14]

In February 2021, the identified remains of 104 victims were finally transferred from Baghdad to Koço in a very dignified ceremony and buried in their homeland. Among those returned in this way was the then mayor and tribal leader Ahmad Jaso. The graves have since been located directly behind the school where the men and women of the village were held.

In the village of Başuk, which used to be inhabited by several hundred members of the Êzîdî-Muslim Mandikan tribe,[15] all Êzîdî could be saved because the Sunni showed solidarity with them and for eight days hid all those who, because of their age or illnesses, were unable to flee to the mountain from the IS fighters patrolling in the village, despite the high risk for themselves that they incurred by doing so.[16]

In other places, the situation was much worse. Whoever didn't make it to the mountain in time and was regarded as a male of fighting age or beyond was executed, while the women and children were taken captive, regarded as spoils of war, raped and enslaved. In this, the women and the girls of Koço were far from being the only ones.

The story of Ali Saleh Qasim (Elî Salch Qasem), community doctor in Koço

Four days before 15 August 2014, the emir of IS, Abu Hamza Salem Yunus Hussein al-Ahmadi, came into our village and told the mayor and Sheikh of Koço, Ahmad Jaso, that he didn't want to convert us to Islam but would take us to the mountain so that we could join the other Êzîdî. From there, he said, we could go to Kurdistan, to our families, or wherever we wanted.

On 15 August between ten and eleven o'clock in the morning, I was in my house and was just giving a boy a pill; I was the community doctor. Then I watched 15 to 20 IS cars enter the village. All of the cars were black. One of them drove up to my house and stopped in front of my door. I told the mother of this boy, 'I think they are coming to kill us.' But she responded, 'No, they won't kill us.' After half an hour, they went to the house of Ahmad Jaso, the Sheikh, and told him that all women and men had to come to the school within half an hour and were only allowed to take their money, mobile phones and some small stuff with them. Thus, we all went to the school. The women and children were brought to the first floor, the men to the ground floor. Abu Hamza stood before Ahmad Jaso, the Sheikh of the Mandikan: 'Give us all the money of your people!' Thus, we collected all our money and handed it to the emir. Five minutes later, he said; 'Give us all your mobile phones!' We then gave him our mobile phones. Yet another five minutes later, he said: 'Give me your gold!' and Ahmad Jaso ordered us to give him the gold, which we all did. After this, Abu Hamza said in Arabic (because he talked to us in Arabic): 'I told you and advised you to become Muslims, but you didn't do that, and you are free not to do it.' We responded, 'Oh, we thank you for this, and may God bless you.' He then said that all those of us who converted to Islam would remain unharmed and would be protected within the borders of the Islamic State.

We didn't say anything to this and kept quiet. We are not Muslims and want to remain Êzîdî, and we remembered that just four days ago, Abu Hamza had promised us to take us to the mountain. But now we were told to come out of the building. At first, twenty to thirty people were escorted outside and huddled onto a small Kia pickup. These were all old and sick men. One of them, his name was Ravo Mukri, was eighty-five years old. He said to the IS fighters, 'We are 30 people and we don't have space enough on such a small car!' But the IS fighters only said, 'Shut up and get up on the car!' A small boy, my little son, wanted to come with me, but the IS fighters told him to go back to his mother.

Outside of Koço, they stopped at a house. Altogether, it was three cars. Then they told us to climb down. One man who was older than 80 had a hard time doing this. They chased us from the car and when we went to the house, in there, we saw four IS fighters with their guns. After a few minutes, one guy took photos of all of us. A man next to me said, 'They take photographs of us and then they will kill us.' The IS fighters shouted, 'Hurry up! Hurry into the line!' One of them was now shouting all the time, 'Allahu akbar! Allahu akbar!' and then they started to shoot at us. None of us was left standing, they killed all of us. I was the only one who was only hit in the left knee. I fell down, but I was not dead.

I lay on the floor beneath the other people, but I didn't move. I kept totally quiet and pretended to be dead. I wanted them to think I was dead. And after a few minutes, they did go away, to another car, and shot the people from that car.

After I hadn't heard anyone move for half an hour, I crawled away and went to the house of my cousin, Naif Jaso, who had been in Dohuk at the time of the arrival of IS. There, I met Raval Ammo, Xidr Hassan Ahmed, Idris Basho Silo, Giço Ammo Silo and Qasim Hafto – we were all in Naif's house. After half an hour, we realised that we had no water. We needed water, and therefore four of us went to the Arab village Biske Jenubi, where we got water. One of the men in this village, Jasem Abdallah, was a friend of mine. Before the arrival of IS, he had often been at my house and he used to eat with us and to sleep at our place. When he saw us, he called Naif Jaso, who was in Dohuk, on his mobile. He told him, 'Your cousin, Ali Saleh Qasim, is here!' But to me, he said that we should go: 'If you are caught here by IS, they will kill us as well, so please, go away from here!' And I responded, 'OK, we are leaving.' We went from one place to another, but none of them was safe. In the end, we holed ourselves up in a field, hiding in such a way that only our heads were sticking out, and after the sun had set at around seven o'clock in the evening and darkness had descended, we went in the direction of the mountain.

When we had reached the east of the village of Hamadan between midnight and one o'clock in the morning, the dogs of the village began to bark and ran in our direction. The IS fighters noticed and once again, we had to act as if no one was there. Then we continued to walk to Gelermi Hirkan, where we drank water. They also gave us food and we walked on towards Çêl Mêra. There, we reached the PKK. They gave us food, water and tea, and provided us with medical care. They took us to Syria with a car, to the hospital in Dêrik. We stayed there for a night and then, on 18 August, I said that I wanted to go back to Dohuk in Kurdistan to another hospital, and thus they brought us back to Kurdistan.

Three of my children, Saleh, Basman and Hassan, and my wife Sahu Issa were killed by IS. My mother, my sister and my five brothers were also killed. The same happened to the three children of my brother. They killed them all. Only one of my sons, Ayas, had marched to the mountain two or three days before IS killed everybody. Another one of my sons, Dilşad, was in Turkey when IS arrived here. Dilşad wanted to go to Germany and therefore he managed to survive in Turkey. And two of my daughters were kidnapped by IS. Now that they have been freed, they are also in Germany.

None of us have returned to Koço. All the survivors either went to Germany or Australia. I, too, have put myself on the list of those who want to go to Australia. Under no circumstances can I live here anymore, next to all the murderers who have killed my children and my wife. After all, many murderers were from here; they used to be our Arab neighbours. When Abu Hamza came here on the first day, he was accompanied by two men from the neighbouring village, people who I've known for a long time. The name of one of them is Khalaf a-Aid, the name of the other Abu Khaled. Nothing has happened to them, and I don't want to encounter these people all the time. No, I can't live here anymore. I came only back here to Koço because I wanted to visit my village one more time before I go to Australia. Nobody will come back to this place.

17
Genocide

The German-Êzîdî jurist Serhat Ortaç has given a detailed explanation for his verdict that the persecution, enslavement and
murder of the Êzîdî by IS has to be regarded as a genocide in the
sense of the genocide convention. Article II of the Convention on
the Prevention and Punishment of the Crime of Genocide, which
was adopted after the destruction of the European Jews by Nazi
Germany and with reference to the genocide of the Armenians in
1915 (a convention which Iraq joined in 1959), says that there is
a genocide if one of the following acts is 'committed with intent
to destroy, in whole or in part, a national, ethnical, racial or religious group':

(a) Killing members of the group;
(b) Causing serious bodily or mental harm to members of the
    group;
(c) Deliberately inflicting on the group conditions of life cal-
    culated to bring about its physical destruction in whole or
    in part;
(d) Imposing measures intended to prevent births within the
    group;
(e) Forcibly transferring children of the group to another
    group.

In the case of the practices of IS, the commitment to destroy the
Êzîdî as a group in whole or in part is undoubtedly present. IS
itself did not leave this in any doubt. Thus, the IS propaganda
magazine *Dabiq*, which appeared from June 2014 (Ramadan
1435) to July 2016 (Shawwal 1437) before it was replaced by its
successor magazine *Rumiyah*, explained very clearly that at the
Last Judgment, the Muslims would be taken to task for having
allowed the continued existence of the 'pagan minority' of the
Êzîdî, given what the verses about the sword in the Quran say about

such groups.[1] The deliberate destruction of cultural and religious sites, the forced conversions, the mass executions, and the jihadist indoctrination of the children are all proof that IS did not just aim at killing individual Êzîdî, but that it targeted the whole group and its religion for destruction. IS is indubitably guilty of four out of five practices mentioned (a, b, c and e), each of which alone would be sufficient to meet the criterion of genocide. Therefore, Ortaç is quite correct in concluding 'that IS has committed a genocide of the Êzîdî in the sense of the genocide convention. Moreover, the United Nations have stated several times that IS has very probably committed multiple additional crimes against humanity as well as war crimes which do not fall under the criterion of genocide.'[2]

In recent years, the 2014 genocide has also been officially recognised as such in various ways by an increasing number of national parliaments and international organisations. Both the United Nations and the European Parliament have used the term genocide in various documents. National parliaments, such as those of Armenia, Belgium or Australia, have also recognised the genocide.

More controversial so far is the question of the concrete naming of the genocide. While the Kurdistan Regional Government, for example, repeatedly emphasises the Kurdish character of the victims, it is not difficult to see that there are essentially political interests behind this. The persecution of IS was clearly directed against the Êzîdî and not against Sunni Kurds – some of whom were even involved in the persecutions. The Êzîdî were definitely not the only victims of IS, which also persecuted Shiites, Christians and members of other religious minorities, as well as political opponents. However, the Êzîdî were systematically persecuted as Êzîdî, and their persecution was justified as such. It was not their Kurdish language or their political views that led to their murder, persecution and enslavement, but solely their membership in the ethno-religious group of the Êzîdî.

18
The reintroduction of slavery and sexual violence

In its glossy magazine *Dabiq*, IS justified the reintroduction of slavery with the claim that the Êzîdî are 'devil worshippers and Satanists', and declared that the Sharia students of IS had been tasked even before the conquest of Sinjar with finding out how this group of 'polytheists' ought to be treated in true Islam.[1] In contrast to Christians and Jews, in the case of the Êzîdî they regarded it as impossible to just have them pay a poll tax (*jizya*) and then allow their continued existence as wards under the rule of Islam. IS argued that because the Êzîdî were actually polytheists and not apostates, and therefore people who had only superficially adopted an Islamic terminology but had never been real Muslims, it was allowed to take their women and children as slaves. For that reason, the argument continued, it was in accord with the Sharia, or with what IS understood by the Sharia, that the captured women and children were divided up between the participants in the attack, while a fifth of the 'spoils' were handed to the authority of IS. IS proudly proclaimed that its assault on Koço resulted in the biggest enslavement of people since the abolition of the Sharia.[2] With these claims, it invoked some classical Islamic voices such as the companion of the prophet Abū Huraira, who is known as the transmitter of the Hadiths (that is, the sayings and acts of the prophet), or the Hanbalite scholar Ibn Rajab.[3] Even though it could not directly base its arguments on the Quran, IS regarded itself as entitled to these measures of enslavement by the long history of Islamic slavery and by the reflections of various Islamic legal scholars.

At first, the kidnapped Êzîdî women and girls were brought to three main registration sites: a school in Tal Afar, the Badush prison in Mosul, and a hall for marriages in Mosul. In these three camps, hundreds or even thousands of women and children were

The story of Şerihan Rajo

In October 2018, Şerihan Rajo told me her story. She explicitly asked to have it disseminated in Europe under her real name, which is why her narration is reproduced here in full and in her own words, translated from Arabic to English. The story of Şerihan Rajo is representative of many stories of many young Êzîdî women enslaved and raped by IS in 2014. Şerihan Rajo is one of the courageous survivors who do not balk from talking about their terrible experiences. Other women – famous ones such as the Peace Nobel Prize winner Nadia Murad and less famous ones who are still living in the tent camps of the expelled – have also told their stories. Still many others have not been able to do this. The suicide rate among surviving former prisoners of IS is alarmingly high. Şerihan Rajo, however, seems to have inherited the courage of her mother, who defended herself and her children against IS and lost her life while doing so. Today, a mural of this resilient woman is on display in the city centre of Sinunê. Şerihan Rajo herself has narrated her story publicly in Iraq and has asked to disseminate it in Europe as well. She wants the whole world to know what was done to her and the other Êzîdî women.

My name is Şerihan Rajo, I come from Sinjar, and I am twenty years old. Because of the genocide of IS against the Êzîdî, I had to flee to the mountains with my mother and my brother. On our way there, a red car of IS followed us and tried to capture us. My mother didn't want to surrender; she wanted to prevent the IS fighters from kidnapping and beating us and from raping me. She didn't give up. She had got a small pistol from my father which was hidden in her bag. At the crossing to Sinunê, my mother took out her pistol and proceeded to shoot one of the IS fighters, wounding another one. After this, my mother was killed by 27 shots right in front of my eyes.

They drove my brother and me to Xanasor, where we stayed for four days. They beat, raped and abused the girls and women, and murdered the men who were with us. My brother was also beaten and murdered. After these four days, they took me to a Syrian school. On the first floor, there were Êzîdî men and boys, on the second the Êzîdî women, girls and children.

We stayed in this school for a month. Then they put the women and girls in buses and sent them to Tal Afar. The older women were brought to another village. The men were also taken there. I was driven to a big farm in Tal Afar together with around fifty to sixty girls. Each day, the IS fighters beat and raped us. Each time, they singled out another group to do this.

I was then brought to Tal Qasab and Tal Banat [two Êzîdî villages in the Sinjar region] together with two girls. Once there, we were again beaten, abused and raped. We were also forced to fast on Ramadan and we got nothing to eat and drink. We stayed there for almost a week; then they brought me to Koço, where I stayed for a month together with other Êzîdî families.

In Koço, little girls were taken away from the breasts of their mothers. Women were beaten. Men were beaten or even murdered. Everyone from ten-year-old girls to fifty-year-old women were raped. Then we were again carted off, this time together with nine girls, to a farm in Raqqa [in Syria]. There were many other Êzîdî prisoners there, more than in Koço. The IS fighters were lodged on the first floor, and the Êzîdî women, girls and children were on the second floor. There were no Êzîdî men and nobody knew anything about them.

After a week, we made preparations to flee, but our plan failed. They didn't give us anything to eat or to drink. Each day, different IS groups arrived from Syria, Mosul and Tal Afar, beating us with sticks and insulting us.

Then I and another girl were taken to a village near Aleppo. She had a broken leg. Her name was Salwa and she came from Xanasor. After a month, they separated her from me. The names of the men who took her away are: Abu Sa'id al-Jasrawī, Abu Abdullah al-Jasrawī, Abu Abdulaziz al-Jasrawī and Abu Zaid al-Jasrawī. Abu Abdulaziz al-Jasrawī took Salwa home with him.

Now I was alone in this house near Aleppo. Abu Sa'id al-Jasrawī tied my hands, tore my clothing and raped me.

I stayed with Abu Sa'id for three months. After that, Ramadan came, but for us, there was no Iftar[4] and no Suhūr.[5]

Whenever I had the chance to find something to eat, I hid the food beneath my clothes and went to the toilet or the bathroom in order to eat surreptitiously. I wasn't able to endure fasting for 30 days.

Each Ramadan, we were beaten and called infidels and insulted by the IS fighters. They said that we and our parents had no religion, no god and no belief, and that they would force us to convert to Islam.

After three months, Abu Sa'id al-Jasrawī decided to sell me. He photographed me and set a price for me.

I was bought by two men, Abu Abdullah al-Iraqi and Abu Anas al-Iraqi. They took me back to Iraq, to the village of Rambussi.[6]

After I had stayed a week with Abu Abdullah and Abu Anas, I was sold again, and this time I ended up in the village of al-Ba'j.[7]

I was bought by Sa'd Talal and Abu Talal Kurdi and stayed with them for about a month. Then Abu Talal sold me to Abu Nasser al-Shami from Mosul. I stayed in his house in Mosul for yet another month.

I got pregnant from Abu Talal. Then came Ramadan. Why was I supposed to fast while I was pregnant?

Each day, Abu Talal beat me and brought groups of IS fighters to his home, some of whom were fifty years old. How can ten-year-old girls put up with a fifty-year-old? Abu Nasser wanted to sell me. During the first three months of my pregnancy, he beat and raped me every day. He presented me daily to his IS group, and he photographed and prepared me for selling me to someone else.

At that time, there were already bombing attacks every day. But the entry door was locked and I wasn't aware of them. He also didn't give me anything to eat.

Because of his abuse, his beatings and his rapes, I lost my child after four months of pregnancy.

Then he sold me to Abu Ahmad al-Jasrawī, who lived in the village al-Nūr near Mosul. I had to stay there for two or three months together with four other girls until he sold me to Abu Ibrahim al-Iraqi.

After a month at Abu Ibrahim Al-Iraqi's place, I was sent back to Raqqa and sold to Abu Sarah Al-Iraqi. Abu Sarah lived in a big building and he already owned two Êzîdî girls. After one or two weeks, he sold me to Abu Mua'z al-Tūnisī.

Abu Mua'z al-Tūnisī brought me to his family house, to his housemaids. I think that he is married to two women. I had to clean the two floors of his house all by myself and I suspect the maids were raped there as well.

Then I was bought by Abu Abdulrahman al-Urduni. He has two wives, with whom I then lived for a year. He is thirty-four years old and he raped a ten-year-old girl. I saw with my own eyes how he went into the room and raped her, while she cried, shouted and begged for help.

The girl is still very young and Abu Abdulrahman is much older than her. How can the girl endure all the things he does to her?

These people don't have any piety at all. We Êzîdî have never killed, abused or harmed anyone. Why are they doing this to us? The Arabs living right around us have perpetrated this genocide against us. During this year together with the other girl, we couldn't escape and got nothing to eat and drink. Then Abu Abdulrahman sold me to his neighbour Abu Omar al-Jasrawī, who took me to his maids but then took me back after a week. He sold me again. This time, I was sold to Abu Huda al-Iraqi of the village Hamadi Omar. I stayed with this man, Abu Huda in Hamadi Omar, for a year. He had many Êzîdî in his house, all were there to be sold. All of us felt like sheep on an animal market: the men always come in to look at us, asking themselves whether to buy us. We rise one after another and they undress us and loosen our hair. Sometimes, they simply come in, beat us and take us with them by force. The even pull us by our hair. Abu Huda sold me to his neighbour Abu Al-Qaʿqaʿ al-Jasrawī, but after two weeks, he took me back.

Then he sold me to Jabhat al-Nusra[8] in Idlib, where I spent a month in prison, totally alone. There was no one and absolutely nothing in this prison. There was only a toilet, but not even a faucet. I had to drink the toilet water because I couldn't stand the hunger and the thirst. I lay down on the floor without a blanket or anything else and couldn't do anything throughout the day. I always heard the noise of men beating other men, but I couldn't distinguish the Êzîdî men from the Muslim men. I suspect that the men being beaten were Êzîdî men.

After a month, they picked me up from the prison and brought me to Abu Abdullah al-Daghestani.[9] After two days I was driven from his place to the Jebel al-Sauieh [near Idlib]. They offered me to a man, but he didn't want to buy me. A second man also declined.[10]

I told them that we are Êzîdî, that we have killed no one, abused no one, and never done any other evil as well: 'You have your religion and we have ours.' They responded: 'No, you are *kuffar* [infidels]. You don't know God and you also don't believe in him! You don't pray and you won't get into paradise. Why are you talking about your people? Do you think that you can escape or kill us?' And then they beat me.

Then I was bought by Omar Abu Abdullah. He is from Baghdad and lives in Jebel al-Sauieh. I stayed with him all alone for three or four months and didn't know how to get away from him. He has two wives, but they were not there. Each day, he either beat me or bound my hands and raped me. He didn't give me anything to eat and thus I had to eat dry bread and drink the toilet water to survive. I didn't know what to do.

There was no way out. Then I had the idea that I could claim I wanted to convert to Islam (but only to save my life and not because I was convinced of it). From then on, I did everything Omar wanted me to do. I prayed, I fasted, and I even memorised half of the Quran. That pleased him very much and he told me, 'You are going back to the Êzîdî!' But my response was, 'No, the Êzîdî are *kuffar* [infidels] and I don't want to go back.'

Then he asked whether I wanted to call my father and my sister. I said that in my opinion all Êzîdî were infidels and that I wanted *them* to come to where we were and to convert to Islam. I figured this was the only way my escape plan could possibly work. He gave me a mobile phone and told me to give my father and my brother a call. But I said that I didn't want to leave Islam and that I didn't want to go back to this infidel religion. He gave me a big iPad and I stored his number and the number of my parents in it.

When he was at home, I prayed, fasted, read the Quran, cleaned and took care of him. He believed me and allowed me to go shopping unaccompanied. I always came back home. Three times, he offered to drive me to my parents, but each time, I rejected and said that my family are *kuffar*. He tested me three times to see whether I wanted to go back to my parents, and he believed me. He allowed me to do all I wanted. Whenever he was in the IS camp, I called there to find out whether he was coming home or not, and then I called my family (my father and my brother) and the other Êzîdî, asking them to help me in getting out of here and ending my suffering. I was fed up with all I had been through: hunger, thirst, suffering, abuse.

But when he came home, I acted as if I were talking about other things when I conversed with my family. Once, he had to go to the camp and told me he was not coming home this day. I then called my family and told them that I was alone at home and I told them where the place was. They now had three days to get me out of there; otherwise, I would somehow escape on my own. I just couldn't take it anymore. I was twenty years old and weighed only twenty kilos.

My family wanted to help me; they asked where my place was and told me they needed a couple of days to plan everything. But I only knew that I was in Jebel al-Sauieh, not what the exact location was. At four o'clock in the morning, I put on my headscarf, went out and photographed a blue generator near the house. I described Abdullah, his friends, the fighters and his house, and told them that right next to it there was a blue generator. I also told my family what Abu Abdullah himself had said about his house, but they didn't find it.

I sent my coordinates and the pictures I had taken to my brother and after three days, he called me and told me that the trafficker would be driving either a car or a motorbike. Actually, he drove a Kia. With that trafficker, I rode from Jebel al-Sauieh to Sinjar.

IS didn't only kidnap Êzîdî, but also Christians and Muslims. I can remember that it was in Raqqa that I got to know Christians for the first time. There were several Christian women there, among them an older Christian named Mariam who came from Iraq and had also been sold, just like the Êzîdî. Once, all of us were in the same room and then a woman sent by the IS fighters came and complained that the women plucked their eyebrows, and did not want to pray, fast and convert to Islam, and that all of this was against their Sharia. Her husband, Abu Huda al-Iraqi, who had bought me from Abu Abdulrahman al-Urduni, came in and beat Mariam so violently with a stick that the stick broke into four pieces on her arm.

held captive and guarded by fighters of IS.[11] In Mosul, Raqqa and Tal Afar, slave markets were organised where the Êzîdî women and girls were sold – for the most part, only after they had first been raped by the fighters.[12] They buyers also included civilians. Both young and old women were raped, kept as sex slaves and forced to do extremely hard domestic work. Girls who were later liberated told of extreme sexual practices. Many women were severely mistreated. Young women were found with shards of glass in their vaginas. There are reports about multiple rapes and forced abortions. Even nine- or ten-year-old girls had been made pregnant by their abusers.

But in the Islamic State, the enslaved women were also turned into a capitalist commodity. Because family members and Western NGOs tried to ransom women and were willing to pay up to $30,000 per woman, the slave trade became a business from which both IS and the middlemen (aka 'slave liberators') profited nicely.[13] How much money IS was able to rake in from these sales is not known; in 2016, UN Secretary-General Ban Ki-moon estimated that IS had extorted at least $45 million from trafficking in women and girls in 2014 alone.[14]

Many families had to go deeply into debt to liberate their female relatives from their existence as slaves. Apart from family networks, several Canadian and US charities and NGOs that had taken up the cause of saving Êzîdî and Christian children and women took action. In August 2015, Steve Maman, a businessman from Toronto, announced that he had collected $200,000 as ransom for enslaved children and women, and for that he was immediately called the 'Jewish Schindler' by the Canadian press.[15]

The government of the Kurdistan Region also established a fund supposed to serve the liberation of the slaves. Where that money actually went was never really checked or monitored. In any case, after the destruction of IS no attempts were made at reconstructing the financial flows and retaking the money from the traffickers. Many families who bought the freedom of their relatives are still deeply in debt as I write.

The kidnapped children were systematically brainwashed and converted to a form of Islam that followed the jihadist interpretation of IS. During my field research in the camps of the refugees from Sinjar, I have more than once encountered children who had been in IS for a while. Some of them were extremely violent towards other children and pointed to the sky with their forefingers up in the style of the followers of IS, and in one case, I heard a child declare that he wanted to murder all these 'devil worshippers'.

While the Islamic State lost its last territory on 22 March 2019, and was destroyed by the YPG and their allies in the Syrian Democratic Forces (SDF), the whereabouts of more than 2,000 women and children were still unknown. Though it must be assumed that many of these people were murdered or lost their lives in the course of the fighting, there is clear evidence that a number of Êzîdî women and children are still held captive by IS supporters both in Iraq and Syria, and that several women were sold to 'owners' in various Gulf states or in Afghanistan. Every now and then, their relatives are getting text messages from them. In 2019, it was suspected that some Êzîdî women and children were prisoners of Sunni families in Mosul because at least one of the women in question contacted her family via text message, but then the contact broke off again.

Since the publication of the German-language original of this book in summer 2019, several women have been found detained by Sunni families in Iraq and Syria, but also in Turkey. It was therefore possible for IS members to bring their 'slaves' across the border to Turkey and live there with these women for months without being bothered. No one knows how many such women are still with their tormentors as slaves.

Also, in the detention camps in Syria where the relatives of IS fighters are held, women who were looted and enslaved by the jihadists in 2014 still turned up in 2021. In the al-Hawl camp in particular there is an atmosphere of fear that has made it seem too dangerous for many Êzîdî to reveal their identity to the Syrian Democratic Forces. After all, the structures of the IS continue to exist there. Murders of apostates and strict adherence to IS's version of Sharia continue to be the order of the day there.

Some women may also fear honour killings, or at least rejection by their own family members. Although the religious authoritarians, intellectuals and political forces of the Êzîdî have clearly spoken out in favour of the affected women being taken back by their families, the imprisoned women do not know this. They themselves were exposed to IS propaganda for years and have their own memories of their families' ideas of honour. This combination leads some women to fear not only their jihadist tormentors, but also their own families and community. This is even more extreme in the case of affected Shiite women – for example, the Turkmen Shiite women from Tal Afar, who are in fact mostly rejected by their families and who have no choice but to continue to associate with the women of IS.

As of mid-2021, around 2,900 Êzîdî were still missing. Even though a considerable number of these women and children are probably no longer alive, there are still indications today that survivors are in the grip of their tormentors, and not only within Iraq and Syria. At the end of February 2021, a seven-year-old girl was freed who had been taken to Turkey by her IS slaveholders and offered for sale on the Internet. In addition to Turkey, there is also evidence that women and children have been trafficked to several Gulf states. To date, little commitment has been shown by these states to find and free these women.

The surviving women and children have to cope with serious psychological problems. Even though the political and religious leaders of the Êzîdî have advocated for the readmission of the women in question into the community, and even though the Baba Sheikh has developed a special cleansing ritual for the women for this particular purpose, many of them are now confronted with the rejection of their traditional patriarchal families or blame themselves for having been 'sullied' by the fighters of IS. The suicide rate among the freed women is extremely high.

Many women have given birth to children of their rapists during their captivity and are now afraid that these will not be accepted by the Êzîdî community, or they reject their children themselves because they remind them of their martyrdom during their time in slavery. Therefore, they frequently leave their children behind in Syria, which often makes the psychological wounds of the women even worse, especially if the decision is taken because they are afraid of their own community. Though there are families who take such children in, and there are signals from the Êzîdî clergy that these children should also be accepted into the community, the number of children left behind – who are then taken in by Kurdish or Arab families in Syria and will possible never learn that they are the product of a rape – is very high.

According to current Iraqi law, all children of Muslim fathers are registered as Muslims. By this rule, the children of raped Êzîdî women are also automatically Muslims. It was only in April 2019 that the president of Iraq, Barham Salih, suggested to change the Iraqi personal status law in such a way that the mothers of such children can demand that they be registered not as Muslims but as Êzîdî.[16]

In the kidnapped Êzîdî children, IS has inculcated an enormous hatred of the Êzîdî religion and its members. During my visits to the refugee camps I spoke with little children who had just been freed, but who openly told me that they wanted to kill all these 'infidel Êzîdî' and that their parents deserved to die. Other children were arrested by the Iraqi army and treated as IS fighters. At the end of 2019, the Bavê Çawîş went to Syria to look for Êzîdî children among the people captured in the last IS enclave Baghouz, and indeed he found a number of these children in the prison camp in al-Hawl.

Even though an Institute for Psychotherapy initiated by the German-Êzîdî trauma therapist Jan İlhan Kızılhan was opened at the University of Dohuk in October 2017 in order to train local psychotherapists,[17] appropriate mechanisms to supply the survivors in Iraq with professional care are sorely lacking. It will take years until any remotely adequate work with the survivors will be possible.

19
Struggle for liberation
Regional conflicts in the smallest spaces

Several militias involved in the liberation of the Sinjar region since autumn 2014 continued to stay in the region even after the victory over IS, a fact that has led to a division of the settlement area. Three or even four groups can be identified which cooperated or competed with each other, depending on the situation: a block close to the PKK, a block close to the Iraqi government, and another block close to the PDK, which temporarily swallowed the fourth group around Haydar Shesho which originated in the PUK but then tried to become independent. All these blocks pursued different political projects and conceptions of identity. But most of all, they were dependent on actors from the outside, a fact that projected various regional conflicts onto the scene in Sinjar.

In August 2014, the summer offensive of IS led to the formation of the Defence Force of Sinjar (Hêza Parastina Şingal, HPŞ) under the command of Haydar Shesho. The Shesho family had already acquired a certain reputation in the region under Saddam Hussein. The refusal of Haydar Shesho's uncle Qasim Shesho to collaborate with the Saddam regime and the fact that he had liquidated a negotiator of the Iraqi secret service won the family a certain fame, but also had the consequence that large parts of the family were forced to go into exile in Syria already in 1982. At the same time, families in the region that were faithful to Saddam formed an alliance against the Shesho clan. Many family members later emigrated to Germany and continue to live there, but Qasim and Haydar Shesho returned to Iraq after the fall of Saddam Hussein in 2003.

While keeping his distance to the ruling PDK in the beginning, the family patriarch Qasim Shesho later joined this faction, probably not least because a family with which the Sheshos had been in conflict for decades had, just like many other collaborators of the Saddam regime, drawn closer to the PDK and because the Shesho family did not want to give up on their influence in the region. Whatever the exact background of these political developments in the mid-2000s may have been, Qasim Shesho now became one of the most important allies of Barzani's PDK.[1]

His nephew Haydar Shesho, however, joined the other large Kurdish party and was elected to the first post-Saddam Hussein Iraqi national convention in January 2005 as a PUK delegate. Even though the nephew and the uncle belonged to rival political parties, the family ties remained important: in the course of the retreat of the Peshmerga and the struggle against IS, the two once again found common ground with each other.

In August 2014, Qasim Shesho dissociated himself from the PDK and aided his nephew in building the HPŞ. In an interview with *Voice of America* in September 2014, Shesho did not only ask for heavy weapons for the Êzîdî fighters, but also clearly dissociated himself from the (Muslim) Kurds of the PDK by referring, instead of Kurdistan, to 'Êzîdxan', the explicitly Êzîdî settlement areas: 'I am serving only Êzîdxan, and our goal and the goal of our brave fighters is the defence of our honour there.'[2]

A couple of months later, this criticism of the PDK had all but disappeared: Qasim Shesho became the commander of newly established Êzîdî Peshmerga units of the PDK and was now able to get arms and salaries from the Peshmerga Ministry of the Kurdistan Regional Government.

Haydar Shesho on his part also urgently sought support for his insufficiently armed fighters; in contrast to his uncle, he didn't find it in Erbil, but in Baghdad, where he had his HPŞ registered as a People's Mobilisation Unit (al-hašd aš-ša'bī). The People's Mobilisation Units were an umbrella organisation which was supported by the Iraqi government since June 2014 and consisted of around 40 militia fighting against IS. In the European media, these units were often summarily described as 'Shiite militia', but this description is misleading. Even though most of these formations were indeed confessional Shiite militia which had followed the call of the Great Ayatollah Ali al-Sistani to save Iraq from the anti-Shiite IS, there were also Sunni, Christian and Êzîdî militia which did not only win legal status, but also equipment, arms, ammunition and pay for their soldiers through their status as People's Mobilisation Units.

The first groups of the Resistance Units of Sinjar (Yekîneyên Berxwedana Şingal, YBŞ) had already been trained by the Kurdish Popular Defence Units YPG in Syria in July 2014, that is, before IS's attack on Sinjar, but after it had captured Mosul and Tal Afar. The YBŞ now also registered as a People's Mobilisation Unit to gain legal status and support. In addition to the aid from Baghdad, the YBŞ could count on the military and logistic support of the YPG and the YPJ from the nearby Rojava area in Syrian Kurdistan. The presence of experienced commanders and fighters of the PKK guerrilla HPG who acted as advisors and trainers on the ground turned out to be helpful as well. Moreover, the YBŞ could draw on the political structures of the Free Democratic Êzîdî movement (Tevgera Azadiya Demokrat Êzîdiyan, TEV-DE) founded in 2004. Its first field commander, Sheikh Xairî Xidr, had already built a small self-protection unit called Tausî Melek after the attacks of 2007. After his death in the struggle against IS in October 2014, Mazlum Şingalî became the field commander of the unit, while Said Hassan Said functioned as the commander in-chief and was mainly responsible for the political tasks of the YBŞ.

But the commanders of the YBŞ did not include only local Êzîdî, but also fighters from the Êzîdî diaspora such as İsmail Özden from Batman in Turkey, who was killed on 18 August 2018 by a Turkish air strike. He was known in Sinjar under the name Zekî Şengalî and was the most important contact of the YBŞ to the other Êzîdî militia. Just as most Êzîdî in Turkey, İsmail Özden and his family had emigrated to Germany in the 1980s. He took up residence in Celle in Lower Saxony, the same place where the first Êzîdî EU representative (and later HDP MP in the Turkish parliament) Feleknas Uca was born. From Germany, İsmail Özden went to Iraq, where he helped to build the YBŞ in Sinjar in 2014.

This is another example for the importance of Germany within the Êzîdî diaspora. In autumn 2014, men who had spent many years of their lives in Germany found themselves in the top positions of the three most important military units which resisted IS in Sinjar: Qasim Shesho, the commander of the Peshmerga, had long worked as a gardener in Bad Oeynhausen in North Rhine-Westphalia, Haydar Shesho, the commander of the HPŞ, had lived in Hanover and Wolfsburg (where his family lives to this day), and Zekî Şengalî had lived in Celle before he became politically active in Hamburg.

Faced with the superiority of IS, in 2014 and 2015 the various military forces cooperated with each other fairly well, forming a united front against the jihadists. Nevertheless, it became clear already in autumn 2014 that the government of the Kurdistan Region, that is, the ruling PDK, would help the Êzîdî only if they were ready to submit to the PDK's command. In September 2014, Haydar Shesho, who was then defending Şerfedîn, the most important Êzîdî sanctuary in Sinjar, with his HPŞ, received a call from Mîr Tehsîn Beg. The Mîr of the Êzîdî told him:

> You have to leave Sinjar! As long as you are there, the Peshmerga will not go there. As long as the five villages on the mountain are still controlled by you and the PKK, nobody will come to help the people there. You must leave, then help will be sent, but otherwise, it won't![3]

The backgrounds and the secret agreements which had probably been concluded between the various actors in the summer of 2014 will hardly come into the open anytime soon. It is, however, an undisputable fact that not only did the Peshmerga of the PDK retreat without a fight in August 2014, but that they also hesitated for a long time to advance into the direction of the mountain regions after these were again cordoned off following the closure of the corridor previously opened by the YPG. Both on the mountain and in Şerfedîn at the bottom of the mountain, which had never been captured by IS, more than 5,000 civilians and fighters of the various resistance groups continued to hold out until the end of August 2014. Until October 2014, the presence of IS on the northern side of the mountain range was relatively weak. It almost seems as if the conquest of this area had not been a part of the original plan of IS, but just so happened because of the surprising flight of the Peshmerga. It is quite possible that IS initially wanted to take only Sinjar City and the passageways south of the mountain and that the north fell into their hands against their own expectations because of the retreat of the Peshmerga. In any case, until October 2014 several villages on the northern side including a large part of the town of Sinunê were still not under the control of IS. In the course of that month, IS took the offensive on the plain north of the mountains, conquered the villages still under Êzîdî control, and carried out attacks on Şerfedîn, which could probably be defended only because IS mistook a small, determined group of HPŞ fighters in the town for a much larger and much better armed contingent. Apart from Şerfedîn, from the end of October until the middle of December 2014 the fighters of the YBŞ and the HPŞ were able to keep only the tent camps in the mountains and the mountain villages Kerse, Qobane and Kolko.

In August 2014, the Peshmerga had taken up position in the Arab border town of Rabi'a, which is located only 50 kilometres from the eastern end of the Sinjar Mountains, and had brought it under their control.[4] From Rabi'a, it is only a one hour's drive to Sinunê, the most important town on the northern side of the Sinjar Mountains. But nevertheless, between August and December 2014 the Peshmerga made no attempt to advance further to the west from Rabi'a. Only on 17 December did they begin an offensive under the direct command of Masoud Barzani (who deftly used the opportunity as a media prop), during which 8,000 troops marched from the northeast in the direction of Sinjar. Already on the first day, the advance was supported by altogether 45 air raids of the US air force.[5] The UK supplied military advisors[6] and Germany delivered arms, a step that was supported by a large majority of the German parliament but was voted against by the left.[7]

With this kind of support, it was easy for the Peshmerga to advance from Rabi'a and, a little further to the south, Zummar to the north side of the mountain already on December 18, breaking the encirclement by IS in the process. Given the massive military superiority of the Peshmerga, there were no real battles during this offensive. Because of the air strikes of the US air force, the fighters of IS largely retreated to Tal Afar. Already on 21 December, the Peshmerga and fighters of the YBŞ and the HPŞ entered Sinjar City on the southern side of the mountain, but were then unable to keep the city.

Almost simultaneously with the attack of the Peshmerga, namely, on 19 December, the Syrian-Kurdish YPG started an offensive against the IS positions close to the border to the north of Sinjar. From Jeza (Kurdish: Ceza), an Arab place near the border which the YPG had captured in February 2014 after violent and costly fighting, three additional Arab villages on the Syrian side and four villages on the Iraqi side were taken within two days, securing the supply of the YBŞ from Syria and re-establishing the connection to Rojava.

At the end of the offensive, almost the whole northern side of the mountain range was under the control of Kurdish and Êzîdî forces and the connection to both Iraqi Kurdistan and Rojava in Syrian Kurdistan had been re-established. Among the liberated small towns on the northern side of the mountains were Sinunê and Xanasor whose inhabitants began to return already in 2015 and which became the quasi-capitals of the two regions. Xanasor became the centre of the part controlled by the YBŞ, that is, the pro-PKK forces, and Sinunê became the stronghold of the part of Sinjar under the control of the Peshmerga, that is, the PDK. The HPŞ was basically limited to Şerfedîn and a few smaller villages in the northeast of the mountains. But with the reconquest of the north and a few positions at the outskirts above the centre of Sinjar City, the front came to a standstill.

Meanwhile, the Êzîdî who had fled to the Kurdistan Region and were housed in the tent camps in the province of Dohuk became increasingly critical of the behaviour of the Peshmerga in August 2014 and their own treatment as refugees in Kurdistan. The ruling PDK attempted to respond to this criticism with repression and intimidation. At the beginning of August 2015, three prominent Êzîdî intellectuals, the poet Hecî Qeyranî, the singer Dakhil Osman and the former TV journalist Berekat Isa fled from the Kurdistan Region. By their account, these three men from Sinjar had received death threats from circles of Masoud Barzani's ruling party PDK because of their activities. On 4 April 2015, the young internet activist and member of the 'Worldwide Initiative for the Êzîdî' Kheri Ali Ibrahim from Dohuk was arrested because he had posted comments on Facebook that were critical of the repression of Êzîdî activists.[8]

The climax of the repression was reached on 5 April 2015, when Haydar Shesho, the commander of the Defence Force of Sinjar (HPŞ), was arrested in Kurdistan.[9] The background to this was that Shesho had refused to subordinate himself to the PDK and its Peshmerga and to dissociate himself from the People's Mobilisation Units. Haydar Shesho pursued the aim to build an autonomous political force of the Êzîdî which was to have nothing to do with either the PDK or with his own former party, the PUK, and was to be independent of both Baghdad and Erbil. But this was not just about politics, but also about very concrete questions: Who was to supply the pay of the fighters? In an interview with me, Shesho told me that he would have been ready to subordinate himself to the Peshmerga Ministry if the latter had paid the salary of his soldiers. But the Kurdistan Regional Government would not do this. Moreover, Masrour Barzani (Kurdish: Mesrûr Barzanî), the son and crown prince of Masoud Barzani who, as the chairman of the security council of the government of the Kurdistan Region, was the supreme commander of the Peshmerga, the secret service and the police forces of the PDK, also demanded that Shesho return all arms and equipment he been given by Baghdad. Since he refused to agree, he was thrown into jail. There, he first found himself in a cell together with imprisoned IS fighters; then he was threatened with a charge of espionage and was finally released without charge after eight days. But as a precondition, Shesho had to declare that from now on his fighters were subordinated to the Peshmerga Ministry and that his connections with the People's Mobilisation Units were henceforth cut.

Nevertheless, Haydar Shesho tried to retain a certain autonomy for the HPŞ. Among other things, this showed itself in the remaming of his militia into Defence Force of Êzîdxan (Hêza Parastina Êzîdxanê, HPÊ) in November 2015. Êzîdxan is one of the designations of the traditional Êzîdî settlement areas and the name of the autonomous Êzîdî entity propagated by Êzîdî nationalists: It can be understood both in a territorial sense and in terms of identity politics. Even in June 2016, Shesho still stressed his good relationship to the other Êzîdî militia while underlining his distance to 'the Kurds'. But the pressure by the PDK continued and became so massive with the heightened tensions between Baghdad and Erbil towards the end of the war against IS in 2017 that Shesho attempt to build a militia independent of both capitals finally failed. In March 2017, he put his troops officially under the command of the Peshmerga Ministry of the government of the Kurdistan Region. While the HPÊ continues to exist, since that time it has not been under the command of the Iraqi central government in Baghdad anymore.[10]

More stable than the alliances of the HPÊ were those of the Resistance Units of the YBŞ. It has been supported by the YPG, the YPJ and the PKK since its founding, even though it temporarily lost its status as a People's Mobilisation Unit registered in Baghdad due to pressure from Turkey. Similar to all armed units in the political ambit of the PKK, women participated in the YBŞ as active fighters right from the beginning. In January 2015, an autonomous women's unit was formed on the model of other units close to the PKK, which initially acted under the label 'Women's Defence Units of Sinjar' (Yekîneyên Parastina Jin ê Şengalê, YPJŞ), a name that took its cue from the YPJ in Rojava. In April 2016, it was renamed into 'Women's Union of Sinjar' (Yekinêyen Jinên Şengalê, YJŞ).

The rift between the PDK and the HPÊ led to a rapprochement between the latter and groups close to the PKK. But the main line of conflict was still between YBŞ and the YJŞ on the one side and the PDK and Qasim Shesho's Peshmerga on the other side. Haydar Shesho's HPÊ occasionally tried to mediate and maintained its relations to the units of Haydar's uncle despite the HPÊ's conflicts with the PDK as such. Qasim Shesho on his part mediated in the conflict between the PDK and his nephew.

The YBŞ and YJŞ on the one side and the HPÊ on the other side also rivalled with each other, but until 2017 they were united by their hostility to IS and their rejection of the PDK. From October 2015 to the spring of 2017, the HPÊ, the YBŞ and the YJŞ coordinated their activities under the loose umbrella of the 'Sinjar Alliance' (Fermandariya Hevbeş a Şengalê). On 12 November 2015, both the fighters of the Sinjar Alliance and the Peshmerga of the PDK went on the offensive with the support of the US air force to expel IS from the city of Sinjar. Once again, Sinjar was subjected to an air bombardment, which destroyed large parts of the city but also led to its conclusive liberation. In the operation which went down into history under the name 'Anger of the Peacock Angel', the fighters of the YBŞ and their allies, the YPG and the HPG, captured the city on 13 November. The first to march in were the fighters of the units close to the PKK, followed by the Peshmerga. Surprisingly, the fighters of IS neither resisted nor did they engage in house-to-house fighting to keep the city. The film director Carsten Stormer who filmed at the front lines later explained that IS didn't show the slightest sign of resistance.[11] A series of reports confirms that IS had retreated from the city already two days before the offensive.

The day after, several villages to the west of Sinjar City were liberated and the whole region up to the Syrian border was cleansed of IS. Then the offensive was ended even though there had hardly been any losses and IS had already retreated from the region. The Peshmerga and the YBŞ explained that their US allies had asked them to at least temporarily stop the fighting after the operation 'Anger of the Peacock Angel' to avoid political problems with the Iraqi central government. In the refugee camps in Kurdistan, his restraint led to much frustration with the actors; many Êzîdî from the southern villages still occupied by IS began to turn to Baghdad for help.[12]

Moreover, in the course of 2016 the tensions between the YBŞ and the Peshmerga of the PDK began to intensify; the HPÊ found itself in the crossfire and came under increasing pressure. The conflicts between the factions and the repressive policy of the PDK vis-à-vis any criticism within its territory also had consequences for the most important US–Êzîdî NGO, Yazda, which was engaged in the reconstruction of Sinjar with a number of small ventures and had projects for the support of abducted and raped women in the province of Dohuk. On 2 January, the government of the Kurdistan Region summarily closed Yazda down after the NGO had issued critical statements.[13] After international protests, the NGO was able to resume its work two weeks later, but the warning was certainly understood. Since then, Yazda has exercised restraint with regard to any open criticism of the Kurdistan Regional Government.

The political and military tensions between the rival Êzîdî militia came to a head at the beginning of March 2017, when Barzani sent a group of allies of the Peshmerga of the PDK, the so-called Roj Peshmerga, to Sinjar to assume control of the border between Iraq and Syria. The official name of the Rojava Peshmerga is Units of the Kurdish National Council in Syria (Encûmena Niştimanî ya Kurdî li Sûriyeyê, ENKS), which means that they are units of the Kurdish opposition parties in Syria which are allied with Barzani's PDK and sharply opposed to the PYD which rules Rojava, and therefore, also to the PKK, the YPG, the YBŞ and the YJŞ. Had the Roj Peshmerga succeeded in bringing the whole Iraqi–Syria border under their control, they would have cut off the villages controlled by the YBŞ and the YJŞ from their supply from Rojava and would have made a decisive step in the expulsion of the PKK allies from Sinjar.

The conflict between the Roj Peshmerga and the YBŞ escalated in the early morning hours of 3 March 2017 in the area between the PDK-held village Sinunê and Xanasor, which was held by the YBŞ. So far, the exact sequence of the military clashes could not be confirmed by independent sources. While the Roj Peshmerga claim that they had only wanted to drive through the area and were blocked by the YBŞ, the YBŞ accuses the Roj Peshmerga of an attack on their positions near Xanasor. It is, however, undisputed that the skirmishes caused several deaths including civilians and came to a standstill only after the mediation of the US in the course of the day.[14]

Even after the ceasefire, the political situation remained tense and both sides intensified their propaganda. On 14 April 2017, Nazê Naif Qaval, a seventeen-year-old activist of the Free Women's Movement of Êzîdxan (TAJÊ), was shot and killed by Roj Peshmerga during a civil demonstration against the PDK.[15] The PKK-leaning media reacted to the death of this young woman with a massive attack on the PDK. The PDK in its turn exploited the switch of a small group of former YBŞ fighters to the Peshmerga for its propaganda. While local Êzîdî talk about a small group of around a dozen YBŞ fighters who switched to the PDK in April 2017, the media close to the PDK boasted about hundreds of former YBŞ fighters who had allegedly defected. These high numbers are not confirmed by any independent media outlets. In private conversation, even Êzîdî PDK members from the region admit that the switch of a small group of YBŞ fighters had been grossly embellished.

This complex situation got even more complicated in the course of May 2017 when more and more Êzîdî from the southern villages of Sinjar joined the Shiite-dominated People's Mobilisation Units and founded their own Êzîdî units. Among the commanders of the new units allied with Baghdad was, among others, Naif Jaso, the brother of the mayor of Koço who had been murdered by IS in August 2014. After the death of his brother, Naif Jaso had succeeded him in the position of the traditional tribal head. The survivors in the villages in the south of Sinjar had waited for the liberation of their own villages since the reconquest of Sinjar City in November 2015 and were now, one and a half years later, losing patience.

In addition to many men from the then-unliberated south of the region, a young YBŞ commander from Xanasor also transferred from the north side to the People's Mobilisation Units. A former smuggler, Xal Ali (Uncle Ali), as he is known in the region, had fallen out with some of his former friends and was therefore one of the founders of the People's Mobilisation Units as a former YBŞ fighter.

Between 12 and 29 May, 2017 and with the support of the central government in Baghdad and the Iraqi army, the People's Mobilisation Units liberated the southern parts of the region up to then still under the rule of IS: Tal Ezeir, Rambus, Ger Zerik, Tal Qasab, Tal Banat and Koço, the place which had become a symbol for the massacres of the Islamic State on 15 August 2014.

Barzani's PDK reacted to the new rival with virtual panic, the arrest of the supporters of the newly founded Êzîdî People's Mobilisation Units and the expulsion of their families from Kurdistan. Êzîdî PDK functionaries gave speeches in the refugee camps in the province of Dohuk which were full of threats against the supporters of the PKK and the People's Mobilisation Units. During these days, inhabitants of the camps would tell me about their fear that the rivalries between the Peshmerga, the People's Mobilisation Units, the HPÊ and the YBŞ could lead to a civil war in Sinjar or to a division of the region between Baghdad and Erbil. [16]

In December 2017, Human Rights Watch (HRW) accused the Êzîdî People's Mobilisation Units of having killed 52 civilians of the Sunni Imteywit tribe in July 2017 in an act of revenge.[17] The case was never solved. What we know is that in the first weeks after the liberation of South Sinjar, there were acts of revenge against Arabs who had cooperated with IS – similar to what happened in other former IS regions in Iraq. In July 2017, a large group of Sunni IS sympathisers or fighters was killed by People's Mobilisation Units. It is, however, entirely unclear whether this was done by the *Êzîdî*

People's Mobilisation Units founded only very shortly before the events or by the *Shiite* allies of these new units: Shiite People's Mobilisation Units sustained by local Shiites and supported by Iran had also been active in the region since at least May 2017. Just as unclear is who gave the order for the massacre and how many people were actually killed. The belated publication of the massacre suggests that the event was also exploited to put pressure on the leaders of the Êzîdî People's Mobilisation Units, particularly Naif Jaso. At the time when the massacre was made public by HRW, Naif Jaso was having massive problems with the PDK.

In the north of the region, too, there had been a massacre of the Arab Juhayish tribe after the recapture by the Peshmerga, whose sheikh had been one of the most important local notables of IS and had urged the local Muslim sheikhs in his house to take the oath to the 'Khalif'. In this case, however, the perpetrators were not the Popular Mobilisation Units, but the Peshmerga of the PDK. Like the acts of revenge in the south, this one was never really solved.

It is, however, also indisputable that the participation of local Arab and Kurdish Sunnis in the massacres of IS and the lack of prosecution of these crimes have brought about a relation between the various ethnoreligious groups in the region that is characterised by massive conflicts to this day.

The hard frontier between Êzîdî and Muslims, which did not exist in this form until 2014, was drawn by the genocide. The economic relations between Êzîdî and Arabs, especially in smuggling or the godfather relations of Êzîdî with their Muslim-Arab *krivs*, which were established via circumcision, suffered a harsh interruption as a result of the genocide. Especially in the first years after the genocide, many Êzîdî collectively blamed 'the Muslims' for the genocide, which can probably be seen as a consequence of the collective trauma and as a success of the propaganda of IS. Since the return of many Êzîdî (but also Arabs), especially to the north of the region, more differentiated views can be heard again. If you ask long enough, you will receive much more differentiated answers to the question of the perpetrators in 2021 than you did immediately after the genocide. Meanwhile, distinctions are being made between the behaviour of different Arab and Kurdish-Muslim tribes. The fact that some 200 inhabitants of Xanasor alone were able to escape to Syria with the help of their Muslim *krivs* is now also discussed by some survivors. Arabs from the villages in the far western region controlled by the YBŞ have now also been integrated into the YBŞ and the old smuggling relations between the Arab border villages in the far north on the Syrian border and the Êzîdî are being resumed.

The fear of a new civil war got worse during the summer of 2017 after Masoud Barzani had proclaimed, on 7 June, his intention to carry out a referendum on the independence of Kurdistan on 25 September 2017. This referendum was supposed to include the 'Controversial Areas' under the control of the Peshmerga. When I drove through the parts of the region ruled by the Peshmerga during one of my field trips in September 2017 a couple of days before the votes were to be cast, the posters for the referendum and Kurdish flags were just as prominent in these regions as in the core areas of the Kurdistan Region. Sinunê was full of posters advertising the plebiscite. Even between the tents of the civilians still holding out on the mountain, posters told about the brighter future in an independent Kurdistan. But in the parts of the region dominated by the People's Mobilisation Units and the YBŞ, nothing of the sort was detectable.

The partition of this small region into three or even four parts was never more in evidence than in these days before the referendum: Because the southern parts were under the control of the People's Mobilisation Units and the Iraqi army, the YBŞ and the Autonomy Council it had founded in February 2015 hoisted both the Iraqi flag and the banner of the Council (a yellow sun on a green background and a red stripe with seven stars on top of it), plus the flags of the YBŞ and the YJŞ. In Şerfedîn, where Haydar Shesho's HPÊ continued to be present, one could see the flag of Êzîdxan: a yellow sun on a red background with two white stripes at both the top and the bottom end. And in the areas ruled by the PDK, the Kurdish flag with its green-white stripes and a yellow sun in the middle was the dominant one.

In the days before the referendum, the atmosphere between the rival groups was particularly tense. But the retreat of the PDK Peshmerga after the referendum took place in a surprisingly orderly fashion. In the early morning hours of 17 October 2017, one day after the evacuation of Kirkuk by the Kurdish Peshmerga, the retreat of the Peshmerga from Sinjar City began. Around noon, the Peshmerga of the PDK also withdrew from the north of Sinjar. Some families close to the PDK from the small town of Sinûnê fled in the direction of Kurdistan, but others stayed in the town, which was later taken over by the PKK ally YBŞ and their Women's Units of Sinjar (Yekinêyen Jinên Şengalê, YJŞ).[18]

But the Muslim units of the PDK Peshmerga, among them the Rojava Peshmerga which had engaged in an armed clash with the YBŞ in March 2017, were the only ones to retreat. Haydar Shesho's HPÊ retained its presence in its stronghold Şerfedîn and in the villages Gohbal, Borik and Zorava. After the retreat of the PDK, the HPÊ dissociated itself from the Peshmerga Ministry of the government of the Kurdistan Region, and its presence in Şerfedîn is tolerated by the Iraqi government. The town is under the full control of the HPÊ. On the principal road from Golat to Sinunê, there is a checkpoint of the Iraqi army at the turnoff to Şerfedîn, but the road leading to Şerfedîn itself is under the exclusive control of the HPÊ.

Qasim Shesho, the former commander of the PDK Peshmerga and some of his Êzîdî Peshmerga fled to Shesho's nephew Haydar. Because this disregarded the order of the Peshmerga Ministry to retreat, he was dishonourably discharged. But the connection to the PDK was not entirely broken. Even though Shesho sharply criticised the withdrawal decision of the PDK, he holds Masoud Barzani still in high esteem and is ostentatiously loyal to him. The PKK and the YBŞ still seem to be his main enemy. The number of the (former) Peshmerga still under his command is difficult to estimate. In autumn 2017, his family talked about 1,000 fighters, but on the ground, the number looks much smaller. Moreover, such a big unit could hardly be accommodated in Şerfedîn. In October 2018, Qasim Shesho even claimed that he had 'altogether 5,000 Peshmerga registered', though he also added that they did not get a regular salary from the ministry anymore, but were only paid 200 dollars each.[19] This meagre pay might be the very reason for announcing such inflated numbers. Peshmerga commanders have frequently resorted to this ploy to increase both their personal income and that of their troops.

The PKK-leaning groups YBŞ and YJŞ also continue to be present in the northwest of Sinjar and are cooperating with the Iraqi army and the Êzîdî People's Mobilisation Units. For a short while, the YBŞ was even able to extend the area under its control and took Sinûnê as well as the village Duguri from the Peshmerga, but at the beginning of 2018, most of the checkpoints it had occupied were handed to the Iraqi army. Since that time, the most important checkpoints at the entry of Sinûnê are jointly manned and controlled by Iraqi soldiers and YBŞ fighters.

There is no clear frontier between the regions controlled by the Iraqi army and the Popular Mobilisation Units, on the one hand, and those controlled by the YBŞ, on the other. Many checkpoints are mixed. The Iraqi police also move in areas under YBŞ control, and conversely, the police force established by the YBŞ, the Asayîşa Êzîdxanê, is also active in areas more tightly controlled by the Iraqi army. The small area around Şerfedîn, which continues to be held by Haydar Shesho's HPÊ and to which the last PDK Peshmerga around his uncle Qasim Shesho have retreated, occupies a special position in this regard. However, the HPÊ fighters are also able to move freely in the areas controlled by the Iraqi army.

However, the PKK-leaning groups in the region came under pressure when Turkey began its offensive against Efrîn in Syria in January 2018 and, in March 2018, also started military attacks against the PKK in the Iraqi-Kurdish province of Dohuk. The Turkish president Erdoğan openly and with increasing frequency threatened to attack Sinjar. On 24 March, the KCK, the umbrella organisation of the groups associated with the PKK, explained that the guerrillas would withdraw from Sinjar because the population there was now sufficiently organised to defend itself against attacks like the one by IS in 2014. According to the KCK, the guerrillas thus retreated in the safe knowledge that it had reached its goal.[20] But on the very next day, 25 March, Erdoğan used a congress of the ruling party AKP in Trabzon as his platform to declare that the operations of the Turkish army would not end with Efrîn: 'The PKK terrorists went to Sinjar. We have said that we would go there as well. The operations there have already started.'[21]

Erdoğan's speech turned out to be no more than an empty threat: populist electoral rhetoric. The HPG and the YPG were indeed withdrawn, but the local forces of the YBŞ and the YJŞ continue to control the northwest of the region to this very day. On 27 March 2018, the YBŞ and the Iraqi army agreed to a joint control regime at the border to Syria, an agreement which had consequences for the civil population. Before the agreement, the two supply roads that had been established after the liberation of the area had been under the exclusive control of the YBŞ and had been open for civilians. Since the untarred tarmac to the north of the Khatuniyya lake on Syrian territory which leads to the west of Sinjar was put under the joint supervision of the army and units of the YBŞ, it has still been open for fighters of the YBŞ and the YJŞ and their supply, but is frequently closed for civilians. This has led to regular conflicts between the local Êzîdî population and the Iraqi army, in part because many inhabitants of the villages under YBŞ control can reach the hospitals in Syria easier and faster than those in Iraqi Kurdistan.

But generally, the relations between the Iraqi army, the Êzîdî People's Mobilisation Units, and the YBŞ can be described as fairly good. One example for this is that in October 2018, the People's Mobilisation Units handed two villages, Tel Ezeir and Siba Shex Xidir, in the southwest of Sinjar to the YBŞ and the Autonomy Council of Sinjar.[22]

With the elections of 12 May 2018, three Êzîdî candidates from three different lists became members of the Iraqi parliament. The quorum mandate for the Êzîdî minority was won by Saib Khidir of the Êzîdî Progress Party (HTY). This party is independent, but has historically been more or less close to the PUK. Khidir is a respected personality with many international contacts and great political experience. But actually, he doesn't come from Sinjar, but belongs to the Arabic-speaking minority of the Êzîdî of Bashiqa in the Nineveh Governorate. His organisation does not have a Kurdish name, only an Arabic one. The other two Êzîdî representatives, Khalida Khalil of the PDK and Hussein Hassan Narmo of the PUK also do not come from Sinjar. Khalida Khalil was born in Şêxan but later lived in Mosul, while Hussein Hassan Narmo hails from a village near the Christian-Assyrian city of al-Qosh. The previous Êzîdî deputies, like the well-known Vian Dakhil (PDK) who had given the internationally noted desperate speech described above, were no longer represented in the parliament. Haydar Shesho's Democratic Êzîdî Party (PÊD), which has strong roots in Sinjar itself, and the Êzîdî Party for Freedom and Democracy (PADÊ), which is close to the PKK and the YBŞ/YJŞ, did not win any seats. Thus, Sinjar itself was not directly represented in the 2018 parliament.[23]

At the beginning of June 2018, a few US military units were stationed in Sinjar to establish stability and to protect the local Êzîdî should the need arise. They coordinated with the 15th brigade of the Iraqi army in Sinjar City and Sinûnê. With this, the US returned to Iraq with ground forces in Sinjar almost ten years after its withdrawal from the country.

But the presence of these units did not prevent the Turkish president Erdoğan from finally making good on his previous threats. On 15 August 2018, he used, of all things, a memorial event in Koço in remembrance of the IS massacre four years before to have a car with high-level commanders of the YBŞ bombarded on their way back from the commemoration. In the operation, Zekî Şengalî (İsmail Özden), one of the most important commanders of the YBŞ, was killed, while field commander Mazlum Şengalî was seriously wounded.

Even though the cooperation of the Iraqi army with the Autonomy Council of Sinjar established by the YBŞ amounts to a certain degree of recognition of the special status of the region, this doesn't change the fact that no decision has yet been taken on Singal's future. Officially, Sinjar continues to be part of the Iraqi province Ninawa (with Mosul as its capital) and has no special legal status whatsoever, even though this is exactly what all the relevant Êzîdî forces demand. The only thing that is controversial among them is what status a self-administration of the region should have and whether it should be part of the Kurdistan Region of Iraq or not.

Diplomatic support for the autonomy or at least some form of regional self-administration of Sinjar came from Brussels in the form of an EU report published at the end of June 2018. In the report, the EU parliament encouraged the international community and the EU itself to support the protection of the diversity of ethnic and cultural identities of Iraq and local forms of self-administration in the larger frame of the Iraqi constitution for Sinjar and the Nineveh Governorate.[24]

In March 2019, the good relations between the Iraqi army and the YBŞ suffered a serious blow. On Sunday 17 March, near Xanasor there erupted a gunfight between the YBŞ and the Iraqi army after YBŞ fighters had refused to stop at a checkpoint of the 15th brigade of the Iraqi army and the soldiers had allegedly mistaken them for smugglers, who are indeed very active in this region. A gun battle ensued, which led to two fatalities on each side. After the incident, both parties blamed each other but also declared that they wanted to solve the problem through talks. Nevertheless, the situation escalated again two days later when a delegation of Êzîdî YBŞ fighters and representatives of the Iraqi army met in the village of Medîban east of the Sinjar Mountains and after a few minutes opened fire on each other. According to Iraqi accounts, two Iraqi soldiers were wounded in the process. The gunfight lasted only a few minutes before the two sides again agreed to continue the talks.

Even though it was a misunderstanding that triggered this tension, the incident makes clear how difficult the conditions on the ground actually are. Without a clarification of the political status of the region and a transformation of the political and military structures established during the struggle against IS into a legal form that is also recognised by the Iraqi government and a clarification of the relationship between the Êzîdî and the neighbouring groups which have collaborated with IS against them and participated in the genocide, the security situation of the region will remain precarious.

Since the beginning of 2021, the Iraqi army has cut off the border between the YBŞ-dominated area and Syria with a new fence. An October 2020 agreement between the governments in Baghdad and Erbil, which was reached without the YBŞ, has not yet been implemented. An ultimatum to disarm the police of the YBŞ-affiliated self-administration in the spring of 2021 passed. On 24 April 2021 protests by local supporters of the YBŞ prevented the implementation of the agreement and the Iraqi prime minister Mustafa al-Kadhimi let it be known through intermediaries that there would be no armed attack by the Iraqi army on the YBŞ or its police. Meanwhile, such an attempt to forcibly conquer the areas under YBŞ control in the western Sinjar region would also be relatively difficult. The YBŞ has used the last few years to massively fortify the mountainous region. Anyone who has visited the interior of the mountains in 2021 will find caves with military positions everywhere, roadways to supply military installations, and YBŞ fighters who would be willing to fight for every square metre of ground. Large parts of the YBŞ military installations have now gone underground due to the constant threat of Turkish air attacks, and any fighting unit that the YBS would want to forcibly remove from there would have to fight a bloody battle for every peak and canyon. At present, the focus appears to be more on containing the YBŞ than on military confrontation.

Although the PDK failed to return to Sinjar even one year after the agreement between Erbil and Baghdad, the ruling party of the Kurdistan Autonomous Region managed to achieve political success in the Iraqi parliamentary elections on 10 October 2021. In the run-up to the elections, the PDK's campaign in the Sinjar region itself was obstructed, while the PDK made it impossible for other parties to campaign in IDP camps in Kurdistan. In the run-up to the elections, there were therefore debates about depriving IDPs of their right to vote at all, but this proved unfeasible. In the end, current demographics decided the outcome of the elections. Since a majority of the Êzîdî still reside in IDP camps in Kurdistan, the PDK managed to win all three mandates in Sinjar, two for Êzîdî and one for a Muslim Kurd. The mandate reserved for the minority was won by Naif Khalaf Seydou of the Êzîdî Progressive Party (PPÊ). The YBŞ-affiliated PADÊ and Haydar Sheshos PÊD didn't win a mandate.

20

The life of the displaced

The insecurity and the sluggish pace of the reconstruction of the region are the reasons why the majority of the Êzîdî who fled in 2014 have not returned to Sinjar, although parts of the population returned in 2020 in the wake of the COVID-19 crisis. However, the majority of those who fled in 2014 still live in the camps in the Kurdistan Region of Iraq. Returnees are found almost exclusively on the northern side of the mountains. Several thousand civilians continue to live on the mountain where they fled in August 2014. The tents have become weather-worn and some people are now building solid dwellings. Thus, it is actually possible that the flight of 2014 will lead to the resettlement of the mountain from which the Êzîdî were expelled during the Ba'th regime.

By now, almost 50,000 Êzîdî refugees from Sinjar live in Europe, most of them in Germany, but thousands of them continue to be stuck in camps in Greece. The road to Europe mostly leads through Turkey, where the refugees are initially received by the Kurdish population in the southeast of the country. The various emergency camps that were established in the municipalities ruled by the pro-Kurdish party HDP in Roboski, Şenoba, Şirnak, the village of Koçer near Siirt, Mardin, Batman and several villages near Batman in 2014[1] were in part abandoned by their residents in 2014 and 2015. The remaining Êzîdî refugees were then accommodated in the better organised camp in the Fidanlık Park near Diyarbakır. The Turkish government ran only a single camp in Midyat. Because the refugees were not allowed to leave and because it was under the control of armed Jandarma, many called it a 'prison camp'.[2] All the other camps were run by the HDP municipalities.

When I visited the camp in the Fidanlık Park for the first time in autumn 2015, it was supported very actively by the HDP and the Kurdish population. At the same time, within the camp the tensions between the groups which sympathised with the Kurdish movement close to the PKK and thought that the Êzîdî should remain in Kurdistan and those who wanted to continue their flight to Europe were impossible to overlook.[3] The camp was supported by the Yenişehir district of Diyarbakır. In autumn 2016, 4,000 Êzîdî still lived there, many of whom intended to go onward to Europe but had already been blocked by the EU border security several times. The camp was relatively well organised and also included a school. The only disadvantage was that the camp was located pretty far from the centre. But even so, minivans (Dolmuş) were available which the refugees could use to commute to the city.

After the two HDP co-mayors of the Yenişehir district were arrested on 6 December 2016 in the course of the renewed escalation of the conflict in Turkish Kurdistan and the city had been put under the receivership of the government, the Êzîdî refugees lost their support. The Turkish Presidium for Emergency and Catastrophe Management (Afet ve Acil Durum Yönetimi Başkanlığı, AFAD) proclaimed that it would resettle the 1,029 refugees still remaining at that point into official state camps of the AFAD and that it would also dissolve the camp in the Fidanlık Park, the protests of the HDP notwithstanding.[4] At the beginning of January 2017, this plan was put into practise.

The refugee camps of the AFAD which were established in border regions since the beginning of the Syrian civil war are guarded, can be entered and left only with permission, and are under the direct control of the Turkish government. One of the reasons why these camps could not be a long-term option for the Êzîdî refugees is the fact that they also hosted many conservative and jihadist Muslims who were clearly perceived as a threat by the often heavily traumatised refugees. Therefore, the Êzîdî in the camps tried to get to the EU as quickly as possible or – if they couldn't come up with the money for traffickers – to return to Iraq.

A part of the refugees of the year 2014 initially remained in Syrian Kurdistan and was housed in the Newroz Camp in the north of the small town of Dêrik in the far northeast of Syria. When I visited this camp in the summer of 2016, 450 families still lived there, some of whose members were fighting in the YBŞ in Sinjar. The camp was decorated with pictures of the PKK leader Abdullah Öcalan and flags of the Resistance Units of the

YBŞ and YJŞ. The Autonomy Council of Sinjar also had an office there. During my last visit in January 2019, the camp was already being dissolved and more than half of the tents had already been removed. In the course of the last two years, most families have returned to the area of Sinjar ruled by the YBŞ, while some have emigrated to Europe.

The majority of the expelled still live in the camps in the Kurdistan Region of Iraq. Irene Dulz estimates that between 286,500 and 345,000 Êzîdî from Sinjar and the Nineveh Governorate[5] have found refuge in Dohuk and the 'Controversial Areas' administered by the Kurds. In these camps, the political outlook of the local administration is also very clearly visible in the form of party symbols of the PDK and pictures of Masoud Barzani. Those who do not come to terms with the PDK are often treated less favourably. There were even instances where relatives of the members of the Êzîdî People's Mobilisation Units founded in May 2017 were expelled from both the camps and the Kurdistan Region. The camps are managed by the Board of Relief and Humanitarian Affairs (BRHA) of the government of the Kurdistan Region. Most of the internally displaced people (IDP) from Sinjar live in these camps. According to a statistic published by the BRHA in February 2016, 189,321 refugees lived in formally established camps in the province Dohuk, and an additional 32,306 lived in the provinces Erbil and Silêmanî. The statistic further says that 325,178 people live in informal settlements, dwellings, or shells of buildings outside of the camps of the BRHA.[6] No comprehensive statistics on this have been published since 2016. Since then, a small part of the refugees have returned while some of them have succeeded in emigrating to Europe. But the general picture has not changed. For the visitor of the camps in Iraq in 2019, no improvement was detectable. Both the formal and the informal camps are massively overcrowded. Four years after they were expelled from their homes, a large part of the people are still forced to live in tents. The children of the camps go to school for a couple of hours each day. Speaking to the teachers, one learns that many students have big psychological problems and are hardly able to follow the lessons. In March 2017, a teacher in the camp Xanke told me, 'We are actually doing some sort of therapy with the children and we're trying to help them to kill time.' Of course, even here there are also children who are eager and hungry for knowledge, but in general, the learning conditions in the camps are very problematic.

People formerly employed by the state still receive their salaries even if their jobs in Sinjar no longer exist. These salaries are feeding whole extended families. Poorer groups are forced to rely on aid deliveries or donations by family members abroad. Since 2014, the social differences within the camps have increased, and in part, they depend on political compliance. Loyal members of the PDK enjoy political advantages over families which are perceived as political opponents.

Between January 2015 and January 2019, I was able to visit refugee camps in the province Dohuk seven times. There was little change during that period. In some places, schools originally housed in tents were relocated in containers, or playgrounds were built. Some of the tents now have concrete floors. But the quality of the flysheets has suffered in the course of these years. In the informal camps, some of the residents have started to tend chickens or sheep and to establish small gardens. Even the beekeeping that used to be widespread in Sinjar was restarted by some of the refugees in Kurdistan.

In talking to survivors, one is confronted with an extremely intense frustration and little hope for a return to and the reconstruction of Sinjar. During a research trip to the Xanke camp in May 2017, a thirty-year-old man from Sinjar City told me, 'The situation in the camp is even worse than in 2015. We are getting less food than before, and after three years, our tents are broken. We have been forsaken by the rest of the world and Europe doesn't want us.' [7] He does not see any future for the Êzîdî in Iraq: 'We can't live here anymore. I would very much like to go to Germany. But I can't afford the traffickers, and so I have to stay here.'

Despite this precarious situation, the expelled are not returning to Sinjar. According to the International Organization for Migration (IOM), until May 2016 only 3,220 families had again settled in Sinjar, most of them in the larger villages and towns on the northern side of the mountain range. [8] Apparently, Sinjar City isn't very attractive for the Êzîdî, in contrast to a sizable number of Babawat. The latter's Shiite flags are on prominent display in the city and the reconstructed Sayyida Zaynab Mosque on a hill at the edge of the town catches the eye. Sinjar's Christians, however, have not returned, and the Christian churches are still lying in ruins.

During my field research in Xanke, I was able to carry out 42 qualitative interviews with residents of the camp administered by the BRHA and with refugees of the informal camp next to the BRHA camp, and almost half of my interviewees told me that they had stayed in Iraq only because they had not yet found a way to get to either Europe or a non-European country and that they simply could not afford to pay a trafficker for the transit to Europe. Even the people who did want to go back to Sinjar told me that for them, this depended on certain preconditions. For most of them, the main problem was the lack of security. Here, not only did they fear a revitalisation of the jihadis, but also armed conflicts between the various Êzîdî militia. In 34 of the 42 interviews, the rivalry of the parties and militias was identified as one of the biggest problems, while only ten per cent of the respondents said that they didn't trust the Muslims in Iraq anymore. This strong emphasis on the rivalry of the militias may also have to do with the particular period in which the interviews were carried out – that is, after the liberation of South Sinjar by the Êzîdî People's Mobilisation Units and the ensuing pressure exerted by the PDK on all rival militias. But the conflicts between the various groups continued to be mentioned even after the withdrawal of the PDK Peshmerga in October 2017 and the takeover of the area by the Iraqi army. The last time I was able to talk to the refugees in Kurdistan was in January 2019. The people I spoke with also regarded the unsettled status of the region and the conflicts between the central government, the government of the Kurdistan Region and the various militias as the main obstacles for their own return to the region. Apart from this, the lack of reconstruction, the lacking infrastructure, and the continuing omnipresence of mines were mentioned as important causes for not wanting to live in Sinjar again.

To this day, Sinjar City has only one school and no hospital. There are doctors and teachers from Sinjar who now all live in Kurdistan and continue to receive their salary, but do not work in Sinjar. It is a vicious circle: The people don't come back because there is no infrastructure. And there is no infrastructure because the people aren't coming back.

In our conversation with her, a sixty-year-old woman from Sinunê mentioned the lack of security as one of the main reasons why she and her family felt unable to return to the region: 'The murderers and rapists are still around. They used to be our Arab neighbours.'[9]

A fifty-year-old man said:

I have lived my whole life in Tal Banat and used to be a peasant. I had never wanted to leave. But IS forced me to do so, and I can only return once the Kurds finally leave the Êzîdî alone and stop fighting out their party conflicts to our detriment. In this regard, the Kurds are no better than the Arabs. All Muslims have killed Êzîdî, and the PDK has done nothing for us.

After the takeover of the region by the Iraqi army in October 2017, yet another factor emerged that made a return of the Êzîdî more difficult: The most important thoroughfare between Sinjar and the Kurdistan Region, which runs via Rabī'a relatively close to the border, was closed because of a conflict between Baghdad and Erbil. Since then, the only road from Kurdistan to Sinjar is the one through Mosul. The drive to Sinjar is now not only longer but also more dangerous, because Mosul is still a stronghold of Sunni Muslims, among whom there are many followers and underground networks of IS.

Most of the refugees felt betrayed by Europe. In an interview in May 2017, a forty-year-old family father from Borik lamented:

We are losing Sinjar, and the Êzîdî will leave Iraq. We have already lost Şêxan. After that, what will remain? The Kurds and the Arabs both want to get rid of us. In Iraq, there is no place for non-Muslims. It is a shame that Europe rejects the Êzîdî. We have fled without any worldly goods and cannot afford to pay traffickers.[10]

This confessionalised interpretation according to which 'the Muslims' wanted to get rid of them goes back to the long history of persecution of the Êzîdî even before the IS attack and confessionalised persecution and is strengthened by the negative experiences of the Êzîdî in the Kurdistan Region of Iraq. Many Êzîdî felt forsaken by everyone: by the Muslim Kurds, by the Arabs, but also by the international community, and most of all, the EU.

The sealing of the borders of Europe for refugees from the Middle East has hit the Êzîdî from Sinjar particularly hard because in 2014, they mostly had to flee in a hurry and without any financial means at their disposal. In contrast to some other refugees from Syria or Iraq, they don't have the money to pay the increasingly expensive traffickers that could take them to an EU country. Special reception programmes such as the one in Baden-Württemberg were designed exclusively for women and children, a fact which has contributed to the isolation of many women and has torn many families apart.[11]

Many of the refugees ask for international protection in Sinjar and the establishment of their own administration as an autonomous province or an autonomous region. Actually, a large percentage of my 2017 interviewees mentioned this as a precondition for their return to the region.

Altogether, in the first years after 2014 we find the picture of a highly unsettled population which, in the immediate wake of a genocidal experience, became enmeshed in political power struggles which have deprived it of the opportunity to regain their inner security and to come to terms with the traumas of the genocide.

However, when the authorities of the Kurdistan Autonomous Region began imposing a curfew on refugee camps in Kurdistan in the spring of 2020 due to the COVID-19 pandemic, thousands of displaced people decided to return. By then, only Sinunê and Xanasor had been partially repopulated. Now, however, people were returning to other towns on the north side of the mountain, and some even ventured into the towns on the south side. This wave of return was not the result of an improvement in the situation in the Sinjar region, but of deterioration in the camps. The cordoning-off of the camps had deprived people of income-generating opportunities and, in a sense, kept them trapped in precarious tent camps. Relatively many then preferred to return. However, this does not mean that the entire north has been repopulated or that the camps in Kurdistan have been dissolved. Sinunê and Xanasor are still the most densely populated places. In Dugure, further east, no more than a quarter of the population has returned. The picture is similar in some of the other towns in the north. In the south, the situation is even more precarious. Only a few families have returned to the villages there, and they now live in ghost towns, some of which have been destroyed. There is a lack of any infrastructure and income opportunities. Some of the returnees from 2020 therefore returned to the tent camps in Kurdistan as early as 2021. Others are considering this step. In the spring of 2021, I was able to speak with a returnee to Tal Kassab who, despite a university degree and knowledge of English, was unable to find a job, and explained to me that he was on the verge of leaving the region again and settling back in the camps in Kurdistan, as there were at least prospects of a job there and at least the electricity supply was halfway secured.

In fact, NGOs and international organisations are often more present in the camps in Kurdistan than in the Sinjar Region itself. Many Êzîdî accuse the PDK, which is in power in Dohuk, of wanting to keep the displaced in the camps for political reasons, because this would enable it to force the loyalty of thousands of voters in Nineveh Governorate in elections. Providing for the displaced has also become a lucrative business for some.

At the same time, any initiative in the camps is destroyed. Meanwhile, a whole generation of young people are growing up in the camps in Kurdistan who have already spent seven years in tents and have only learned to read and write in provisional schools run by the Kurdistan Regional Government. Many of these young people no longer know Arabic, but are learning only Kurdish, which further reduces later job prospects in Sinjar. Salaries of state employees continue to be paid in the camps without them even having to do anything in return. This, too, contributes to a dependence on an auxiliary economy that stifles any personal initiative. In the long term, the majority of the Êzîdî are thus turned into passive recipients of aid.

The fact that for many IDPs neither the camps in the autonomous region of Kurdistan nor the return to Sinjar offers a desired perspective was demonstrated once again in the autumn of 2021, after the Belarusian dictator Lukashenko tried to put pressure on the EU by means of asylum seekers from the Middle East. Among the refugees brought to Minsk to be herded to Poland, Lithuania and Latvia in the direction of the EU were many Êzîdî from IDP camps in Kurdistan. They became a pawn in the conflict between the EU and Belarus. When the English version of this book was completed, no statistics existed about those thousands of asylum seekers who were stuck in the cold autumn forests at the EU's external borders and were sometimes brutally driven back to Belarus by the Polish police and army with illegal pushbacks. However, the author of this book is aware of quite a number of families from Sinjar who disappeared from their relatives at the EU external border after the Polish, Latvian or Lithuanian police officers took away their mobile phones.

These people deliberately take the risks in the forests and swamps at Europe's external borders and are well aware that they may not survive such an escape. For many Êzîdî from the IDP camps, however, the threat of death at the European borders is now less threatening than the hopeless existence in the IDP camps where they have been living for over seven years.

21
Regional conflicts
Sinjar in the crosshairs of Turkey and Iran

Because of its strategic position between the parts of Syria and Iraq controlled by the Syrian Democratic Forces, since 2018 Sinjar has increasingly become one of the regions where an intense Turkish–Iranian rivalry is palpable. Since then, Turkish air strikes have posed one of the greatest security risks in the region. On 15 August 2018, Zekî Şengalî, one of the most important Êzîdî leaders within YBŞ, was assassinated in a Turkish attack. The Turkish President Erdoğan has repeatedly declared Sinjar to be the second Qandil and a threat to the security of his country.

Turkish air raids do not only kill commanders and fighters of the YBŞ. On 5 November 2019, three civilians were injured by Turkish air attacks. On 15 January 2020, Zerdaşt Şengali, yet another local commander of YBŞ and its press spokesman, was killed together with other fighters of YBŞ. Zerdeşt Şengalî, who I came to know better during my research for this book, was a child of Sinjar through and through and not a PKK fighter from Turkey. Born in 1991 under the name Nezar Bapîr Murad in the village of Borik in the northeastern Sinjar region, he had joined YBŞ only in 2014 in the course of the IS attack.

Such Turkish air attacks do not only serve to combat the YBŞ, but also to intimidate the population. Apparently, the aim is to prevent the civilians displaced in 2014 from returning to their villages. In spring 2020, when the situation of displaced persons in Kurdistan had massively deteriorated due to the spread of COVID-19 and the strict lockdown by the Kurdistan Regional Geverment, more and more families decided to return to Sinjar after all. Living in the ruins of their villages now seemed to be more attractive than the lockdown in the tent camps. On 14 June 2020, shortly after about 2,050 families had returned to Sinjar,

Turkey finally started the most violent bombing of the region since the end of the fighting with IS.

Although Turkish pressure has officially led to a withdrawal of the PKK from the region, the regional PKK-related militia YBŞ has remained present and still controls the northwest of the region. In 2019, the relationship between the YBŞ and the Iraqi army also suffered significant cracks: as mentioned earlier, on Sunday 17 March 2019, a shooting occurred near Xanasor between fighters of the YBŞ and the Iraqi army. The YBŞ fighters had refused to stop at an Iraqi army checkpoint, allegedly leading the Iraqi soldiers to regard them as smugglers. In fact, smuggling between Syria and Iraq has become an important business in this region. The portrayal of a mix-up is therefore quite plausible. In the end, two people were left dead on each side. Subsequently, the situation escalated again on 19 March during peace talks between the two sides, when both sides opened fire on each other after a few minutes. The problem was finally resolved through negotiations, but such conflicts contribute to the insecurity of the population, as do the attacks by Turkey.

In October 2020 the government in Baghdad and the government of the Kurdistan Region finally agreed on a security and administrative agreement on the Sinjar district. The agreement, which bypassed all local forces and was negotiated exclusively between Erbil and Baghdad, envisages the withdrawal of all local militias, including the YBŞ and all other People's Mobilisation Units. In the future, only the local police, the National Security Service and the intelligence service will be responsible for the security of the region. The office of Iraqi Prime Minister Mustafa al-Kadhimi and the Iraqi Ministry of the Interior are to employ 2,500 local police officers, including 1,500 from the IDP camps.

However, this bilateral agreement between Erbil and Baghdad was reached not only without the local actors, but also without the consent of any of the militias that are now expected to withdraw from the region.

Until the completion of the English version of this book in the summer of 2021, the agreement between Erbil and Baghdad could not be implemented. The YBŞ, which has massively fortified the parts of the mountains under its control with underground fortifications, will certainly not simply leave the region voluntarily at the request of Baghdad and Erbil.

While travelling in the western part of the mountainous region in spring 2021 I could observe that the mountains are full of huge tunnels and underground positions of the YBŞ. If anybody, whether Iraqi or the Turkish army, would want to conquer that region, there would be heavy fighting about every metre of land against fighters who know the territory extremely well, as most of the YBŞ fighters are locals who have close connections to civilians. And the YBŞ is not only an Êzîdî force anymore; Sunni Arabs from the villages in the far west and the northwest of the region also joined YBŞ. Thus it would be really difficult to wipe out such a locally rooted militia.

As a result of this strength it seems that the Iraqi army rather tries to contain than to fight the YBŞ. In early 2021 the Iraqi army erected a new border fence between Syria and the YBŞ-controlled regions in Sinjar. This does not necessarily mean that there is no more smuggling going on at that border, but it only happens if the local commanders of the Iraqi army are included and get their share of the profit.

The YBŞ itself has always raised the Iraqi flag on its checkpoints as well since 2019. A stronger integration of the YBŞ into the Iraqi security structures is also in the interest of the YBŞ itself in view of the repeated Turkish drone attacks. Prime Minister al-Kadhimi, in office since May 2020, assured the YBŞ through intermediaries in April 2021 that the Iraqi army would not attack the YBŞ or disarm its police forces by force. Although no one knows whether future governments will see themselves bound by such a merely informal promise, a major military confrontation between the Iraqi army and the YBŞ is unlikely in the medium term. Nor do the YBŞ fighters in the region necessarily regard the Iraqi army as enemies. Fear reigns above all from Turkish drone attacks.

The region is of strategic importance not only for Turkey, but also for Iran and the pro-Iranian militias in Iraq and Syria. Many of the supplies for the pro-Iranian militias fighting on the side of the Syrian regime in Syria run through the region. In particular, the strait from Mosul via the Shiite militia-controlled Tal Afar via Sinjar City to Syria is an important route for Iran and its allies.

And finally, the region, in which smuggling has always played an important economic role, has meanwhile also become part of transnational smuggling routes. Not only sheep and cigarettes, but also much more lucrative goods such as drugs are now smuggled here between Iraq and Syria on their way to Europe and the Gulf States. Those who earn money from it also belong to those groups that are not interested in stabilising the region.

22
Marginalised and instrumentalised
Is there a future for the Êzîdî in Iraq?

The fact that a part of the Êzîdî population of Sinjar has survived the genocide of IS and that IS was militarily defeated as a para state, if not necessarily as an organisation, in March 2019 does not mean that the suffering of the survivors has ended and that the Êzîdî in Iraq can now hope for a better future. Rather, they have been drawn into the inner-Iraqi and supra-regional conflicts. The war against IS intensified the dependency of the two parties (PDK and PUK) that dominate the Kurdistan Region on the rival regional powers of Turkey and Iran, repeating the alliances of the intra-Kurdish fratricidal war of the 1990s in which the PDK was supported by Turkey and the PUK by Iran.[1] This kind of dependency also has its effects on the clients of these parties in Sinjar. The lack of an autonomous economic basis has pushed all military actors in Sinjar into a dependency on external funders and external political and military allies. But this also means that the conflicts between the US and Iran, between Erbil and Baghdad, between the PDK and the PKK, or between the PDK and the PUK have immediate effects on the relations between the local Êzîdî militias. Even though the militias occasionally pursue their own respective self-interests and local disputes also play their role, this dependency on arms deliveries, military training, and financial donations from the outside creates a situation in which Sinjar increasingly turns into a stage for proxy conflicts between the big actors in the Middle East.

These conflicts and the failure to make decisions with regard to the future political status largely contribute to the delay of any reconstruction in the region. This means a lack of doctors, teachers and other personnel necessary for the welfare of potential returnees. The lack of infrastructure and supply as well as the politically motivated blockade of the most important connecting road between Sinjar and Kurdistan are part of the reason why so few people are returning.

This feeling of insecurity is also amplified by the insufficient legal accounting for the crimes of the past. Even though membership in IS is sanctioned with the death penalty in Iraq, the sentencing of defendants is often executed with undue haste and without detailed legal accounting. Well-connected and wealthy perpetrators frequently manage to buy their way out in a highly corrupt system. Moreover, to this day there is evidence that Êzîdî women and children are still held captive by Sunni families in Mosul, some other towns in the region and even in Turkey or the Gulf states.

In this situation, many Êzîdî call for the support of the international community, but so far, that community has shown little interest. A military presence of international troops would require the approval of the Iraqi government, but humanitarian aid and diplomatic initiatives are also few and far between. This is so despite the fact that even an unarmed mediating mission might contribute to an easing of the situation and to finding a political solution for the region. But given the big conflicts in Iraq and in the neighbouring Syria, Sinjar already seems to have been forgotten again. Even though the Nobel Peace Prize for Nadia Murad focused international attention on the situation of the women kidnapped and raped by IS, this has not led to greater efforts to reach a political solution for the region and a reconstruction. Sinjar thus remains both conflicted and economically and politically marginalised.

Many Êzîdî believe that they have no future in Iraq anymore. At the same time, they know that Europe has closed its doors, and in Sinjar itself many of them are struggling to prevent a mass exodus and to rebuild the region. But this can succeed only if both the Iraqi government and the international community see to it that the Êzîdî are no longer played against one another, if the attacks by Turkey come to an end, and if the regional powers stop slugging out their conflicts at the cost of the Êzîdî. Some kind of self-management of the region as a unified area which is recognised by the Iraqi government and enables the local population to autonomously decide its political future is not just the wish of most Êzîdî, but would also be an adequate form for all inhabitants of the

region, quite independently of their language or religion, to rene-
gotiate the ways in which they want to live together in the future.

Developments since the publication of the German edition of
this book have been contradictory and by no means all negative.
The weakening of the migration movement to Europe could
be related to the fact that it has become even more difficult to
cross the borders into Europe since 2020 due to the COVID-19
pandemic and the associated border closures. As described earlier,
the return of part of the population to the region was also related
to the COVID-19 crisis or the closures of IDP camps in the autonomous region of Kurdistan in spring 2020.

However, during my most recent visits to the region, in the spring
of 2021, I also had the impression that civilians' subjective sense
of security had improved, especially in northern Sinjar. Although
I did not conduct an empirical study on this, the Conflict and Sta-
bilization Monitoring Framework (CSMF) of the United States
Institute for Peace also came to a similar conclusion in June 2021.
It concluded that in the conflict-affected areas in Nineveh Governorate, 'ISIS is no longer the main security concern. Instead, it is
rampant unemployment that is at the top of people's minds.'[2]

This issue of unemployment, plus the lack of public services
(e.g. electricity and water supply), were repeatedly mentioned to
me during my last visits in 2021 as the main problems. These are
particularly problematic in those regions that lie outside the easily
accessible and again heavily populated villages in the north of the
mountains.

One of the most interesting aspects of the last few years is that
the IDP camps on the mountain itself have become more permanent and ultimately many of the villages on the mountain that
were desettled in the 1970s are now being repopulated. There is
a certain irony in that the genocide of IS, of all things, has partially reversed the development that the modernising dictatorship
of the Ba'th Party of the 1970s had imposed. Some people have
returned from the collective towns (*mujama'at*) of the Ba'th regime
to their villages on the mountains. Of course, not all of the former
villages have been repopulated, and the former *mujama'at* (at least
in the north) are by no means abandoned. However, some of the
old villages have re-emerged. In addition, one can find individual
homesteads scattered across the mountain in lonely high valleys

and mountain slopes, some of which were built in former villages and to which people have retreated who feel safer there.

However, the security thus gained is often exchanged for an even more precarious supply situation with public services. While a minimum of infrastructure is provided by NGOs and international organisations in the newly established or rebuilt villages south of Şerfedîn, and those along the paved road over the mountain between Kerse and Sinjar City, the situation is much worse in even more remote side valleys. For example, the mud houses in the high valley of Bardahele have no access to drinking water or electricity. A family visited during a hike who returned here in 2014 from Tîl Êzêr, the former collective town of Al-Qahtaniyya, told us that none of their seven children could attend school. None of the children speaks Arabic. No one in the family can read or write. Drinking water has to be fetched with great difficulty, and for electricity she has only a very small solar panel at her disposal, which is barely enough to charge her mobile phone.

Of course, there are no jobs either. Most families in Bardahele live from subsistence farming. What was common in this region two generations ago, however, is now perceived as poverty, so that many of those affected hope for outside help to alleviate the situation.

At least there is reason for hope for the surviving victims of the genocide on a legal level. After a long political struggle, a Survivors' Bill was passed on 1 March 2021. The law defines the atrocities against the Êzîdî, Christians, Shabak and (Shiite) Turkmen as genocide, and regulates assistance for survivors. It recognises 3 August as a national day of remembrance of victims and survivors of the genocide, and focuses on survivors of sexual violence. The Bill furthermore focuses on the need to prosecute the perpetrators for their crimes and that they shall not benefit from amnesty.[3]

However, it remains to be seen how much such a law will change the situation of the survivors. This will depend on the ability of the Iraqi state to function and to guarantee not only security in the region, but also a certain rule of law that enables survivors to insist on their rights.

In 2021 the underground networks of the so-called 'Islamic State' were regaining influence. As the civil war in Syria continues and as the political stability in Iraq is still precarious, the situation in the Sinjar region still cannot be considered safe and stable. There is hope, but for a highly traumatised population this might not be enough to permanently return home. Thus the future of the Êzîdî in Iraq is still uncertain.

PART II

Photographs

1. The Sinjar Mountains from the northwest with the village of Bara, January 2019.

2. Şerfedîn, one of the most important Êzîdî shrines in Sinjar, June 2016.

3. One of more than 70 mass graves of IS victims in the Sinjar region, June 2016.

4. Koço school, October 2018. In this school women and children were locked in on the first floor while men were shot.

5. Tents of the displaced on the plateau at Mount Sinjar, June 2016.

6. Displaced people at the tent camps on Mount Sinjar, September 2017.

7. Children from Sinjar at Xanke camp, one of the largest IDP camps in the Kurdistan Region of Iraq, May 2017.

8. Zerdaşt Şengali, YBŞ press officer at YBŞ headquarters west of Xanasor, January 2019. He was killed by a Turkish attack one year after this picture.

9. The well-known cleric Feqîr Cerdo on Mount Sinjar, September 2017.

10. Axîn Intiqam, commander of the Women's Units of Sinjar (YJŞ), January 2019.

11. Haydar Shesho, commander of HPÊ in Şerfedîn, June 2016.

12. Qasim Shesho as commander of the PDK's peshmerga in Sinjar, June 2016.

13. Advertisement for the Kurdistan Region government's independence referendum in Sinunê, September 2017.

14. Command of the Êzîdî Popular Mobilisation Units in the city of Sinjar, October 2018.

15. Memorial plaque for Zekî Şengalî in front of the Xanasor People's Council, October 2018.

16. HPÊ checkpoint at the entrance to Şerfedin, October 2018.

17. Sinjar City centre in April 2021 looks almost the same as it did after the recapture in 2015: the ruins of the city are full of explosives.

18. The Shiite Sîti Zayinab mosque in Sinjar City, April 2021. It was destroyed by IS, but has since been rebuilt.

19. The Shiite Ahl ul-Bayt mosque next to the Pîr Zekr shrine in Sinjar City was blown up by IS and could not be rebuilt as of April 2021, when this photograph was taken.

20. The Pîr Zekr shrine with its ancient sacred mulberry tree in Sinjar City, shown here in April 2021, is considered one of the holiest places of the Shiite Babawat, who in the past were often described as a heterodox group and sometimes celebrated religious festivals in common with the Êzîdî. The Islamic State also destroyed this shrine. In 2021, it was under reconstruction.

21. Êzîdî *ziyaret* on the highest peak of the Sinjar Mountains, Çêl Mêra (1463 m), April 2021.

22. Religious festival of the Êzîdî at the *ziyaret* of Sheikh Mend, April 2021.

23. The *ziyaret* of Sheikh Gureish, May 2021. It is located in a Sunni Muslim cemetery where members of the Kurdish-Sunni Tatan are buried, but is now visited and maintained by the Êzîdî. Until 2014, the *ziyaret* was visited by both Muslims and Êzîdî.

24. The cemetery at the *ziyaret* of Shebel Qasim, May 2021. This is one of the largest Êzîdî cemeteries. Wishes and problems are woven into the cloths on this sacred tree.

25. The *mazar* of Sheikh Mahamma, May 2021. It commemorates a Muslim sheikh who is said to have died here. However, it is an Êzîdî *ziyaret* near the village of Bara in the far west of the Sinjar Mountains. After its destruction by IS, the Ziyaret was not rebuilt until 2019.

26. The second *ziyaret* near Bara, Daqi Mera, May 2021. This was reportedly saved by a ransom payment made by local fighters to IS and thus remained in its original form.

27. *Ziyaret* Serê Kaniyê, May 2021. Not to be confused with the Kurdish town of the same name in Syria, it is also called 'little Lališ' because of its beautiful location in a mountain valley.

28. In addition to the large *ziyaret*, there are also so-called *nişangeh* (literally: place that symbolises something) in the region. These are small shrines that refer to a *ziyaret*. These can also be erected at significant natural phenomena, like this rock, May 2021.

29. The YBŞ municipality of Xanasor has created some sports facilities in the centre of the city, which are also used by mixed-gender groups, April 2021.

30. The villages in the south of the mountains, which were inhabited by Êzîdî until 2014, are still largely abandoned; only a few families returned to Tal Kassab in 2020, for example. Some have returned to the IDP camps in Kurdistan after a few months, May 2021.

31. Dugure in the north of the mountain has been slowly repopulated since 2020. However, the majority of residents were still in IDP camps in Kurdistan in 2021.

32. Cafe in Gohbal with various political symbols on the wall: the Iraqi flag, a martyr of the YBŞ and the flag of Ezîdxan as used by the supporters of HPÊ.

33. Most of the houses in the village of Bara are still built in the traditional style as mud houses, May 2021.

34. One of the worst massacres of IS took place in the village of Hardan. Most of the men of the village are still buried in an anonymous mass grave at the road junction towards Hardan, shown here in May 2021.

35. Of the old mountain village of Smoky, only the cemetery and some sheep pens remain in May 2021, when this photograph was taken. Smoky was one of the villages that Saddam Hussein had destroyed in the 1970s in order to settle the people in collective towns.

36. Some of the villages that were desettled in the 1970s became refuges in the wake of the IS attack and have since been partially rebuilt. This photo shows a reconstructed mud farmhouse in Bardahele in the central Sinjar Mountains, May 2021.

37. Only a few locals have returned to the small village of Karke, May 2021.

38. New fighters are sworn in for the YBŞ on the Zerdaşt plateau on Mount Sinjar, May 2021.

39–40. The Arab village of Wadi Bir Jari in the northwest on the Syrian border, May 2021. Wadi Bir Jari is a former collective town. Arabs have always lived here in the border region. Under Saddam Hussein, however, Arab nomads were also forcibly resettled because the Arab nationalist regime at the border preferred the Arab population to the Kurdish-speaking Yezidi. After the collapse of the regime in 2003, smuggling was the only source of income left for the people here.

41. The Arab village of Umm al-Dhiban in western Sinjar, May 2021. The village has been under the control of the YBŞ, which has also integrated Arab fighters into its ranks, since 2015.

42. Many villages of the De'ud Arab tribe around the small town of Qairawan, whose sheikhs were among the main supporters of IS in the region, remain semi-deserted to this day. However, members of the tribe who have not committed any serious crimes have been allowed to return, as here in the village of Sibayat Harush, May 2021.

PART III

Interviews

The interviews in this section were mainly conducted in the course of several field trips, partly in Arabic, but also in English, German or with the help of a translation into Kurdish. Some of the shorter interviews were also conducted by telephone, especially when it was not possible to travel to the region due to the war situation. Most of the interviews were conducted in Sinjar or in the IDP camps. A few were also conducted in Erbil or in the diaspora. However, all interviews provide an authentic snapshot from the respective personal perspective of the interviewees.

Baba Sheikh (Bavê Şêx) Khurto Haci Ismail, also called Keto (Xeto)
Born 1933, supreme cleric of the Êzîdî since 1995
10 September 2010

In the course of the last few years, the Êzîdî have come more and more under the pressure of jihadist forces. The attacks in two villages in Sinjar in August 2007 were certainly the climax of this violence. How do you assess the situation of your religious community in Iraq?

The situation is difficult for everyone in Iraq and the violence affects many people, but for us as Êzîdî it is particularly hard because we are a relatively small group which cannot defend itself. The larger groups dominate their own areas, whereas we depend on the protection of the state and if the state is unable to protect us, the situation for the smaller religious communities will simply become even more difficult. Here in the Şêxan region, we are a bit safer because here, the Kurdish Peshmerga is in control, but in Mosul, Sinjar and the Nineveh Governorate it is much more dangerous for us. Even here in Şêxan, we are frequently having problems.

What exactly are these problems?

This region used to be inhabited almost exclusively by Êzîdî, but then, under Saddam, many Êzîdî were expelled because he wanted to Arabise the region. But now, we are experiencing a Kurdisation and many [Muslim] Kurds have been settled here. We are once again a minority in our area. The conflict between the government in Baghdad and the Kurdish government in Erbil also doesn't make it easier for us because most of the Êzîdî live in the contested areas, which sometimes even makes it difficult to get from Sinjar to Şêxan. Of course, the situation is better than under Saddam Hussein, but without a solution for these conflicts, it remains hard. Therefore, more and more Êzîdî are emigrating to Germany, which weakens our community here even more.

You just mentioned yourself that more and more Êzîdî are leaving Iraq and emigrating to Europe, particularly Germany. One of your brothers also lives in Germany with his family; that is, you know the situation there well. In Germany, it is often difficult for young Êzîdî to keep the commandments of their religion, particularly the marriage rules. Êzîdî in Germany also fall in love with non-Êzîdî, and for the members of Şêx and Pîr families it is particularly difficult to find legitimate partners for a marriage. Are there considerations on your part to reform the strict marriage rules of the Êzîdî?

There are many discussions about this in our community, but such things can't be changed from one day to the next. In the past, these rules have helped to protect us in a hostile environment. Whether they are still appropriate today, we need to discuss openly. But such things need time and also cannot be decided just by myself.

But what do you then say, for example, to a young woman from a Pîr family in Germany? Who is supposed to marry her if there are at best one or two men in all of Germany who also come from Pîr families and are the same age?

She could also marry a man from Iraq. There are enough Êzîdî here who would be only too happy to go to Germany, and probably she would be able to select her future husband from these at will.

In Germany, this strict approach leads to a situation in which more and more young Êzîdî completely turn away from the religious community or are expelled from it, just because they insist on marrying someone else. It makes a difference whether someone grows up in an Êzîdî village or in the diaspora, where he or she primarily gets to know non-Êzîdî.

We Êzîdî here have already survived many massacres and genocides and we will also survive the current situation. Of course,
some things will change when more and more of our people are
in Europe, but our social order and our marriage rules belong to
the core of our society and even in Germany, they cannot simply
be changed.

*Let's get back to the situation in Iraq. As you know, the jihadist
propaganda against the Êzîdî constantly uses the terrible lynching
of Du'a Khalil Aswad, who was murdered because of her romantic
relationship with a Muslim in April 2007, in order to present the
Êzîdî as barbaric and anti-Muslim. Of course, this murder doesn't
justify any of the deeds of the jihadists and I am perfectly aware of
the fact that it is being misused for propaganda. But even so, the
murder happened. The policemen who were standing by did not
prevent the family from murdering their own daughter. The people
there even filmed the event. What did you as the religious leader of
the Êzîdî say about it?*

I have condemned this terrible act right from the beginning and
have publicly declared that parents are not allowed to kill their
children, and that this of course also holds in a case like this. As
for myself, I even hosted Du'a Khalil here in this house to protect
her. She lived here right under my roof. But then the family
claimed they had forgiven their daughter and that they wouldn't
do her any harm. Therefore, she went back. In Bashiqa, I was no
longer able to protect her and I don't understand why the police in
this case simply stood by without intervening. I have clearly condemned this after it happened. Such behaviour goes against our
religion and I was really horrified that the family lied to me when
they claimed they had forgiven their daughter.

*Despite your clear stance in this regard, such cases continue to
happen, even in Germany.*

Yes, this has to do with tradition and a wrong concept of family
honour, but it cannot be justified on the basis of our religion.
Both I and the other clerics have always clearly condemned such

murders. Unfortunately, not everyone is listening to us, neither in Iraq nor in Germany.

With people leaving for Europe, many things change. Can the religion of the Êzîdî adapt to the needs of a diaspora community?

Our religion differs from the dogmatic book religions in that we have always transmitted our most important contents and religious instructions orally, which is why we have remained more flexible and are less prone to dogmatism. But given the hostile environment, we have also cut ourselves off from others to a relatively high degree. This was necessary to survive in a world in which we were denounced and persecuted. In Europe, we are not persecuted and because of that, certain things that have developed here in response to our persecution may perhaps no longer be necessary there. We Êzîdî are looking back at a millennia-old history during which we have frequently changed. In this regard, one only needs to remember the reforms introduced by Sheikh Adî. After him, Yazidism has had a different outlook in many respects. Therefore, in a changed world changes are certainly possible. But all of this requires time and many discussions; one cannot expect a minority to change if it is under a lot of pressure.

Sheikh Khairy Khedr (Şêx Xêrî Xidir)
Founder and first commander of the Tawûsê Melek Units, the predecessor group of the YBŞ; fatally wounded in battle on 22 October 2014
7 August 2014

How does the current situation on the Sinjar Mountains look like?

It is a catastrophe! Tens of thousands of women, men and children have fled here from IS. The supply situation is disastrous. We have only very little food and water. In August, it is very hot here and there is very little shadow on the mountain. The old and the sick are dying. We are supplied with helicopters and they also fly people out, but it is still far too little.

Will you be able to defend the mountain?

Yes, we will keep the mountain. So far, the fighters of IS haven't seriously tried to conquer the mountain itself and I think we are able to defend ourselves here. The problem is the supply situation, including arms and ammunition, as the Peshmerga have retreated with all their weapons. This means that we have to defend ourselves with our own weapons. Because the Iraqi army has also collapsed, we urgently need international support.

Did the Peshmerga of the PDK really retreat overnight?

Yes, on 3 August. The Peshmerga didn't even wait to give the civil population an opportunity to flee. In this situation, the people had no other choice but to flee to the mountain, while otherwise, they would at least have been able to take their cars and drive to Kurdistan. For the same reason, thousands of people were trapped in the south of Sinjar who could not flee to the mountain in time and have now fallen into the hands of IS in the village of Koço. The retreat of the Peshmerga was a betrayal of the Êzîdî which we will not forget.

What do you expect from the international community in this situation?

We urgently need military and humanitarian support! We need food, water, arms, ammunition and air attacks on the positions of the jihadists!

Naif Jaso
Brother of the mayor of Koço and traditional tribal leader of his village
9 January 2015

You are one of the few men to have survived the massacre of Koço. How did that happen?

When IS came, I happened to be in Dohuk and that is the reason why I survived. In Dohuk, I was in constant contact with my brother, mayor Ahmad Jaso, and I kept talking to him on the phone. Therefore, I knew the situation and could pass the information on to the Americans and the media. Unfortunately, it was of no use.

Why did so many Êzîdî fall into the hands of IS in Koço? Why were so few of them able to save themselves?

Koço used to have a population of about 1,700 people. The geographical situation of Koço is different from the one in the Sinjar Mountains. Koço is south of the city of Sinjar. We are at a distance of about 22 km from the mountain and of 13 km from a group of other Êzîdî villages. Koço is encircled by Arab villages, one of them directly next to it and two as you approach our village. To the west, there are even more Arab villages. When most of the Êzîdî fled on 3 August, the people in Koço also hoped to flee, but the distance was too great. Some people managed to reach the mountain behind Sinjar, but some were captured. The others remained in the village.

What happened to the people in the village? After all, your brother gave you a 'live' description of the situation on the phone.

The people who stayed in the village waited there until three o'clock in the afternoon. Then, Arabs from the neighbouring village came and told them, 'Collect your weapons and stay here in the village. You are safe here.' Then they came and collected the weapons and took them with them. One of them told the Êzîdî, 'I will come back tomorrow.' On the next day, he came again and said, 'We are giving you three days. Either you accept Islam or we will kill you!' In the course of these three days, people asked for help among the Arabs, among friends, colleagues, the Sheikhs of the region, in order to win time to decide what to do. The succeeded in getting the deadline extended to eleven days. We tried to win time to find a solution and to change the situation.

What did you do with this information?

We frantically tried to find a solution for ourselves. We pleaded with both Baghdad and America. We contacted Prime Minister

Maliki himself and we asked Ayatollah Sistani for help. We implored [the chief of staff of the Iraqi army] General Babeker Zebari. But none of them did anything. All of them, America and all of the others, were eagerly awaiting the attack to see what would happen.

How did the massacre of 15 August come about?

On 14 August, when the time we had been given had run out, they brought some food to the village. On the morning of 15 August, they came back. At around 10:30 a.m., they encircled the village and said: 'All of you have to go to the school!' This was a two-storey school into which they herded all of us. I told my brother, 'Today they will decide on your fate!' The IS fighters gathered everyone in the school and said to the villagers, 'Come on, we will take you to the Sinjar Mountains.' The people thus gathered in the school on the northern side of the village. They separated the women from the men. They took the women and the children including the boys up to the age of ten to the first floor and left the men and the older boys on the ground floor. When they gathered the people in the school, Kheri Bozani was with me and we contacted the air base of the Americans. I said to Kheri: 'The American fighter planes are flying above us. If they refuse to do anything, they will kill all of the men and kidnap all of the women. The best thing would be for the planes to attack the school and bring all of this to an end.' But someone in the American base said, 'That is against human rights.' I said, 'There are no human rights. We don't need any human rights, neither for ourselves nor for them.' I pleaded with him to attack our village, my sons, my brothers, my mothers, my sisters, because for us, that would still have been more honourable. Let them attack both us and IS. The American fighter planes were in striking distance from Koço. But the planes did nothing. Therefore, the IS fighters could bring their cars and tell the people, 'Come here and climb up. We'll take you to the mountain.' And before that, they told us, 'Collect your gold.' They collected more than three sacks of gold from the women and they said, 'Bring us your money!' And the people brought their money. I haven't seen it myself, but they said that it was more than seven sacks with money. The people were in a hurry to make their way to the mountains. They were supposed to take the people from the school to the mountain. But they brought them to a different place. They took a group that had been loaded onto a car to a waterhole and massacred them all. I knew a man from an Arab village near Koço, two kilometres from there. After they had collected all the mobile phones of the people in the school, I called him and told him, 'Sultan, they will kill them all!' I said to him, 'Please, leave the phone on, I want to hear your voice.' After a quarter of an hour, the man began to weep. I asked him, 'What happened?' He said, 'I've heard the sound of an explosion.' After they had brought the men from the ground floor of the school to the cars, it was the turn of the women. They have decorated Koço with cemeteries instead of gardens.

How many people fell victim to this massacre?

Altogether, 420 people were murdered. We know the exact number because they murdered all boys and men from ten to eighty years. Seventeen of the men managed to survive beneath the dead bodies. They were alive and were beneath four groups that were not buried immediately. All the other groups were buried instantly and thus nobody had a chance to survive. Two or three of the survivors later died of their wounds.

Right now, Koço is still under the control of IS, even after the liberation of the northern side of the mountain. Do you know anything about the fate of the women that were kidnapped at the time?

Most of the women and girls are still in the clutches of IS. From those who were liberated, we are hearing terrible stories about what was done to them. Their liberation must have the highest priority. But we are also waiting for the liberation of our village and for the moment when we can at least have access to our dead again.

Zekî Şengalî (İsmail Özden)
Important Êzîdî commander of YBŞ from the Turkish part of Kurdistan; killed by a Turkish air attack on 18 August 2018
14 November 2015

Yesterday, the news came in that you have reconquered Sinjar City together with the HPŞ and the Peshmerga. Is that true?

Yes, yesterday we advanced to the centre of the Sinjar and were able to capture the larger part of the city. Today, we also captured several villages to the west of it. We from the YBŞ were at the very front line and were the first to capture the city. The Peshmerga moved into the city only after us.

How did the battle for the city develop? In the end, the events really went unexpectedly fast.

Actually, IS already retreated right at the beginning of our offensive. These cowards simply fled without a fight.

How well does the cooperation with the other groups, that is, the HPŞ and the Peshmerga of the PDK, go?

At the moment, we are all fighting against the same enemy. But in fact it is really often our people who are at the front lines while the Peshmerga often only form the rear-guard and secure the supplies. But one must also not forget that many *heval*[1] from Rojava[2] and Bakur[3] are fighting on our side.

What is the current supply situation of the civilians and the fighters?

After the northern side of Sinjar was re-liberated in December 2014 and the connection to Rojava and Kurdistan was secured, the situation here has markedly improved, to the extent that the first civilians have already returned to the northern side of the mountain.

How are the liberated areas administered at the moment, and what kind of administration of the region do you want to see in the future?

Right now, Sinjar is administered by us, the Peshmerga and the HPŞ. The Peshmerga would like to subordinate the area to the government in Erbil, but we regard some kind of self-administration of the region as the better option. But in the end, this is something for the people here to decide for themselves.

Haydar Shesho (Heydar Şeşo) – 1st interview
Commander of HPÊ (known as HPŞ until November 2015)
2 June 2016

What is your take on the current situation here?

In December 2015, we liberated the whole northern part of the mountain and Sinjar City together with the Peshmerga and the YBŞ. But since the end of 2015, the front line has come to a stand-still. Here in the north, in Şerfedîn, the situation is very secure by now, which is shown by the fact that the people have finally returned. But in the south, the situation is completely different and as long as IS is so close, everything remains very insecure and most of the Êzîdî will not come back.

Your unit began in 2014 under the name Defence Force of Sinjar (Hêza Parastina Şingalê) and then in November 2015 renamed itself into Defence Force of Êzîdxan (Hêza Parastina Êzîdxanê). Why? What is that supposed to mean?

Today, we do not only work in Sinjar anymore, but want to be present for the Êzîdî everywhere. We work in all of Êzîdxan. Not just as a military force, but also, as a political and humanitarian one. We are dependent on no one else and are obliged only to the Êzîdî. And what we do is no longer just about Sinjar, but about all Êzîdî and our whole settlement area of Êzîdxan.

Does that mean that you are for some sort of cross-territorial Êzîdî area?

No, not necessarily. We only see ourselves as a pan-Êzîdî movement which wants to be available for all Êzîdî, even if they are in Armenia, Turkey or Syria.

*The HPŞ was previously registered as a People's Mobilisation Unit.
Then you were arrested in Kurdistan by the police of the PDK in April
2015 and dissociated yourself from the government in Baghdad. How
do you fund these units now? Are you paid by Baghdad or by Erbil?*

At the moment, we are getting no real support from either side
and are forced to rely on the support of Êzîdî donors. We already
have some support from Germany, but that is of course not sufficient to pay our fighters. We have many more young men who
want to fight for us than we can pay. Those who fight for us must
bring their own weapons and uniforms. Even though we see to it
that all members of our units have to eat, what we can give them
is certainly not sufficient for their families. My goal has always
been to build a really independent Êzîdî force which is dependent
neither on Bagdad nor Erbil. But this is of course a goal which is
very hard to finance.

*By now, there are two additional Êzîdî military actors apart from
the HPÊ, namely, the YBŞ and the Peshmerga of the PDK under the
command of your uncle, Qasim Shesho. What is your relationship
with these actors?*

We try to get along well with both and sometimes also act as medi-
ators between the Peshmerga and the YBŞ. But we are also often
caught in the middle and because we are those with the worst
equipment and the smallest financial resources, this is not an easy
situation.

*I would like to also ask you some questions about your family
history. After all, you are not the only family member active here,
but there is also your uncle Qasim, the commander of the Peshmerga of the PDK. How did your family become involved in the
politics of this region? After all, this reaches back into the history of
the Ba'th regime.*

My father Qaso Shesho and my uncle Qasim Shesho were members
of the PDK already at the end of the 1960s and we got into trouble
with the Ba'th regime already then, during the first rebellion of
Mullah Mustafa Barzani. Until 1975, they destroyed our villages

Rashid and Nusewan two times. In 1974, they arrested my father, my uncle Qasim and another uncle, as well as their cousins.

That was the time when the villages in Sinjar were destroyed?

Yes, it happened once before the arrest, and then a second time, when they destroyed all the villages in Sinjar and put all the people into twelve large collective settlements. At that time, my father and my uncle were sentenced to fifteen years in prison and remained in jail until the end of 1979. After this, we tried to live entirely normal lives just like all Iraqis and wanted to stay here in the region. But they did not leave our family alone, and finally, my father and my mother said that it was best for us to just leave Iraq, and thus, in 1982 we went to Syria, where we remained in exile trying to fight against the regime. At that time, we were not the only Êzîdî in Syria. Altogether, there were around 200 Êzîdî families in Syria who came from Iraq. Most of them were from Sinjar. At that time, Syria and Iraq were enemies. Syria had good contacts with Iran, and for that reason, it was totally at odds with Iraq during the war between Iraq and Iran. But nevertheless, in 1987 the Syrians arrested us as well as 13 or 14 other people and kept us in prison for two years. But due to the help of Jalal Talabani and his direct contacts with the Syrian president Hafiz al-Assad, we were able to get out of jail. I don't know what would have happened had Talabani not directly intervened with Assad.

At that time, Talabani was on good terms with Iran and Assad.

Yes, but immediately after our time in prison, my uncle came to the conclusion that we could no longer stay in Syria and then we went from Syria to Germany pretty quickly, in December 1989. Actually, we had wanted to go to Sweden, but we ended up being in Germany. Fortunately, we didn't have any problems there until we left in 2003.

You lived in Bad Oeynhausen, didn't you?

Before that, we lived in Hanover, and then my uncle Qasim moved to Bad Oeynhausen. I still have a second residence in Wolfsburg.

How have things developed since 2003?

In 2003, my uncle said, 'The regime is finished, what do you think? Shall we go back?' Most of our relatives wanted to stay in Germany, but at the time, I also wanted to go back, and then we went back to Iraq even before 9 April, the liberation of Baghdad. We were trained in Hungary by the Americans and then we were the second group of Iraqis who were brought back by the Americans. On 13 April, we were already in Sinjar. At that time, there were many Arabs here because before, the Êzîdî were not allowed to live in the city of Sinjar. Back then, we were permitted to live only in the villages. The only people allowed to live in the city were the ones who had lost a family member in the Iraq-Iran war. But in 2003, many of the Arabs who had worked with the regime against the Kurds for many years left the area because they were afraid of the revenge of the Kurds. These Arabs then all went to Ba'aj and other Arab places south of Sinjar.

That is already part of the prehistory of what happened in 2014.

Yes, after the Arabs had moved out, the Êzîdî could return to the city, and we thought that the Arabs had left for good. But unfortunately, after two weeks there was an order by Barzani that all those who hadn't killed any Peshmerga were allowed to come back. Many of the Arabs came back, but many Êzîdî now also moved to the city. After all, now we had again a government and a law that allowed us to live in the city. And this also meant that, if there were problems, these were supposed to be solved by law and not by vigilante justice. We were then under Kurdish control for one or two years, but after this, Sinjar increasingly came under Arab rule. I could see this, as I became a member of the Iraqi parliament in 2005.

You were then a member of Jalal Talabani's PUK.

Yes, exactly, until 2014 I was a member of the PUK and I always worked with the PUK, not the PDK. I was in parliament for a year, during which we agreed on the constitution. This was also the time when I was wounded by an attack.

When and where exactly did that happen?

That was on 17 September 2005 when there was an attack on our car in which three people lost their lives and I was wounded. And this terror attack happened in Mashahada, a small town between Baghdad and Samarra. At the time, this was still al-Qaida. We had already had a problem with al-Qaida before because they had set up a checkpoint in the street, but on that occasion, fortunately nothing serious happened. But after the attack in September 2005, I had to go back to Germany for two years, for medical treatment. In Germany, I had to undergo three surgeries on my hand. Then the terror here in Iraq continued. You have heard what the terrorists did in 2007.[4]

What was your relationship to the PDK and the Kurdistan Regional Government at that time? After all, your uncle Qasim Shesho became one of the most important PDK functionaries among the Êzîdî in Sinjar, but you were then still a member of the PUK, which was much less important here than in Silêmanî or Kirkuk.

Throughout this whole time, I didn't have a good relation with the PDK even though they always tried to pressure me to work with them. I always told them that if they wanted to help the Êzîdî people just as much as the Kurdish people, fine, but apart from that, we will be working only for our own people. Different from me, my uncle has almost always been on good terms with the PDK, almost always, not all the time. Sometimes, there were also problems between him and the PDK. My uncle is not like the other Êzîdî members of the PDK who go along with everything the PDK tells them. When there is something that he thinks is good for the Êzîdî, he will do it, but if he thinks something is not good for us, he will not go along. My uncle has always been in the presidium of the PDK of Sinjar, but he was only one among several others.

But these family ties to the PDK didn't help once it came to the defence of the region in 2014?

In the days leading up to 3 August 2014, we became aware that things would become very dangerous for us because after the conquest of Mosul by IS, only the road via Rabī'a remained open and everything else between us and Kurdistan was already under the control of IS. At the time, we organised a meeting in Şerfedîn together with my uncle which was attended by 500 young Êzîdî, and we said, we have to do something because the larger part of the Nineveh Governorate was already under IS control. We were almost encircled by IS and really only had the connecting road via Rabī'a left. At this meeting, my uncle said to me, 'What do you think you want to do?' In response, I told him, 'Even though it is good that the Peshmerga are here, I don't think that the Peshmerga alone are able to protect us. We have to arm ourselves and must take our protection into our own hands.' Then my uncle said, 'OK, then do that.' More than 3,500 young men entered their names on my list. And I took this list and went to the most important man of the PDK in Sinjar, Sarbast Baiperi, together with my uncle and told him that more than 3,500 young Êzîdî stood at the ready to protect Sinjar together with the Peshmerga, come what may. But Sarbast Baiperi stated in no unclear terms that the protection of Sinjar was the exclusive task of the Peshmerga and that they didn't need any help. We said, 'OK, no problem, whether you think you need us or not is up to you. But this is our own matter and we must protect ourselves.' Then he prohibited this and told us we couldn't do this because the people had registered themselves for the defence of 'the Êzîdî'. I then told him that if a Muslim were to register, I would be happy to write 'the people of Sinjar' on the list, but it was only Êzîdî who had registered with not a single Muslim among them. He then again told me quite unequivocally that this was not allowed but that he could guarantee that nothing would happen in Sinjar and if it did, they, the Peshmerga, would take care of it. Then I said, 'OK, but we beg to differ. After all, we are encircled from all sides.' He then again prohibited us from defending ourselves, and I said, 'Well, I will do what I think is right and you will do what you think is right.' He then once more prohibited our plan and this was the end of our talk in July. At that time, many Êzîdî who had been in the Iraqi army were coming back to Sinjar. After all, in June whole army units simply dissolved when IS captured Mosul and many of the Êzîdî soldiers took their weapons, came back to Sinjar, and had their weapons with them. But what did the Peshmerga do now? They established checkpoints everywhere, searched the people for arms and took the arms away from them. In this way, the Êzîdî soldiers lost their weapons. We told the Peshmerga over and over and again, 'Why do you take the weapons from these people? Leave them at least their weapons so that they can defend themselves!' But the Peshmerga did not listen to us. They probably took away 80 per cent of the weapons of the Êzîdî. At the time, we had cars and weapons. The Peshmerga took all of that away from us, even though they already had the very same weapons themselves. That is something I have already said in public more than once: The fact that the Peshmerga fled on 3 August had nothing to do with any lack of arms. In addition to their own weapons, they now also had ours and they could have easily held their ground against IS, preventing the terrorists from entering Sinjar. But unfortunately, they didn't do this. Militarily, the retreat of the Peshmerga in August was totally unnecessary. I then told Sarbast Baiperi that I would go to both the Kurdish parliament in Erbil and to Silêmanî with this list to enable us to build our self-defence as planned. Right on 2 August, I reached Duhok and in the night after that day everything happened. I then stayed overnight in Xanke[5] and in the middle of the night, a couple of minutes after half past three, a relative called me; his name is Daud Khafer, he is a friend of my uncle. He asked, 'Haydar, where are you?' I told him I was in Xanke and he asked why. And I was like, 'You were present at our meeting, and that's why I am now going to the Kurdish parliament.' But he said, 'No, it's too late, because IS is already on the way to Sinjar. Can you call Qasim Shesho and tell him? I have repeatedly tried to call him, but his phone was switched off. Can you let him know?' After this, I immediately called my uncle and that was the right thing to do because his phone was not available. Therefore, I called a boy I knew and asked him to hurry to my uncle and let him know. My uncle called me back and I told him that IS was attacking Sinjar and that it was doing so via a place called Ger Zerek. We both agreed that we had to do something. My uncle called the Peshmerga, that is, Sarbast Baiperi and several commanders. The told him, yes, go there and we will join you once our Peshmerga are ready. He took ten men and drove there, and he called Sarbast Baiperi every 30 minutes and asked where the Peshmerga were, until 5:30 or 6 a.m.

That is, he called and asked about the whereabouts of the Peshmerga from 3 a.m. to 6 a.m.?

Exactly, for three hours. And the distance is not great, just about 15 kilometres from Sinjar to Ger Zerek. Each time, Sarbast Baiperi said that the Peshmerga would be there right away. At 5:30, the men in Ger Zerek said, we only have a few light weapons and it is better for the women and children to leave for the mountain, while we will stay here as long as we manage to stay alive. Then the women and the children fled to the mountain and the men continued to defend the village. During that defence, about 40 to 50 men died, but the children and the women could escape. After this, Qasim Shesho went to Tel Azer. It was already empty as the people had fled to the mountain. And then he drove to Sarbast Baiperi in Sinjar and confronted him, asking why the Peshmerga hadn't shown up. Baiperi said that he hadn't got the permission to send them and that they would now leave Sinjar and Qasim should come with him. But my uncle responded, 'No, I'm staying here!' Then Sarbast Baiperi ordered him to come with him as the Peshmerga were all ready to leave Sinjar. But my uncle stayed behind and was able to see how the IS people went into the offices even before the Peshmerga had left and took the papers there, without the Peshmerga doing anything about it.

That is, the administration was handed to IS without a fight?

Yes, that's what my uncle saw. There were also local Muslims who cooperated with IS, and they took over the offices even before the fighters of IS had actually arrived. When my uncle saw that the city was handed over without any resistance, he went to the mountains to fight. He said, 'Yes, I have understood now. This was a big lie to the detriment of the Êzîdî.' Today, the PDK claims to have done things for the Êzîdî, but for that time, that isn't true at all. Back then, the PDK didn't do anything for the Êzîdî. We don't know the exact background behind all of this, but this is the way it was. In any case, Sarbast Baiperi and the Peshmerga withdrew and left us hanging on a limb.

Sarbast Baiperi himself was not a local Êzîdî, was he?

No, Sarbast Baiperi is a Muslim from Duhok. But he was the local PDK boss, and whenever the Êzîdî wanted something, they had to ask him for permission.

How did things develop on a local level after this?

Qasim Shesho went outside of the city and into the mountains for about one or two kilometres but got the order that it was useless to stay there, and then he realised that it was over and retreated to the mountains for good. He called me and told me I should stay in Dohuk because Sinjar was lost, and he described to me how the Peshmerga had done nothing and handed Sinjar to IS instead. He said I couldn't go there, but I answered that I would do despite his objections. He tried to talk me out of it and argued IS would arrest me if I did. But I wouldn't allow him to talk me out of it and decided to drive back all the same. I wanted to go back and early in the morning at seven o'clock I told my driver about my plan, but also, that we could die if we went. I wanted to leave it to him whether he wanted to do this as it was really dangerous. But my driver simply said, 'If you go, I will drive you!' Then, the two brothers of your friend Mirza Dinnayi, Khalaf and Qasim, called me and told me that their families were still there, but that they themselves were right here in Duhok. They also wanted to go back to Sinjar and thus we agreed to try it together. In Sêmêl,[6] I waited for them for twenty minutes and then we went off together. But now I didn't need the driver anymore and I told him to stay behind. We had only our small arms with us, nothing else. Then we came to the Peshmerga checkpoint in Suhela, where we were asked where we wanted to go. When I said that we wanted to go to Sinjar, they said, 'Sinjar is finished! All the people are leaving Sinjar for Kurdistan.' I told them, 'We have 300,000 people in Sinjar; I must go back to them. How is it possible for the Peshmerga to simply leave like that?' He says, 'I don't know. If you go there, you have to take care of your safety yourself. We won't do it and don't accept any responsibility. Just wait for a group of Peshmerga; some of them want to go to Sinjar. You can go with them!' We then waited for these Peshmerga for about 40 minutes, but no one came. Ahmed Şingali, a young journalist who works for the PUK, was also there and waited together with us. He also thought that all of this was out of kilter and told us that, under the circumstances, he would join us. Then there arrived around 50 Peshmerga with a lot of heavy weapons, hummers, and other army vehicles. They were driving in the direction of Rabī'a, and we went with them. But the Peshmerga then stayed behind in Rabī'a, and Ahmed Şingali stayed behind with them whereas I drove on together with Khalaf and Qasim. After 10 kilometres, there was a road, and there, we encountered droves of Peshmerga who were all driving in the opposite direction. But when we asked them what was up, they wouldn't tell us. The street was so crowded that we often had to wait on the side-lines. Altogether, it took us five hours to get from Sêmêl to Sinunê, a distance which normally takes two or three hours. At 2 p.m., we arrived in Sinunê. In the course of these five hours, I saw many, many Peshmerga with many arms, including heavy arms, like Doshka[7] and everything. I asked a number of them why they hadn't stayed in Sinjar, but I never got an answer. I also even met the head of the Asayîş in Sinjar whose name is Qasim Simmu and who was alone in his office. I wanted to talk to him, but he only looked away and refused to speak with me. When we came to Sinunê at two o'clock in the afternoon, the police were still there, the Peshmerga, they were all still here, the whole city was still under Kurdish control and no IS was to be seen anywhere. At the same time, the people were fleeing the place. I then asked the Peshmerga what they were waiting for, and they told me that they were waiting for Sarbast Baiperi and the other leaders of the Peshmerga. And I said to them, 'But nothing has happened here so far, so why do you want the people to flee and leave the area even though as of yet not a single IS fighter has shown up?' The Peshmerga admitted that they didn't have an answer to this and were simply waiting for orders from above. We didn't get any answers from anyone. Khalaf Bahri, who at the time was working with the YPG but is now with the Şerfedîn temple,[8] also came and joined our discussion about what to do now. I then split from Dr Mirza's brothers because they drove on to Xanasor and I decided to stay in the area together with Khalaf Bahri. Thereafter, I drove to Şerfedîn where I met our people. But there were only ten men there and they had hidden their weapons because we had been told by Sheikh Ismail[9] that all people who were found with weapons would be executed. Then I said to them, 'If we do nothing, we are also finished, so go and get your arms!' Then everyone of them went to fetch their arms, that is, their Kalashnikovs, because that's all we had, and then we were finally armed again. We then decided to set up a checkpoint right there and that we would allow nobody to enter Şerfedîn. Then Sheikh Ismail came back and asked what we were doing here. And we told him that we were staying because we had many families here and we had to defend them. But Sheikh Ismail said, 'What can anyone do here with only a few fighters and Kalashnikovs when all the Peshmerga are gone. We must all get out of here!' I retorted that it didn't matter whether there were Peshmerga or not. But Sheikh Ismail responded, 'We have many families here. You may be able to defend yourselves here for a day or two, but that will be it. We need to get the families out of here.' I called my uncle Qasim and asked him where he was. He answered that they were in the mountains and that there were so many people there that it was almost impossible to move. I explained the situation and told him that IS had not yet arrived where we were. He then said, 'Try to stay there until we come.' But Sheikh Ismail said that we could not stay with our weapons. We then said, 'OK, for starters, we will go to the mountains. There are many families here, and if something happens, we actually can't do anything.' Thus, we first went to our old village in the mountains. There were so many people there! We waited for my uncle for two or three hours and then we deliberated with him. We concluded that we couldn't defend ourselves in the place where we were. In order to do so, we had to go to our house and to try to stay there and to simply defend ourselves as long as we were alive, and to try to defend the temple.

And your house is there right in front of the temple and therefore, you could establish a line of defence there?

Exactly, that was the plan. My uncle then also wanted to join us, and thus, we began to defend Şerfedîn. When we came back home, we were 16 people. We began with just 16 people. Many of the residents had already left and we told Sheikh Ismail that he could now also leave. We would stay as long as we were alive and defend the temple of Şerfedîn. On the first day, we collected everything that was left here into a stockpile and accommodated ourselves. Then two or three cars of IS came which had about 50 hostages with them, and one of the cars took a turn to Şerfedîn. The IS fighters apparently thought that everybody had already left. I told my people that they were only allowed to shoot once I did. The IS people came closer and we said to ourselves that we had many families here and if they turned around, we wouldn't do anything. Right at the place where I live now, right at the corner of the house, they tried to enter a house that was still in construction. We waited and they climbed onto their car again with their weapons, and then I began to shoot and was joined by the others. We hit and killed one of their fighters right away and then the car immediately turned around. When the other fighters saw this, they instantly abandoned the 50 hostages and bolted. These 50 people all joined us and augmented our force. The IS cars drove on to Sinunê, and some of our people there who had stayed behind later told us that after this, the IS people would always tell other IS people to be cautious when they got to Şerfedîn. But these first three days were terrible. There are some things that I will never forget. We saw many women who simply left their children behind in Şerfedîn, or old people who couldn't go on anymore. These are images I can't forget. But then, more and more people came to us until we were altogether more than 1,000 people, not just in Şerfedîn, but also in Kerse, in the mountain, where many civilians had fled. Between 3 August and the opening of the corridor to Syria by the PKK, everything was simply a catastrophe. These few days were the worst thing I had seen in my whole life until then. After this, the PKK came, and Qasim Shirwan and a few others, the YPG from Syria. And so far, I still say that no matter how the corridor of the PKK came about at the time, the main thing is that the PKK did establish it and that more than 30,000, maybe 50,000 people could flee via Syria. I will not forget what the PKK did at that time. It doesn't matter whether IS got money for this; later, someone from the People's Mobilisation Units told me that they paid IS millions to allow the PKK to establish the corridors. Abu Mahdi al-Muhandis[10] told me at the time that they had paid IS several million dollars to make this possible. But regardless of how exactly this happened, I will be eternally grateful to the PKK for saving tens of thousands lives in this place.

But back then, a sizable number of fighters of the YPG and the PKK also died when they opened this corridor.

Not at that time, the corridor was opened without the use of arms.

But the YPG and the YBŞ tell a different story.

They opened the corridor without military force and then, after about 20 days, they closed it, again without using force. Everyone agreed to this, both IS and the PKK, and the PDK, the PUK and the Iraqi government as well. The goal back then was for all Êzîdî to leave Sinjar, and when we and some others said that we would not leave Sinjar, they closed the corridor again. After this, IS often tried to capture Sinjar, but they never succeeded. Of course, we also lost people, but we were able to keep Sinjar. One month later, Mîr Tehsîn Beg[11] called me, but I didn't want to talk to him because I said if he tried to get in touch one month after the massacre, I didn't feel like talking to him, and I passed him on to Daud who spoke with him for almost 15 minutes. Then Daud passed him back to me, saying he couldn't understand a word and I should talk to him. And then Mîr Tehsîn Beg told me, 'Haydar, can you hear me? You have to leave Sinjar! As long as you are there, the Peshmerga will not go there. As long as the five villages on the mountain are still controlled by you and the PKK, nobody will come to help the people there. You must leave, then help will be sent, but otherwise, it won't.' I answered that I would not do this.

That was at the beginning of September 2014?

Yes, thereabouts. At that time, we were also visited by a politician of the PUK. It was then possible to get through to us and I was really told that the Peshmerga would not come here as long as the big Êzîdî villages were under the control of the Êzîdî. Then the Peshmerga finally did advance towards the west, but after that, they waited for a full 73 days in Rabi'a and did not advance any further. Until 20 October, all the bigger places in the north were under our control. Only Xanasor, Xerdan and parts of Sinunê were under the control of IS. Other parts of Sinunê were under the control of the PKK. But we had far too few arms and too little ammunition and we also didn't get any supply. On 20 October, we had to leave the bigger places in the north and were dislodged by IS. We retreated to the mountains and to Şerfedîn. And after Mîr Tehsîn Beg's claim that the Peshmerga wouldn't come as long as we were here turned out to be correct, we had to give up the villages in the north to get them to come here. It would have taken the Peshmerga only two hours to get here, but they didn't do so until the end of October, even though IS was temporarily very weak. The Peshmerga even promised to my uncle several times that they would come, but they never kept their promise.

And when did the Peshmerga finally come?

That was only in December. At that time, they simply drove in. But by then, IS has already ceased fighting. Anyone who claims that the Peshmerga even fired a single shot between Rabi'a and Xanasor is simply lying. IS retreated just as peacefully as the Peshmerga did in August 2014. When IS retreated, the PKK advanced simultaneously with the Peshmerga. The PKK captured Xanasor and told us it was ours, while the Peshmerga took Sinunê. The US planes also didn't have to bomb anything. It is true that they were flying, but IS simply retreated. Later, Masoud Barzani also came to see my uncle in Şerfedîn and my uncle wanted me to meet him, but I told I was not interested. Another one who came was Nêçîrvan Barzanî,[12] but I didn't want to meet him either. If the Peshmerga had fought and if they had sacrificed just a hundred of their people, they could have saved a thousand people and we would have been spared a lot of terrible things.

There is an enormous difference between the behaviour of the Peshmerga in the Nineveh Governorate and that of those here in Sinjar. In the plain, where there are Christians, they warned the people before their retreat and gave them the opportunity to escape. Here, they didn't do that. What is your take on that? Why didn't they fight here in Sinjar at least for two days to enable the population to flee?

In Bashiqa and Bahzani,[13] the Peshmerga also didn't do this; they only did it in the Christian villages.

That is, you think that this was specifically directed against the Êzîdî.

I wouldn't say it so bluntly. But the Êzîdî were an easy sacrifice. At that time, nobody supported the Êzîdî. The Christians had the Europeans and the Turkmens had Turkey, but we Êzîdî had no one. We believe that the PDK were quite content to leave Sinjar and that there was an agreement with IS allowing it to take it over. The PDK back then thought that IS could be a good neighbour for the Kurdistan Region. Actually, the Peshmerga didn't have any problem with IS.

I still remember that in July, after the capture of Mosul and the massacre in Sinjar, a number of PDK followers were actually quite happy to see IS destroy Iraq for them. They hoped that this would enable them to attain an independent Kurdistan very quickly.

Yes, unfortunately this is the way they thought back then. But after that, other groups of IS entered the picture that didn't feel bound by any such agreements. There certainly was some kind of agreement with regard to Sinjar.

As far as I know, none of the commanders of the Peshmerga has ever been taken to task, right?

No, no one was ever held accountable for this. If the Peshmerga had fought at that time, IS wouldn't have had a chance. But from somewhere on high there was an order to retreat; otherwise, this could not have happened.

Qasim Shesho (Qasim Şeşo) – 1st interview
Organiser of the self-defence of local Êzîdî in 2014 and commander of the PDK Peshmerga in Sinjar from 2015 to October 2017
2 June 2016

You are now the commander of the PDK Peshmerga here in Sinjar. In 2014, after the retreat of the PDK Peshmerga, you sharply criticised the government of the Kurdistan Region and you began to build your own units. What is your current relationship with the Kurdish ruling party PDK?

I am now the commander of the official Peshmerga here. That is, I am subordinated to the Peshmerga Ministry, which also pays my troops. What happened in 2014 was a gigantic mistake. At that time, the Peshmerga completely turned their backs on us. But at that time, the Peshmerga here were Muslims from other parts of Kurdistan and even the head of the PDK here was a Muslim from Duhok. They all ran away and didn't fight. But now the Peshmerga are from here and mostly Êzîdî from this region. The Peshmerga back then betrayed us, but that was not the fault of President Barzani himself, and he was the only one who helped in the aftermath. Now, the Êzîdî are themselves Peshmerga and we would never turn our backs on our own people.

You don't only get salaries from the Peshmerga Ministry, but Germany also supplies weapons to the Peshmerga to help them fight IS.

So far, we haven't got any weapons from Germany. We are sorely lacking in arms and ammunition. We haven't seen any arms from Germany here.

But where do these weapons go if they don't reach you at the front?

I don't know. We are certainly not getting any.

How is the cooperation with the other military groups here going, with the HPÊ of your nephew Haydar Shesho and the YBŞ?

My relationship with my nephew is fine; after all, back then we went to Syria and then Germany together and have a long common history. While it is true that Haydar joined the PUK and that we have our political differences, we work together and understand each other well. We have also fought against IS here together.

But now he has his own militia and my men are part of the Peshmerga. But with the PKK, we are having really big problems. They regard Sinjar as an extension of their region in Rojava, and that, we cannot put up with. We see ourselves as part of the Kurdistan Region of Iraq and I think we Êzîdî will have a future here only as a part of this autonomous region.

When this city was recaptured in November 2015, IS hardly even put up a defence. Why is it that the front hasn't moved forward since? Why have the southern villages of the Êzîdî such as, for example, Koço, still not been liberated?

The Americans prohibited us from doing that because they fear complications with the Iraqi government if too large an area is recaptured from IS by us Kurds. They are afraid that this could lead to fissures in the alliance against IS. Personally, I would very much like to liberate the rest of the region, but because we depend on the support of the US, we have to go along, unfortunately.

Mazlum Shengali (Mazlum Şengalî)
Field commander of the Resistance Units of Sinjar (Yekîneyên Berxwedana Şengalê, YBŞ)
2 June 2016

What is the current situation of the YBŞ here on the ground?

The problem is that even though we bore the brunt of the struggle against IS, the powers that be are now trying to push us aside. In 2014, the Peshmerga of the PDK simply fled and left everybody out on a limb. We were here at that time and we fought, and now we are certainly not simply going away. The massacre in August 2014 could only take place because we didn't have our own defence units. Then, neither the Iraqi army nor the Peshmerga gave us any help. Had it not been for a veto by the others, we would have been able to liberate the remaining parts of Sinjar as well. But both the Iraqi and the Kurdish government were against that. We cleansed the whole western side of Sinjar from IS and did that with our own forces. Nobody supported us in this. We are getting no arms supplies from Germany or the US. These supplies all go to the Peshmerga. But the latter actually hardly do any fighting. Until December 2014, not a single Peshmerga was to be found here. We were the only ones who actually fought, and now they are trying to steal the fruits of our labour.

What is your official legal status here in Iraq at the moment?

Since 2014, we have been registered as a People's Mobilisation Unit and are therefore a legal military entity in Iraq.

But you also understand your struggle as an ideological struggle.

Yes, we are fighting here against fascism, we don't just fight for ourselves. We are fighting for all of humanity. In fighting against IS, we are also fighting for Germany, Austria and Europe. Our fight against IS is for all of humanity, but nobody supports us.

But the YBŞ was not the only force that fought here; another was Haydar Shesho's HPŞ, which was present here already in August 2014. What, then, is the relation between your units?

They were not really present on the ground; it was only a few people in Şerfedîn, but we were the ones who defended the mountain. They may claim that they were also here even if all they do is loiter in hotels. For some of the alleged defenders of the Êzîdî, the whole thing was more like doing business. But right here, we were the only ones who fought. Now they are talking big, but in the first months, we were the defenders of the mountain.

But why has the front against IS not been moving forward since November 2015? In my conversations with the refugees from the southern villages during the last months, they have expressed a lot of dissatisfaction with the sluggish pace of the liberation of the rest of the region.

We would have continued the struggle right away. But first, there are disagreements between the various groups here, and second, the US has told the Peshmerga and the Êzîdî units in no uncertain terms that it doesn't support any further advances at the moment and that it wants to support the Iraqi army in central Iraq first. They probably fear that an advance could create a fait accompli which in turn could lead to conflicts with the Iraqi government.

How, then, does your own concept for the future of Sinjar look like?

We want our own autonomy for Sinjar and we are not going to ask anyone for permission but are already building it right now with the Autonomy Council we founded already in February 2015. We Êzîdî should be allowed the manage and defend ourselves in the larger frame of Iraq.

Mahma Khalil (Mahma Xelîl)
Mayor of Sinjar City, appointed by the PDK in 2015; deposed in October 2017 after the retreat of the Peshmerga
2 June 2016

You are the mayor of a city which is largely in ruins and practically empty. Why has nobody returned to it so far?

You can see for yourself how much has been destroyed here. The battles in 2015 destroyed almost the whole town. To this day, there is no infrastructure, no school, no water and power supply and no hospital, no medical care. But the main problem is that the front line still runs directly along the southern border of the city and that IS fighters still occasionally shoot directly into the city. Moreover, many of the houses are still full of mines. Actually, one cannot go anywhere without being afraid that something is about to explode somewhere. This is simply no safe place for civilians.

Will the city be rebuilt at all?

There have already been voices that wanted to keep the city as it is as a memorial. But we here would still like to rebuild it because we want to enable the refugees to return. But for that, we need international aid and support. We cannot succeed in this alone.

But the problem with the front line could actually be solved if the south of the Sinjar region were finally liberated as well. Why has the front line there not moved for more than a half year?

This is a politically delicate matter. Ultimately, it was the Americans who prohibited the Kurds from advancing further to the south because they didn't want to anger the central government, which they still need in the struggle against IS. Unfortunately, this has stopped the liberation of South Sinjar and led to a situation where my city is still directly at the front line.

Khansad Ali (Xansad Elî)
Doctor and director of the hospital in Zerdaşt, the high plateau where most of the expelled live
18 September 2017

When did you come here as a doctor?

That was on 15 September 2014. The mountain was then still encircled by IS and I was flown in by helicopter.

How was the work back then so briefly after the genocide, when the mountain was still under siege?

In the first months, I was still working in a tent and actually didn't have any equipment, and the supply of drugs was very difficult. Now there is this little clinic here and there are at least enough drugs, and now the streets are open for real emergency cases.

You are the only doctor here on the mountain. How many patients per day do you treat on average?

Today, I had 130 patients and this was an entirely normal day. The people come to me with all sorts of ailments as I am their only access to medical treatment.

You, as a doctor, are wearing a uniform of the Peshmerga of the PDK. Why?

The Peshmerga have fought against IS and they protect us. They are supporting my work and thus, I see no reason not to wear a uniform.

But there are also opponents of the Peshmerga in this area. Do you only treat supporters of the PDK or do you also treat others?

I treat everyone who comes to see me as a matter of principle.

Faqir Jerdo (Feqîr Cerdo)
Prestigious Êzîdî cleric who lives on the mountain as a refugee
18 September 2017

The people here on the mountain have been living in tents for more than three years and still can't go back to their villages. You are living here yourself, know many families, and enjoy a high esteem among many Êzîdî. How have the lives of the people changed in the course of the last few years in your view?

The supply situation has become much better by now. There are now wells which were drilled by the Barzani Charity Foundation. We are supplied with food and are now also growing our own vegetables. But it is still very difficult for people to live in tents for such a long time and not to be able to return to their villages.

Why can't the people return to their villages?

Many of the villages are destroyed and mined. In addition, many people are still worried about their safety. We have many conflicts here and many of the IS terrorists are also still at large.

You are a man of religion. How does the religious infrastructure for the refugees look like here on the mountain?

Well, here, around the tent settlements, there are of course no temples. The people here go to the temples in Şerfedîn and the Çêl

Mêra temple on the highest peak of the mountain range. But we Êzîdî do not really need a temple to practise our religion. I pray my sun prayer each day both at sunrise and at sunset. For this, I only need the sun and no temple.

Qasim Shesho (Qasim Şeşo) – 2nd interview
Organiser of the self-defence of local Êzîdî in 2014 and commander of the PDK Peshmerga in Sinjar from 2015 to October 2017
19 September 2017

In several days, we will be witnessing the referendum on the independence of Kurdistan. Why will this referendum also be carried out in the areas of Sinjar held by the Peshmerga?

Actually, we wanted to hold the referendum in all of Sinjar. But the PKK and the People's Mobilisation Units tried to prevent this. We Êzîdî speak Kurdish and belong to the Kurds. Seen from there, it is only logical that we also want to participate in the plebiscite here.

That is, you are hoping that Sinjar will become part of an independent Kurdistan?

Yes, of course. Within Kurdistan, we will be much safer than as a part of Iraq.

Given the real relations of force here, that is, the fact that parts of Sinjar are dominated by the YBŞ and, since May, also by the People's Mobilisation Units, isn't there a risk that Sinjar could be divided and that the future border between Iraq and Kurdistan will run right through the Êzîdî settlement area?

First of all, we have to carry out the referendum. After that, the Kurdish government will negotiate with Baghdad, and then we will see what borders we can agree on. In any case, we want all of Sinjar to become part of Kurdistan; we don't want a partition of the region.

Naif Saido
The mayor of Sinunê in the north of Sinjar; appointed by the PDK, he was deposed after the takeover by the Iraqi army and the YBŞ in October 2017
19 September 2017

Here in Sinunê, there are many posters advertising the referendum for the independence of Kurdistan even though the whole region belongs to the 'Controversial Areas' and not to the three provinces that are uncontestably part of Kurdistan. Do you really also want to carry out the referendum here next week?

Of course, we will conduct the referendum here as well, just as in all other areas under the control of our Peshmerga. The population of Sinunê has the same right as others to decide whether their city is to be part of an independent Kurdistan.

But does that not risk a division of the settlement area of the Êzîdî here in the region? After all, the west of the Sinjar region is under the control of the YBŞ and the south is controlled by the People's Mobilisation Units.

Of course, we do not want a division of the region – we want the whole region to become a part of Kurdistan. We are grateful to the PKK for its intervention against IS on our behalf in August 2014, but now, they should withdraw and leave the region to the Êzîdî of this area.

Right here, the relation between the Peshmerga and the YBŞ is particularly tense. On 2 March, there was an armed clash in the area between your city, Sinunê, and the small town of Xanasor under the control of the YBŞ that cost the lives of several people. How has your relationship with the YBŞ developed since then in your view?

That was only a small incident and should not be taken too seriously. We will be able to solve these problems. But for us, it is clear that the PKK has to withdraw from here at some point.

Let's talk about your city, Sinunê. In contrast to Sinjar City and the other settlements in the south of the region, life seems to have returned to relative normalcy here. What is the situation with regard to the return of the civilians?

Yes, Sinunê is indeed the place where most of the expelled have returned. My guess would be that around 90 per cent of the population has returned, while all the villages in the south – and some of the villages in the north – all still completely empty. Sinunê did not remain under the control of IS for long and has suffered less destruction than many of the villages. Moreover, IS didn't have the time to mine everything. Therefore, the people could simply return to their houses. In addition, since December 2014 we have been separated from IS by the mountain. For that reason, the people felt safer here than in the south.

How do things look with the infrastructure of the city, such as water and power supply? Has it been restored by now?

There are still problems, particularly with the power supply, which still often fails. But the schools and hospital are open again. The situation in the city is slowly normalising. But the situation in the villages is still very different.

Haydar Shesho (Heydar Şeşo) – 2nd interview
Commander of HPÊ (known as HPŞ until November 2015)
15 October 2018

You have criticised the behaviour of the PDK and its Peshmerga in August 2014 sharply and you have given me your view on how the struggle on the ground developed at the time. But after that, you continued to have problems with the PDK.

After the Peshmerga had returned here, I first thought, 'OK, once everything here is said and done here, I can go back to my family, but only once the struggle here is finished and all of Sinjar is safe.' Since 20 December 2014, the Peshmerga again tried to subject the people here to their control. My relationship with them was not particularly good. In February 2015, I met with Mesrûr Barzanî[14] and he told me, 'You have contacts with the People's Mobilisation Units. You really shouldn't be doing this!'

Because you were then registered as a People's Mobilisation Unit?

Yes, because they had helped us at the time. But that doesn't mean I'm against the Peshmerga. And I told him that I wouldn't mind turning my 1,000 people over to him for the Peshmerga and returning to my private life. Mesrûr Barzanî then reacted by telling me I should break with the People's Mobilisation Units. But we only got the pay for our soldiers and a little money for arms and cars from the People's Mobilisation Units. Mesrûr Barzanî demanded that I return everything we had got from Baghdad. But I didn't want to do that, and I was like: I, too, am an Iraqi citizen, so why should I give it back? And as long as he can't tell me whether he is going to pay my people, I cannot do this. My men have families to eat and they need their pay. Then he said to me: 'I'll give you two months, and if you haven't cut your contact with the People's Mobilisation Units by then, you will only have yourself to blame for what happens then.'

And then you were arrested?

Yes, at the beginning of April 2015, I was arrested. Mesrûr Barzanî had called me two or three times and each time I told him, 'As long as you don't tell me whether you'll take my men in and pay them, I will continue.' When I was arrested, I was in Xanke. I was staying in a house there in the evening when three or four cars of the Asayîş[15] came to the place. Initially, they wanted to question my host, who then approached me and told me about it. I went out and rode with the Asayîş. They said they had only a few questions and would bring me back after I had answered them. Then, in Duhok, they told me right away, 'We have given you two months to cut off your contacts with the People's Mobilisation Units and you have done nothing. Either you sign this paper saying that you won't be in contact with those units anymore, our you will stay here as our visitor.' I then decided to stay as their 'visitor' instead of signing. In the first two or three days they locked me into a cell together with five IS prisoners. I complained to the head of the Asayîş and they gave me a new cell. During the questioning, the interrogator was always talking to somebody on the phone. I don't know who was on the other end of the line but he always checked back with someone. But I refused to sign the interrogation report. They wanted to force me to confess that I was in contact with the People's Mobilisation Units via the PUK, of which I was a central committee member. But I didn't sign this. I was completely isolated and didn't know anything about what was happening outside of the prison during those eight days. I had no idea that there were protests by the PUK and even international protests. But apparently, the PDK had come under considerable pressure in the course of these days and wanted to release me. On the eighth day, the head of the Asayîş said, 'You have to do something when you get out. Simply tell your people that they can join the Peshmerga, and we'll let you go', And I answered, 'I would have told them that anyway, you wouldn't have had to lock me up for that.' Then they brought me to court to arrange my release. Normally, on Fridays the court is open only until 2 p.m., but they took me there at 3 p.m. lest anyone noticed what was happening. Then I was suddenly accused of having violated §156 and §157, that is, to have cooperated with other countries against Iraq. And the punishment for that is life in prison or death.

Did §156 and §157 refer to espionage?

Yes. And therefore, I asked what exactly I was supposed to have done to be accused of espionage. The people in court responded, 'You were in contact with the People's Mobilisation Units!' I answered, 'The People's Mobilisation Units are units of the Iraqi government and are fighting against IS. This is not an institution of a foreign state. They are Iraqis.' They continued to try to talk me into signing their document, saying they would release me if I did. Then I addressed the judge: 'On the one hand, you are telling me I will be released if I sign this, and on the other, you are threatening me with the death penalty. This can only mean that I am not here for legal reasons, but for political ones.' The judge denied this and claimed I had been arrested in accord with the rule of the law. This went back and forth a few times. I demanded an arrest warrant but I was never shown one. Then they brought me back to the prison and released me. They told me to give a statement to the media, after which I would be allowed to go. I insisted on getting an official release by a court order. But the Asayîş told me that the court had nothing to with this matter. Then they asked me again what I would say if my men went to the Peshmerga, and I repeated once more that that was fine with me. Then they finally let me go. But in addition to me, they had also arrested two of my men. I asked about them and insisted that they had to be released as well. Only after all this, we could finally leave. But in the meantime, they had bugged our cars and we had to get new ones.

How did your relation with the PDK and the Peshmerga develop after this episode?

This went back and forth. Sometimes, my uncle mediated. I have always insisted that they have to do something for our people. I don't want anything for myself, but that they have to pay the salary for my men. At that time, we were altogether 7,000 men, many of whom had families to feed. Barzani agreed to initially pay the salary for 1,800 of the men, after which the remaining ones would be gradually added. I waited for two months and nothing happened. I called them and I got nothing. They didn't employ any of them.

Does that mean that the troops didn't receive any pay during that time?

Directly after my release, I went to Abu Mahdi al-Muhandis in Baghdad, thanking him for his help, and I told him that now I didn't need this help anymore. But he responded, 'You still need this aid for your men. If people are putting you under pressure, just tell me.' But I told him that I didn't want any conflict between the Êzîdî. In the end, I got money from Baghdad for four more months, the complete money for two months, and half of it for another two. After that, I got nothing from Baghdad anymore and only a little bit from the government of the Kurdistan Region. Of course, I also got some aid from Êzîdî all over the world, but that was it. I then called Sidat Barzani and told him to let Masoud Barzani know that

I couldn't wait anymore. The people have nothing to eat anymore, it can't go on like this. Sidat Barzani called my uncle and told him I should wait another two or three days until Masoud Barzani was back in Kurdistan, because at that time he was somewhere abroad. Now the message was that he could only take 1,000 men instead of 1,800. I said, 'No, then just forget about it; I won't work with you anymore.' I called the US consulate and they talked me into agreeing to a deal in which they would accept 1,000 men right then and another 1,000 the month after. I convened a meeting of my men and asked them what they thought. Since there were no alternatives, my people said it was better to take the offer of 1,000 than having nothing. But until October 2017, that was it. The pay for the additional 1,000 men never materialised.

And what happened in October when the Peshmerga retreated?

Let's first go to May 2017, when the People's Mobilisation Units came here. Quite suddenly, they liberated the south. At the time, my uncle said that his forces also wanted to liberate the south but that he was prohibited from doing so by orders from above. On 16 and 17 October, when the Iraqi army came here, the Peshmerga again withdrew without a fight, just as they had done back then in 2014. Once again, I talked to my uncle because he didn't want to retreat as in 2014 and was afraid to abandon Sinjar. I told him, 'Whatever happens, we won't fight the Iraqi army. This is not IS, this is not a foreign army; they are Iraqi, just as we are, and we won't fight against them.' And we both agreed that we wouldn't do this. At the time, I was back in Xanke, but I went to Şerfedîn from there. When the Êzîdî People's Mobilisation Units arrived, my men called me because they wanted to know what they should do at the checkpoints. I asked whether the arriving forces were from Sinjar or from Baghdad, but they were people from Sinjar, and I said, 'I have no objections to that, let them pass.' At 6:30 in the morning, I was back in Sinjar and saw the Peshmerga retreating. I then met with the Êzîdî People's Mobilisation Units of the Iraqi army and we agreed on cooperating peacefully. But after that, the People's Mobilisation Units simply appointed a new mayor in Sinjar without asking for permission. Since then, we have hardly been in contact with them. But I and my men stayed in Şerfedîn and then my uncle came to me with a few Êzîdî Peshmerga. He, too, hasn't left Sinjar, but he was fired as commander of the Peshmerga and has been with us in Şerfedîn since that time.

Are your troops now only here in Şerfedîn, or also in other villages?

There are some of our people or groups in the whole northeast of the region, but in these places, they always work in tandem with the police or the army. It is only in Şerfedîn and Golat that we have our own checkpoints. The People's Mobilisation Units are present only in the south and in Sinjar City. In the northeast, it is the Iraqi army, the police and us, and in the northwest from Xanasor onwards, the YBŞ. But in Xanasor itself, the Iraqi army is also present.

How does your relation to the other groups that have been here since October 2017 look like?

We pretty much always try to get along with them. Recently, there have been increasing problems with the YBŞ, but I hope that these will soon abate. We have often issued invitations to all groups to build a joint Êzîdî army composed of all of the groups, but so far, these efforts have failed, even though this would of course be the right step to gain more legitimacy, not least with regard to the Kurdish and Iraqi governments. The US consulate has also asked us why we do not do this, and I told them, 'If you want to bring this about, you're welcome to go ahead. You are strong enough and recognised by everyone. But I alone am unable to bring all those people together.' But in fact, they haven't done anything, and I don't have the resources to do this.

And which role does Europe play, or which role could it play?

As it has become the new home for many Êzîdî, Germany would actually be predestined to play such a mediating role. I myself have been a guest of the German parliament two times. But Germany entertains very good relations with both the PDK and the government of the Kurdistan Region and would like to bring the Êzîdî under the umbrella of the PDK, which would in turn create difficulties with Baghdad, the People's Mobilisation Units, and the YBŞ. If only Germany resolved to do so, it could bring the Êzîdî together in a matter of days. Germany could also pressure Turkey to at long last end the bombing of Sinjar. One must either convince the YBŞ to withdraw or convince Turkey to stop the bombing; at present, the population here is in constant danger.

Do you think Turkey is active here only because of the YBŞ?

No, Turkey had a larger plan. Turkey was involved in all the massacres against the Êzîdî and has supported IS in all sorts of ways. Moreover, kidnapped Êzîdî women have been taken to Turkey. For Turkey, there is certainly more at play. But Europe should pressure both sides, Turkey and the PKK, lest Sinjar becomes the venue of the conflict between Turkey and the PKK.

Vian Dakhil Sheikh Said (Vian Daxil Şêx Saîd)
Êzîdî MP in the Iraqi parliament until 2018, winner of the Anna Politkovskaya Award in 2014 and of the Bruno Kreisky Prize for Services to Human Rights in 2015
17 October 2018

You have become globally known for your speech in the Iraqi parliament when you addressed the president of the parliament with the words: 'Mr President, we are being slaughtered under the banner "There is no god but Allah". Our women are being sold in the slave market, there is a genocide of the Êzîdî. We are being exterminated; our religion is about to be destroyed. I am appealing to your human solidarity: Save us!' How did you experience the days when IS started its genocide of the Êzîdî?

On 3 August at around four or five o'clock in the morning, I became aware that something had happened in Sinjar. That was when the first news arrived that Sinjar was under attack and that the women were being killed. I got calls from many people in Sinjar who gave me detailed reports about the attacks on the villages: Women were isolated from the men and raped. Men were shot and killed and many other terrible, criminal acts were reported. On the next morning, I immediately went to Baghdad, where I met with the diplomatic missions and a few politicians to ask them to help the people in Sinjar and to try to stop the IS attack. On 5 August, I made an interpellation in the Iraqi parliament to gain the chamber's support in pressuring the government to take action to stop the genocide. I read my speech in parliament and all my colleagues supported me in my endeavour. The parliament called on the government to act, but the government was completely helpless itself. The international community had already been aware of the IS atrocities for two days, but had remained silent up to that point. I think that in the end the media have played a bigger role than the Iraqi government and the Iraqi parliament. The media published my speech and it was heard all over the world, and on account of that, even the US became very upset and finally intervened both militarily and in humanitarian form.

More than four years after the genocide, most survivors still live in the tent camps in the Kurdistan Region of Iraq or as refugees in Syria or Europe, even though the last part of the Sinjar region was liberated from IS already in spring 2017. Why? What has gone wrong since that time?

The Iraqi government hasn't done anything for the reconstruction in Sinjar at all. In my view, it is really appalling that among the 260 Iraqi delegates to the Reconstruction Conference in Kuwait, there was not a single Êzîdî.[16] The Nineveh Governorate has also completely ignored us. The projects and plans the provincial administration delivered to the Iraqi government do not include a single project for the reconstruction of Sinjar. Seen from that angle, the neglect by the Iraqi government has been the main reason for the continuing inability of the Êzîdî to return. But there is yet another reason, and that is the loss of trust between the Êzîdî society and its neighbours. Everybody knows that IS didn't only have foreign fighters, but that many Iraqis from the Arab neighbouring villages also participated in attacking the Êzîdî women, men and children. This has created a social rift which is far from easy to heal. There is now mistrust and fear between the Êzîdî and the other ethnic groups. I believe that right now, no Êzîdî is able to return to Sinjar to live there, particularly to the south of the region. The Êzîdî are afraid to have to relive the experience of August 2014 once more. Even though the Iraqi government has publicly declared the victorious destruction of IS, there are still sleeper cells of the organisation in Sinjar whose members believe in its ideology and principles. In my view, IS is not a military organisation, but rather, an ideological and spiritual one, which continues to exist. And you can't destroy an ideology by means of arms and war. Perhaps all of this will continue for a whole number of generations. Therefore, I suspect that the worst fear of the Êzîdî is a repetition of the scenario of 2014 and that this fear will remain even when Sinjar is rebuilt in the future.

One problem that was frequently mentioned to me during my conversations and interviews is the presence and rivalry of the many different militias in the region. You are yourself a member of the PDK, whose Peshmerga were forced to withdraw from the area in October 2017. But the former commander of the PDK Peshmerga, Qasim Shesho, is still in the region with some of his fighters and the PDK still demands the integration of the area into Kurdistan. What is your personal view of the situation with the militia in the region?

We as Êzîdî don't see a problem at all with numerous Êzîdî being active in the Iraqi state security, army, police, and border police or the Peshmerga. But if they participate in other, foreign groups such as the YPG and the PKK or the People's Mobilisation Units, this could cause a division, and if we turn into a split society in this precarious region, this could lead to unrest within our society.

What, then, is your political goal for the future of Sinjar?

In the last years, I have concentrated my efforts on trying to turn Sinjar into an autonomous province which is managed by the Êzîdî. This would also give Sinjar the political clout it deserves. Sinjar should have its own budget, a university, hospitals, and all other basic units of a functioning society.

Is that also the position of your party?

Yes, the PDK supports this goal.

Everyone seems to agree that Sinjar should become a province of its own, but the real question appears to be whether this province should be a part of Kurdistan, a part of Iraq under its central government, or a distinct entity. But let's get to the role of the international community you have criticised a few minutes ago. In 2014, the reaction of the international community was indeed far too muted and came too late. What would you expect from the EU in particular?

Here, there are a number of levels. On the political level, the European countries and Germany in particular should pressure the next Iraqi government to allow for more Êzîdî representatives in parliament. The reason for this demand is this: I was in parliament when the Êzîdî were hit by this tragedy a couple of years ago. At that time, the government didn't include a single Êzîdî member. The consequence was that the EU and Germany did more for the Êzîdî than our own government. Therefore, we need Êzîdî members in the cabinet if we want to prevent this from happening again. On a second level, Germany and the EU can also play an important role in the national reconciliation in Iraq. Our Arab Sunni neighbours also had a hand in the genocide of the Êzîdî. Not all of them, but some! We need a national reconciliation with the tribes whose members participated in IS to enable our people to return to Sinjar. To achieve this, the guilty must be convicted and the innocent acquitted. This brings me to the last level, namely, justice in the transitional period. The criminals must be extradited and convicted in accord with the law, and the victims must be compensated. Iraq is already floating this idea, but we need to profit from the experiences the EU already has in this realm. You've had many conflicts in Europe and know about war crimes tribunals and reconciliation processes. We Êzîdî need your help in this. Our surviving Êzîdî women also need help and Germany is the first country that has offered it. Our children need help because they are psychologically affected, and by that, I mean both those who now live in Germany and those who still live here in the camps. They are the new generation of Êzîdî, and we must care for them.

Qasim Shesho (Qasim Şeşo) – 3rd interview
Organiser of the self-defence of local Êzîdî in 2014 and commander of the PDK Peshmerga in Sinjar from 2015 to October
2017
19 October 2018

*The last time I met you, you were still commander of the Peshmerga
and you resided in a big headquarters in the Sinjar City. Now you
are living here in Şerfedîn with your nephew. While your Peshmerga have withdrawn and government of the Kurdistan Region
has conceded the area in October 2017, you are still here. Why?*

I was born here. This is my home and has been the home of my
forefathers and my grand grandparents for millennia. Here are
our sanctuaries, our cemeteries, and our soil. Everything is here.
Why should I leave? In 2014, we became victims of a genocide
for the 74th time, but, thanks be to God, they haven't succeeded
in destroying us. Yes, IS has massacred or kidnapped thousands
of our women, men, girls and boys, but they haven't succeeded
in annihilating us. Now, the Kurds have abandoned us, the Êzîdî,
for a second time, but even so, after this helped us but those very
Kurds, in particular the PDK under the leadership of Masoud
Barzani. But some PDK leaders don't care about us anymore and
are no longer interested in us.

*What exactly happened in October last year when the Peshmerga
withdrew their troops from here?*

On 15 and 16 October, the cowardly Peshmerga retreated from
Kirkuk, and here, we couldn't get any help from anyone either.
Therefore, the leaders put out the order that we had to leave Sinjar
as well. I could give you the names of those leaders, but I prefer
not to do so. But we didn't follow the order and stayed in Sinjar
with four regiments and more than 2,000 fighters to protect our
area. Either we die in battle, or we survive. As long as I live, I will
not leave Sinjar, no matter what orders anyone in Erbil gives. On
17 October, we initially stayed here with three regiments with 400
men each. Some troops retreated, but many stayed put. Our group
only retreated to this place, Şerfedîn. All of the Sunni Peshmerga

withdrew, but the Êzîdî stayed. At the moment, 5,000 Peshmerga are registered in my files, but we don't get a salary anymore, only 200 dollars per head.

Does that mean that your men here are still a part of the Peshmerga – or were you dismissed from them, as the media have reported?

We have been abandoned by the government of the Kurdistan Region and officially, we are no longer Peshmerga, but the Êzîdî fighters have stayed. Since that time, no one has helped us, except President Barzani. He has helped us five or six times in the course of the year, and each time he gave us 650,000 dollars.

How does your relationship with the Iraqi army look like right now?

I must say that we still have a good relationship with the Iraqi army, especially with the 73rd troop leader, General Nazir. He is a good person, and the government of Sinjar is also OK. So far, they haven't done us any harm, and we have told them right in the beginning: People who come to us as friends are welcome. But anyone who attacks us in a hostile manner must be ready for our counterattack. So far, things have been peaceful and no one has bothered us. On the contrary, the local commanders of the Iraqi army have approached us several times offering their help, and they have always treated us well, General Nazir in particular.

In May 2017, the Êzîdî People's Mobilisation Units (al-Hashd ash-Shaabi) became part of the scene. They have liberated the south of Sinjar and cooperate with the Iraqi army. How does your relation to them look like?

The Êzîdî group which cooperates with the People's Mobilisation Units does not represent the Êzîdî. They are opportunists who work against the interests of the Êzîdî. Some of them only want money and are getting enormous sums from Baghdad. One of them was in debt to the tune of 400,000 and is now getting 400,000 dollar per month from Baghdad. With regard to that, there is no difference between the leader of that group and the leaders of IS. He wants the destruction of all Êzîdî and to make a name for himself with that. Such Êzîdî are hypocrites and frauds.

It is obvious that you don't like the Êzîdî People's Mobilisation Units. And how are things with the YBŞ? You were quoted in the Turkish media where you supposedly said that the PKK hasn't left Sinjar and that you could personally show its whereabouts to anyone who is interested. Did you really say that?

Yes, I did say that and I stand by it. Many PKK fighters have come here, to Sinjar, and are now active under another name such as YPG and YPJ. Our relation with them is not at all good. The PKK is still present here, and we don't want that.

But you are certainly aware of the fact that Turkey is using you here as a key witness in order to justify its bombing attacks on Sinjar.

This is not my fault. Should I lie because of it? It is, after all, true that the PKK is here.

Let's talk about the question of the future of Sinjar. What are your ideas about the future administration of Sinjar?

We don't want to be dependent on the central government because they didn't help us when we fought against IS. The central government didn't even support us with equipment and food. The only one who helped us is the one who you secularists refuse to believe in, namely, God – and in addition to him, Şêx Şerfedîn[17] and our Êzîdî fighters. We took our protection into our own hands and fought against IS alone. We were under siege and didn't have any food anymore, and therefore, we had to leave Sinjar.[18] At the time, I called President Barzani and his son Masrur. On 18 December 2014, we found a way out and President Barzani was the only one who helped us. The central government didn't condemn the terror attacks and assassinations of IS and refused to admit that they were criminals and crooks.

But certain Arab units, the Iraqi army and the People's Mobilisation Units also fought against IS, didn't they?

Not a single Arab country has condemned IS and labelled it a terrorist organisation. On the contrary, they think that IS represents the true Islam and is following in the footsteps of Muhammad: God has created them to be terrorists and to kill, terrorise and loot the people.

And what is your take on the international reactions to the situation here?

The US and the EU have done absolutely nothing for us in all of the last four years. Every now and then someone like you comes along and reports on us. But from the governments, there is nothing. Nobody cares about the minorities here. Everyone is working only for their own interests. I have had an apartment in Germany for the last 28 years and was a member of the Human Rights Committee in Geneva for six years. At that time, between 1974 and 1975, I registered and documented all attacks against minorities, but in the committee, people always insisted that there were no assassinations or genocides. Even then, nobody was interested in these matters. Despite all the new technologies – you can reach anyone in the US or the EU with just a call and you can see everything via satellites – no one helped us and saved us from these infidel and unjust criminals. But it doesn't matter what I say; unfortunately, it doesn't help anyway.

I understand and share your criticism of the western lack of interest in the fate of the Êzîdî, but what do you want in concrete terms?

We need international protection; the PKK and the People's Mobilisation Units have to leave Sinjar. We have no problems in getting along with the central government, but as long as the PKK and the People's Mobilisation Units are in Sinjar, there will be no tranquillity and peace, only renewed murder and looting.

Apparently, there are really massive reservations here against the other Êzîdî militia. What about the Arab neighbours?

Two days ago, two of our Shammar[19] brothers were murdered and someone wrote 'Tawūs-e Melek' on their dead bodies to coax the Shammar into blaming the Êzîdî. But we Êzîdî didn't slaughter anyone. We only protect ourselves, as we have been doing for millennia. But there are forces here who want to sow discord between us and the Shammar. Our minority doesn't even have a million members. Our numbers get smaller with each genocide, and each time we say, 'Thank God, we are still surviving', we are confronted with yet another genocide and attempt to destroy us. There are only media reports about us, but nobody is doing anything for us. For Europe, even the death of an animal is more important than our destruction.

Qasim Shirwan (Qasim Şirwan)
Commander of the Lališ Brigade of the Êzîdî People's Mobilisation Units al-Hashd ash-Shaabi
19 October 2018

Why did you create your own Êzîdî People's Mobilisation Units in 2017?

In August 2014, the Peshmerga abandoned us and allowed IS to invade the region. At that time, both the Iraqi government and the government of the Kurdistan Region turned their back on us. Therefore, we formed our own groups to be able to defend ourselves and to end our dependence on the help of the Iraqi or Kurdish government.

But you did not found the Êzîdî People's Mobilisation Units already in 2014, but only in 2017. Why did you choose that particular year?

After 3 August 2014, we had already armed ourselves, way before the People's Mobilisation Units came here. At the time, we had done so spontaneously to fight against IS. But officially, we became a group of the People's Mobilisation Units under the name 'Lališ Brigade' only after the People's Mobilisation Units came here on 27 May 2017.

How many armed fighters do you have at the moment?

Altogether, 1,400 fighters completed the training of the People's Mobilisation Units and were then taken here. But at the moment,

not all of the 1,400 fighters are member of the Lališ Brigade. Since
May 2017, we have been in control of the villages Ger Zerik, Tel
Ezeir, Koço – actually the whole south of Sinjar. There have been
altogether eight martyrs during the liberation of that region.

*I have just read that the Lališ Brigade has handed over Tel Ezeir to
the YBŞ two days ago. Is that correct?*

Yes, that is correct. We have handed Tel Ezeir and Siba Şêx Xidir
to the YBŞ. We entertain good relations with the YBŞ, and the YBŞ
gets its money from the Iraqi government just as we do. Therefore,
it is no problem for us when they control these villages.

*How are your relations with Qasim Shesho and with Haydar Shesho
and his HPÊ?*

I have a good relation to all Êzîdî leaders. On 3 August 2014,
everyone abandoned us and only the local Êzîdî put up a fight.
Because of all this, we have really good relations with each other.

*But nevertheless, there are a number of different militias here which
also have their problems with each other. I have interviewed many
civilians from Sinjar in the IDP camps, and almost all of them said
that the rivalry between the militias is one of the biggest problems
preventing their return. Why is this the case if all of you are getting
along so well?*

The Êzîdî will never again trust another militia or army, but only
their own forces. We want to be able to defend ourselves. But the
problem right now is that we have various military forces here
which are each supported by different governments, and when
there are problems between these governments, these will be
reduplicated by problems between the different militias.

*Why, then, is it not possible to build a joint Êzîdî force? After all, the
leaders of the YBŞ and Haydar Shesho are saying almost the same
thing as you and claim that they are also ready to cooperate.*

It is my firm wish that the Êzîdî leaders join their forces and that
we create a joint military formation. In that case, our command-

ers should simply be those who have some training in the army, and not the various politicians. This would make it possible for all of us to support this non-political military force. But the Êzîdî militias themselves are weak and underfinanced, and in the end, the forces in the background that support the different militias do not want any unity among the Êzîdî. This is a very dangerous situation, because if there is a civil war in Iraq, we will be shooting at each other here in Sinjar; Êzîdî would be shooting at other Êzîdî.

What kind of political solution for Sinjar would you prefer?

We would like to have our own region of Sinjar which is neither a part of Kurdistan nor governed by Mosul. We want an autonomous province directly responding to Baghdad, not Mosul. But for this, we would need the support of the Americans and the Europeans.

How should this support look like?

The most important thing is that Europe protects us when we are unable to do so and that it helps us with our reconstruction. And Europe should support us in our efforts to get our own autonomous region.

But in Europe, this is regarded as an internal matter of Iraq in which Europe can't simply force Iraq to accept its opinion. Nevertheless, here is another question: What do you mean by demanding that Europe should protect you? Do you want European troops on the ground or should Europe support the local forces with arms and equipment?

We want you to support us with training, logistics and arms. Europe will then be able to monitor what we are doing with it until we can protect ourselves and the European advisors can go home again.

Riham and Farida
Co-workers in the Women's Council (Meclîsa Jin) of Sinjar[20]
20 October 2018

204 · THE WORLD HAS FORGOTTEN US

What does the Women's Council of Sinjar do? What kind of activities do you carry out in the women's centres of the Women's Council?

We offer many courses for the women. Many women here cannot read or write and have never learned a trade. We offer them the opportunity to at least learn to write and read and we are also offering other courses. Altogether, we have seven such women's centres in the whole region with voluntary co-workers who are working for the cause without a salary. The Êzîdî women were kidnapped and raped by IS, but we are still here and fight, and in the end, we will emerge from these terrible developments stronger than before.

But for the individual women, these experiences must have often been quite traumatic.

After what they have gone through during their captivity by IS, many women have big psychological problems, and here, too, we try to help the women and to offer them psychological counselling.

Are you also active in cases where there are problems with the families of the women?

Yes, in some families, there are problems, and then we intervene and try to talk to the people and to solve these family problems. We still have the problem that many women get married as minors at a much too young age. We try to convince the families not to marry the girls that early, because this is bound to create problems.

Here in Sinjar, there is a whole number of different militias, which leads to a lot of insecurity in daily life. What does that mean for the women?

Quite generally, we want to get rid of all the militia that didn't help us, as they are only creating problems here. None of these militias include women. For us women, they only cause problems. The only militia that is different is the YBŞ because, after all, they have their own armed women's units, the YJŞ, and they have really helped us.

The society of the Êzîdî is traditionally very patriarchal and conservative. There are even cases of so-called honour killings such as the one of Du'a Khalil Aswad, which became widely known in 2007.

Our religion is very closed and doesn't allow us to marry followers of a different religion. That was the reason why Du'a was killed in 2007. Preventing things from going that far was one of our reasons to start this new kind of family counselling. We are trying to convince the young women not to marry non-Êzîdî, but we also try to convince the families not to kill their children. At the time, the Islamists exploited the murder of Du'a Khalil to portray the Êzîdî as merciless barbarians. We believe that more was behind this story and that it was also used by the PDK to present the Êzîdî in a bad light.

I know that back then the murder was exploited to malign the Êzîdî, and I have also heard these rumours about an involvement of the PDK, even though this was never proven. But whatever the exact background, this doesn't change the fact that there was a brutal murder, that the murder was perpetrated by the Êzîdî family of Du'a Khalil, and that this was not the only murder of its kind, even though such acts are generally not also filmed and posted on the internet. What do you do when you are confronted with a situation in which a girl is threatened by her family?

If there had been a centre such as ours in Bashiqa in 2007, what happened to Du'a Khalil would not have happened. We would have talked to both the family and her and we would have solved the problem. But when the young women go to Baghdad or Kurdistan and mix with the Muslims, such things can happen because we are then unable to intervene.

How do you see the role of Europe and the international community in Sinjar?

We don't get any international support for our work here. We have been abandoned. What we need here is big and sustainable projects which enable us to return to an independent life. We don't need alms to get by day by day, but serious support enabling us to rebuild our country and to live independently once we have done that. Moreover, you shouldn't take the kidnapped women to Europe. We would like them to join us in rebuilding our region here.

But some of these women such as Lamiya Bashar or Nadia Murad have contributed a lot to engendering international attention for your problems. I think these women have also done a lot for this region.

We don't know about that. But if you invested the money that you give to these women here in the region, the results would multiply. You should help us in rebuilding Sinjar instead of organising the emigration of the Êzîdî.

Hodeida Cuge

Mayor of the small town Sinunê in the north of Sinjar who succeeded Naif Saido after the takeover of the Iraqi army and the YBŞ in October 2017
20 October 2018

How long have you been the new mayor, and who appointed you at the time?

In October 2017, after the retreat of the Peshmerga, the mayor of the PDK was also deposed. Thereafter, I was immediately elected as the new mayor on 17 October 2017. I already fought in 2014 when the mountain was under the siege of IS, but I am not a member of any particular unit or political party, which is why I was able to gain the trust of the citizens.

The last time I was here, the Kurdish flag was on display in the city hall of Sinunê, not the Iraqi one, and the mayor, Naif Saido of the PDK, was preparing the city for the Kurdish independence referendum. Now, the Kurdish Peshmerga are gone and instead of them, the Iraqi army and the YBŞ are in control of the city. What else has changed in the city, seen from the perspective of the new mayor?

The primary thing that has changed here is that we have abolished an administration ruled by a single party for thirteen years and that the central government has returned to power, accompanied by the Iraqi flag. The region was contested between Kurdistan and the central government. We have rehoisted the Iraqi flag and we are once again a part of Iraq. We will wait and see what kind of changes the future will bring.

When the Peshmerga withdrew in October 2017, they were at first replaced by the fighters of the YBŞ, and now, the latter are still here, together with the Iraqi army. Who controls Sinunê right now?

The YBŞ troops were here even before the Peshmerga retreated. But to this day, they don't have any influence in the city itself. Until October 2017, Sinjar was divided into three parts, but thankfully by now it is united again. Xanasor was cut off from the north by Barzani's Roj Peshmerga, and it was also cut off from the south and the mountain region. Now, the Iraqi flag is flying again in all of the region, In the beginning, the YPG and the YBŞ exploited the situation because the Iraqi army didn't show up here for six or seven months, and after the October events, they also came to Sinunê. But then they made an arrangement with the Iraqi army and now there is a coordination between the Iraqi army, the YBŞ, Haydar Shesho's HPÊ and the Êzîdî People's Mobilisation Units. Four of five months ago, the Iraqi army came here as well and took control of the Iraqi-Syrian border.

How do things look like regarding the return of the population to Sinunê and the villages around it? After all, the city and the whole northern side of the mountain range were liberated already in December 2014. But yet, the villages are almost completely empty, and as for the city, it seems that many people still haven't returned here either.

Altogether, only a few families have returned, mostly poor families who hardly had a choice. But each day, one or two families are returning. One of the big problems for such a return is that the road to Kurdistan via Rabī'a is still closed because of the political problems and that nowadays, everybody has to take the route via Mosul. It has become very difficult to get back to here from Kurdistan and the whole trip takes four to five hours, especially if the people want to come back here from Kurdistan with all their belongings.

What is the situation with regard to the infrastructure of the city – electricity, water, schools, and so on?

We have all of that. The supply with power has become better after 17 October, after the Iraqi minister of energy visited the city. Because of mobile power plants commuting between Sinjar and Sinunê and between Kerse and Sinunê, power is available most of the time, though not always. But we should be able to do even better than that. With regard to water, the situation is unchanged. The office for water resources has 93 employees, but only two or three are working here. All the others live in Kurdistan and rake in their monthly salaries without doing anything. The educational situation is, unfortunately, very grim. The school year 2017/18 was really very difficult. In the whole district, we have 14 schools that teach in Arabic and 13 schools teaching in Kurdish.[21] Unfortunately, we don't have enough money and qualified teachers. For that reason, we had to employ voluntary teachers. In the Kurdish schools, we have altogether 101 teachers and in the Arabic schools the number is 183. That is, altogether we have 284 teachers who have now worked voluntarily for a whole year without any salary. In the current year, we have the same problem: The government is unable to employ qualified teachers or to bring in teachers from Kurdistan. But we hope to be able to solve this problem in the near future. We have only elementary schools here, no secondary schools. There is a Kurdish school in Borik, but the government doesn't permit us to open a regular middle school here in Sinunê. But most of all, we need Kurdish- and Arabic-speaking teachers. I have complained about this to the Minister of Education and the Educational Office in Mosul and, a couple of days ago, even to the prime minister and I told them that we have a lack of teachers, but so far, none of them has done anything for us. We are now collecting donations together with the parent representation in order to be able to pay the teachers.

How did your election to mayor in October go? It can't have been easy to organise elections in this situation.

Initially, I assumed this office voluntarily and without pay. Then the parties, Sheikhs, and important personalities in the region elected me. But just recently I told the governor when he came here, 'I have been doing this now without pay, without employees, and without security personnel for a whole year. You must either pay someone to do this or let the citizens choose.' I'm not particularly eager to fill this position but am doing this because it is necessary.

Hidr Haji Mirza
Mayor of Siba Shex Xidir and Sheikh of the Qiran tribe
20 October 2018

According to media reports, your village was handed to the YBŞ by the People's Mobilisation Units. Is that correct?

The village was liberated by the People's Liberation Units and then handed over to the YBŞ, but now, both of them are represented at the checkpoint.

You, as the mayor, have not returned to the village? Has nobody returned to it at all?

No, so far nobody has returned.

Why is that the case?

The security situation is still very bad and the services are not working. The problems between the Iraqi and the Kurdish governments are preventing the refugees from returning. All the roads in Iraq are now open again, and only the roads connecting Bashiqa and Kurdistan and those connecting Sinjar and Kurdistan are closed because we are Êzîdî and because Bashiqa, like Sinjar, is a place where Êzîdî live. The road across the bridge at Bajid is a lifeline for us, but it is still kept closed because of the conflict between the government in Baghdad and the government in Erbil. Anyone who wants to go from Kurdistan to Sinjar now has to take a detour via Mosul and risk running into trouble.

You are living here in Xanasor. Where do the other original residents of your village live?

In Xanasor, Sinunê and Sinjar City. Some of them are still in the camps in Kurdistan.

What would have to happen to induce the population to return to Siba Shex Xidir?

The people would return if the international community protected us. We don't trust the Iraqi army and the Kurdish Peshmerga anymore, and much less do we trust our Arab neighbours who supported IS. The people will trust the situation only if they get international support.

What does that mean? Do you want to have international troops here?

We want to be protected by the international community right now, and we want it to aid us in becoming able to defend ourselves in the future.

What do you want for this region in political terms? How should Sinjar be administered in the future?

We want our own autonomous region and province within Iraq.

Omar Saleh
Secretary General of the PADÊ and member of the Êzîdî Autonomy Council of Sinjar
20 October 2018

You are the secretary general of the legal Êzîdî party PADÊ, which is close to the PKK. It is registered in Iraq and it also participates in elections. How have these ideas taken root in Sinjar? What is the history of your movement here in Sinjar?

Even before the massacre of 2014, there had already been a political movement by the name of TEV-DE.[22] We founded this movement on 22 February 2004. But at that time, TEV-DE was not able to do much because the PDK prevented us from doing so. The PDK has always tried to suppress our political and cultural activities.

Did TEV-DE follow the ideas of Abdullah Öcalan already then?

Yes, we followed this ideology already then, but we were working for the Êzîdî community right here.

How big was the movement before 2014?

When we held our first big meeting near the Mosul dam, 450 members were present. At that meeting, we also wanted to unify the Êzîdî in all parts of Kurdistan and in Europe, but at that time, the PDK blocked us and wouldn't allow this to happen. We had to go to Diyarbakır to hold an international meeting of all Êzîdî from different parts of the world because here, we just couldn't do that. Between 2012 and 2014, we were able to send support to Rojava. In those years, we sent altogether 100 tons of food and equipment to Rojava even though the PDK wanted to prevent us from doing so.

I guess that the movement really gained a lot of its strength because of the genocide in 2014 and the struggle of the PKK and the YPG/ YPJ against IS.

When we saw that IS was successful in Mosul and Tal Afar, we told the population here that the group would also come here and proceed mercilessly against the Êzîdî. Before the massacre, in July, we sent two groups to Rojava to get military and political training. The first group had 21 fighters, the second, a little more than 50. Both received good training as sharpshooters and on various guns, on Doshkas[23] and other weapons. I was part of one of those groups and after participating in battles there, we returned to Sinjar. Two of my sons and one of my daughters were also trained in that second group. But the training of these two groups had hardly been completed when IS attacked, and we had to throw ourselves into the battle immediately.

When was the Êzîdî Autonomy Council founded, in which you were active right from the start?

It was founded on 16 February 2015 and I represent PADÊ in it. We have local councils everywhere, and the central council is in Sinjar City.

How are the members of the council determined?

They were elected.

But how did they get elected? After all, this is not easy in such a situation.

There are various tribal leaders and delegates of the various parties and organisations in the council and these each held their meetings in which they determined their delegates.

Who is represented in the Êzîdî Autonomy Council at present? Which other parties are in the Autonomy Council?

Apart from the PADÊ, we have the Êzîdî Progress Party and various representatives of the tribes and villages.

Apart from the Êzîdî, there are other groups that live in Sinjar, such as the Sunni and the Babawat, and until the genocide, there were also Christians here. Are these groups also represented in the Autonomy Council, or does it exclusively consist of Êzîdî?

Lately, members of these groups have also been represented.

What are the tasks of the Autonomy Council? Can you give me a short record of the past three years?

Neither the Iraqi government nor the Kurdish government have done anything for our region. We are the only ones here who are reconstructing the infrastructure, repairing and tarring the streets, or restoring the water supply in the villages.

Do you also run your own schools, or are the schools here run by the Iraqi government?

We have our own schools which teach in Kurdish, different from the schools of the Iraqi government, where all teaching is done in Arabic. We also have a subject 'Arabic', but apart from that, the schools of the Autonomy Council are teaching in Kurdish.

Where are these schools? Only in Xanasor, or also in the smaller villages?

We have a school in every inhabited village, and also in Sinunê and Sinjar City.

Which alphabet do these schools use to teach Kurdish? The Arabic one, as in the Kurdistan Region, or the Latin-based Bedirxan alphabet, which is used for Kurdish in Syria and Turkey?

Like in Rojava, we use the Latin alphabet to teach Kurdish.

Are the school materials also from Rojava or are they produced here?

The schoolbooks come from Rojava. Our financial means are very limited and we can't afford to print our own schoolbooks.

Do you also have religion classes in the schools, teaching the religion of the Êzîdî?

We have a subject which includes the religion, culture and history of the Êzîdî.

The Iraqi government doesn't recognise your Autonomy Council. Officially, all of Sinjar is part of the province Ninawa. How are your relations with the Iraqi state?

We probably meet about ten times per month with the People's Defence Units and the Iraqi army, as well as with representatives of the Iraqi government. We work together and the Iraqi government knows that the propaganda against us is coming from people who have cooperated with IS. As of yet, we haven't been officially recognised, but we hope that at the end of the discussion process, all of Sinjar will become an independent self-managed region. I am optimistic that we can reach an agreement on that.

Many villages here are still in ruins, and even in Sinjar City, one does not see much reconstruction. Why is this going so slowly?

There are many international organisations that would like to help in reconstruction. So far, however, the PDK has blocked everything by disseminating the rumour that it is not safe to work here. Most of the refugees would like to return, but as long as there is no infrastructure here, no one is able to do so.

But in my interviews with refugees in the IDF camps, they did say that one of their reasons for not returning was that they don't trust the security situation because of the competing militias and the remaining structures of IS.

Of course, this instils fear in the people and the PDK consciously stokes these fears to prevent the people from returning. But actually, there haven't been any attacks at all. The only incident was in 2017 when the Roj Peshmerga killed our people of the YBŞ.

That is, you think that the people can safely return?

Absolutely. We have houses here instead of tents, and the infrastructure is certainly better than in the camps. I really advise the people to return.

But in fact, many villages are still mined.

Yes, in some villages, there are still mines, but we have mine clearance teams and we have just cleansed two villages, Tel Ezeir and Siba Shex Xidir, of the mines. We have almost no means to do this, but there is progress.

Sonia Salim Hassan
Lead candidate of the PÊD for the parliamentary elections in May 2018
25 October 2018

You are not from Sinjar, but belong to the Arab minority among the Êzîdî. But still, you were the lead candidate of the party founded by Haydar Shesho and were thus one of the few Êzîdî women who ran on an electable position in the last parliamentary election. How did you get to this position?

I come indeed from Bashiqa and speak only Arabic and no Kurdish. But for me it was important to work with Haydar Shesho because his group was the only one that defended the Êzîdî in Sinjar. And after he had founded his own Êzîdî party in 2016, it was clear for me that I wanted to participate in its work.

But in the end, you were not elected.

70 per cent of the Êzîdî people are in refugee camps in Kurdistan and the rest has fled to Europe or the United States. During the Kurdish parliamentary election, 70 per cent of the Êzîdî votes were not counted because most of them come from Sinjar and were not in the registration rolls. Only the votes from Bashiqa, Bahzani and Şêxan were counted. Around 100,000 votes from abroad and from the refugee camps also went uncounted; otherwise, the PÊD would have won at least one or two parliamentary seats.

How do you see the future of the Êzîdî in Iraq?

Not in a very bright light. There has always been social ostracism against the Êzîdî, and now, there is no future vision either for us or the other minorities. Neither the central government nor the government of the Kurdistan Region care about the minorities, and the reason for this is that we all live in the 'Controversial Areas' which are claimed both by the central government and the Kurdistan Region. Therefore, no one feels any responsibility for the rights of the minorities in these areas and each of the parties tries to pass the responsibilities to the other.

What could a solution look like?

In my view, Sinjar should become a province that also includes the other Êzîdî areas. Sinjar has the right to be an independent province and must be able to make self-managed decisions independently of the central government and the government of the Kurdistan Region. At the moment, there is nothing in Sinjar, no health services, no hospitals. If you get sick, you have to go to Tal Afar. The people can't go to Kurdistan and have to go to a dangerous place like Mosul where there are still kidnappings and rapes. For us Êzîdî, this is very difficult.

How do you see the situation with regard to the legal accounting for the crimes of IS?

After the liberation of Fallujah, Anbar, Mosul and Sinjar, some IS fighters were captured and jailed, but many of them have died in the fighting. Then there are still others who roam around freely. So far, we cannot talk about any real accounting.

How do you see the role of the European states and the EU in this?

Even though many European jihadists fought under the IS flag, the EU has done nothing about it. The EU cares only about itself and its own matters. We're always hearing about the high esteem of the EU for humanity and for the dignity of the human being. But then I'm wondering why the EU receives and accepts the Muslims as refugees and asylum seekers, even though it knows that IS is a Muslim organisation.

But the Muslims who come to Europe as refugees have often fled from IS themselves and are by no means all jihadists.

Here, very many ordinary Muslims participated in the crimes against us Êzîdî. We are the victims of IS, not the Muslim refugees from Syria and Iraq.

You are one of the few female top politicians among the Êzîdî and you come from the town in which Du'a Khalil Aswad, an Êzîdî girl, was stoned in open daylight and with the participation of a part of the population in 2007. This was then exploited by the jihadists, but how do people deal with such a publicly committed crime in your city?

That was of course an absolutely horrible crime and accordingly, the most important perpetrators were punished for it. But that is not sufficient. We are a very patriarchal society and the pressure the young women are subjected to is very strong. Here, Êzîdî society must certainly also change. But you shouldn't forget that such murders are also committed in all other ethnic groups of Iraq. This is nothing specific only for the Êzîdî. The whole of Iraq has still a lot to learn until women are treated the same as men.

Said Hassan Said
Supreme Commander of the YBŞ
14 January 2019

According to the international media, IS is now defeated. The YBŞ was founded to fight against IS. Why is the YBŞ still needed?

The totalitarian regimes always aim at depriving the Êzîdî of their self-determination. This is not only true of IS. It was the same under Saddam Hussein or under the rule of the PDK. They all want to rob the Êzîdî of the opportunity to determine their own future. They all want us to be their subjects. When the PKK and the ideology of Serok Apo[24] came here, the PKK wanted to reacquaint the Êzîdî with their real history and their real culture. It is for exactly this reason that the existing powers have fought this project: because Serok Apo wanted to reinvigorate the old culture of this region. IS was only one phase in the fight against us. Before IS, there had been many massacres against us and we don't want this past to ever return. If we lay down our arms now, we will again be defenceless and under the control of others. From now on, we, the Êzîdî, will never again be caught defenceless and unarmed. If that ever happened, all of our sacrifices would have been in vain.

Part of the ideological basis of your movement is a strongly feminist position. At the same time, the tradition of the Êzîdî is very conservative, not least and even especially with regard to gender roles. How do you deal with this area of conflict?

In our original culture, we Êzîdî had a lot of respect for women, and women could also occupy important social positions. But now we have deviated from our original culture and have changed due to the centuries of oppression by Arabs and Muslims. But in our past, women played important political and military roles, and that is also compatible with our religion – one only has to look at the example of Xatûna Ferxa, the patron saint of women, who was present in our religion as the goddess of the moon. We only need to rediscover the origins of our religion and to liberate them from the influence of Islam, and then we will find a religion which assigns an important role to the women.

What kind of future for Sinjar do you, as the supreme commander of the YBŞ, imagine?

We want some form of self-administration which might take the form of an independent province within Iraq. We want a province which responds directly to the central government in Baghdad and not to Mosul or Erbil. With that, we are not demanding anything that would violate the constitution of Iraq, but something that can be realised within the existing constitutional order of the country. We also want self-defence units under the direct control of Baghdad instead of Mosul.

What do you think about the international reactions to the genocide against the Êzîdî and what would you expect from the international community? What, for example, should Europe or the US do?

I've been to Europe and have seen that human rights are indeed realised within the European states. But outside of Europe, these states don't care about human rights. How else was it possible that such a genocide with all its violence against women and children could happen here in the twenty-first century, right in front of the eyes of the world? It is not enough to award the Nobel Prize to Nadia Murad. The international community must initiate criminal proceedings against the perpetrators of this genocide. But I'm afraid that this is not going to happen. The genocide of the Armenians took place more than a hundred years ago, and even though the Armenians are Christians, most of the European states still haven't recognised this terrible event. And even though the PKK has been fighting here against these terrorists and has contributed a substantial share to the victory over IS, it is still regarded as a terrorist organisation in Europe and by the United States. Europe and the US are supporting Turkey, even though everyone knows that Turkey in turn supports Jabhat al-Nusra[25] or the Muslim Brothers. But the European states and the US still continue to cooperate with Turkey and regard the PKK as a terrorist organisation. We can't count on the Europeans or the Americans in our struggle. When the PKK saved us from IS, we realised that this party has a stance that doesn't only respect us, that is, human beings, but even the animals and nature. After all that the PKK has done for us, it is still denounced as a terrorist organisation. This clearly shows that the policy of the west is not based on ethical positions and that we cannot rely on it.

Mazlum Shengali (Mazlum Şengalî)
Field commander of the YBŞ
14 January 2019

How many fighters does the YBŞ have at the moment?

Right now, we have 4,000 fighters – 3,500 men and 500 women, with the latter organised in the YJŞ.

And officially, you are part of the People's Mobilisation Units?

We are a part of the National Security Forces and are still discussing which units we want to belong to.

Are you getting pay from Baghdad at the moment or not?

Until fourteen months ago, they gave us salaries for 1,200 men, but since then they have stopped this and Baghdad doesn't pay for them anymore. In the last four or five months, we've been getting salaries for 450 fighters.

And these are then distributed to all, or how do you do it?

Yes, it is split among all of them.

This probably means that the pay is very low.

Yes, with that, the salary for each fighter becomes very small. But we are also getting donations from the European diaspora and from people here in the region. But we don't fight for money; we fight for our people. We have a different sort of motivation.

Turkey always accuses the YBŞ to be the same as the PKK, which Tukey claims is a terrorist organisation. What is the relation between the YBŞ and the PKK?

This is the old tactic of Turkey to present us as part of the PKK in order to be able to conquer our territory. We have no organisational connections with the PKK. But even so, the PKK has defended us against IS and saved us. Therefore, we are grateful to it and regard it as a legitimate Kurdish party which has helped us a lot. When IS came, the Iraqi army was here and the Peshmerga were here and they all had weapons and tanks and none of them did anything. It was the PKK and only the PKK that saved us.

But the ideology of Abdullah Öcalan does play a role for you?

Yes, the ideology of Serok Apo is very important to us. It gives us the framework to create a fraternal relation with the other religions and ethnic groups in the region – with Christians, but also with Muslims. We find this idea of brotherhood neither in Barzani nor in the government in Baghdad; we only find it in the thinking of Serok Apo. But this is the same as it is with Jesus Christ. He is neither Italian nor German nor French, but all Christians in Europe follow him. In the same way, Serok Apo is important to all of us, but this doesn't mean that he is the leader of our organisation.

But Turkey uses this time and again as an argument to bomb Sinjar, for example in the last summer, when Zekî Şengalî was killed by the Turkish air force. What do these attacks mean for you on the ground?

They are the continuation of the genocide. Our martyr Zekî Şengalî wanted to bring all Êzîdî together and prevented armed conflicts between the various Êzîdî militias here. It was exactly for that reason that Turkey attacked him. By killing Zekî Şengalî, they wanted to sow chaos and violence, because he always worked for unity. We know the Turks very well, because almost all of the 72 genocides against the Êzîdî had their origin in the Ottoman Empire. At that time, the Ottomans said if you kill six to seven Êzîdî, you go straight to paradise, and therefore, many of them had regrets if they killed only three or four because that was not enough to be elevated to paradise. Such was the extent of their hatred of us back then. Erdoğan is the continuation of this policy and this ideology. IS or al-Qaida, they are all continuations of these genocides by the Ottoman Empire. And that is a danger, not just for us, but also for Europe.

Under normal circumstances, it would be the task of Iraq to defend its national territory. Why is this not happening?

We were at the border for two years and protected it, but now, the Iraqi army is at the border and is in theory responsible for it. According to Iraqi law and international law, Turkey has no right whatsoever to attack us here.

222 · THE WORLD HAS FORGOTTEN US

How is the relation of the YBŞ to the Iraqi army?

Since the beginning of the genocide, the relation to the Iraqi army has been fairly good. We asked the Iraqi army to come here and helped it with hoisting the Iraqi flag. We have regular meetings and we coordinate. There are no problems in this realm.

And how is your relation to the other armed groups here, to the People's Mobilisation Units, to Qasim Shesho, and to Haydar Shesho?

Between the People's Mobilisation Units and us, there is a relation of mutual respect. They respect us and we respect them. The relation to Qasim and Haydar Shesho is difficult. The problem is that the Shesho family is working only for its own interests. Qasim Shesho is with the PDK and Haydar Shesho has no principles; now he works with these people and then he works with some other people. But are still ready to work with him to build a joint military outfit.

That is, you would still be ready to build a joint depoliticised armed force for Sinjar?

Yes, we are ready to do this with all local forces, even with the Êzîdî Peshmerga of Qasim Shesho, but not with the Roj Peshmerga.[26] They do not come from the region, but were trained by Turkey and have no business being here. Turkey only created these Roj Peshmerga so that they could say that they, too, have 'their' Kurds that are loyal to them. These Roj Peshmerga are no local militias of the residents of Sinjar, but the Êzîdî Peshmerga from Sinjar can become part of a joint security force. The Êzîdî Peshmerga are loyal to Barzani, and in the end, Barzani is still a Kurd. We disagree with him in many respects, but he is a Kurd and his Peshmerga are not totally dependent on Turkey like the Roj Peshmerga.

Until 2017, there were not only PDK Peshmerga here but also Peshmerga of the PUK. Not many, but they were still present. How are your relations to these Peshmerga?

We always entertained a good relation to the Peshmerga of the PUK. We don't have any problems with them. The only ones we have a real problem with are the Roj Peshmerga, because they killed our people in Xanasor in spring 2017. But the Kurdish Peshmerga from Iraq, particularly the local Êzîdî Peshmerga, are legitimate forces with which we can cooperate.

What, then, are your ideas for the future of this region?

The future of the region is still totally open. To be able to build something, the local population needs the political rights to do so. We also need the international support of NATO, the EU, and the international community to realise the rights of the local population.

What should the EU and NATO do in concrete terms?

We neither trust the Iraqi government nor the government of Kurdistan Region when it comes to protecting the security of this region. Therefore, we need observers of the UN, the EU, or perhaps even NATO to guarantee the stability and the protection of the region. It is the task of the international community to protect us as we don't trust the two governments here in Iraq anymore since they turned their backs on us in 2014.

What concrete steps would you like to see?

We want diplomatic and political rights, cultural rights, educational rights, economic and ecological rights, self-defence rights, women's rights, and the inclusion of the rights of the Êzîdî in the Iraqi constitution. It is these rights that Europe, the US, the UN and NATO should guarantee for us; these are the rights we want in this region.

But how do you want to achieve that? Do you want the international community to put pressure on Baghdad, or do you want a physical or military presence of Europe or the US on your soil? What exactly do you expect?

Political pressure is good and a military presence would be even better.

And what kind of political structure would you like to see? Do you want an independent province of Sinjar or something different?

We want a local autonomous and decentralised self-administration which is also recognised by Iraq. This could be, but doesn't have to be, a province. It would be up to negotiations whether this will be an independent province or some other structure.

Akhin Intiqam (Axîn Intiqam)
Commander of the YJŞ
14 January 2019

How many fighters does the YJŞ have at present and what is your official status in Iraq?

At the moment, we have 500 women under arms. The YBŞ is registered as part of the National Security Forces, but we don't get any pay from the Iraqi government.

What will change for you with the presence of armed women in Sinjar? After all, this is something completely new for this region.

The YJŞ was founded during the genocide. IS wanted to destroy the Êzîdî by destroying the Êzîdî women and subjecting them to their violence. At the time, we could see what IS does to us women. But the destruction did not only originate in jihadism, but also in the masculinist mentality represented by IS. By raising our arms against IS as women, we are not just fighting against IS and for the Êzîdî, but also against the masculinist mentality of male perpetrators of violence against us as Êzîdî women. Through this, the Êzîdî community has realised that we as women are able to organise and defend ourselves. Once the Êzîdî society saw that we women are able to autonomously defend and organise ourselves, it also began to sympathise with our cause as women. This has changed a lot of things.

Which kind of women became part of the YJŞ? Are they primarily young and unmarried women or women from all age groups? What kind of backgrounds do women have who fight for you?

Only women from the age of eighteen are allowed to participate in actual battle. There are some younger fighters who want to join us, but they can't participate in the fighting. And we don't accept married women in our ranks. Our women have to fight, often far away from their families. That would be impossible for married women. The maximum age for our fighters is thirty-five.

What are the reasons for girls and women to join you? Are they doing so only for political reasons or are there also young women who maybe have problems with their families or who want to escape from a forced marriage and who regard joining the fight as an alternative to patriarchal family structures?

The women and girls who come to us do so for a variety of reasons, which are of course not exclusively political. Personally, I joined the YJŞ in 2014 during the genocide, and I did not want to fight just against IS, but also against the capitalist mentality which degrades women and looks down upon them. I wanted to end the suffering of the women. There were also some women who joined the YJŞ after their liberation because they wanted to fight back against their oppressors. But of course, there were also women who had problems with their families and suffered under the traditions. These were women who saw no other way out: their alternative was either committing suicide or joining the YJŞ. Many of them wanted to fight against this masculinist mentality which humiliates us women and looks down on us. But the main reason was of course the attacks by IS, who assaulted us and who embody the purest form of this masculinist and chauvinist mentality.

The women who were captured by IS and came to you afterwards, who were raped and experienced all sorts of additional violence, certainly often have psychological problems. How do you deal with these problems in your units?

Of course, among the women who were kidnapped and raped by IS or whose children were killed in front of their eyes. There are many who were initially very browbeaten. Many of them also thought that they would have big problems if they joined the YJŞ. Many were afraid that they would no longer be accepted by the Êzîdî as a whole because they had been raped by Muslims. When they came, the first thing we did was to assure them that we accepted them. We enlightened them about women's rights and about how they could win their rights for themselves. After this, they began to trust us more and more and became more self-confident. We also try to take their fear away by fighting for the betterment of the role of women within the Êzîdî society. We try to help them by giving them ideological training and by explaining how the movement views women and what we are fighting for. In this way, the women gradually get rid of their fears and acquire the psychological ability to fight with us.

Just as the other societies of the region, the Êzîdî society is very conservative and patriarchal. Both in Germany or Europe and right here, the marriage rules in particular frequently cause problems that sometimes even take the form of so-called honour killings of young women. In 2007, there was the case of Du'a Khalil Aswad in Bashiqa, who was murdered by the rest of her family because she had fallen in love with a Muslim, a murder that was then exploited for anti-Êzîdî propaganda. Are such problems also a topic in your feminist political work? What do you do if you have a case in which an Êzîdî girl falls in love with someone who she is not allowed to marry according to the Êzîdî tradition?

This conservatism and the strict rules against mixing with one's enemy have allowed the Êzîdî to survive in an antagonistic environment for all those centuries. Therefore, any woman who falls in love with a follower of another religion is regarded as some kind of traitor. In 2007, there was yet another case in Tîl Êzêr in which the family killed their daughter because she had fallen in love with a Muslim. They also wanted to kill her partner, but he managed to escape. He then joined al-Qaida and blew himself up in a car in Tîl Êzêr.

That was the attack of 14 August 2007, right?

Yes, exactly. But the case of the women who were raped by IS men during the recent events is different from this. In this case, many of our religious leaders have acquitted the women of all blame because they didn't do this voluntarily. We support the position of the Êzîdî leaders that this is something completely different.

I have never heard this story – that the perpetrator of the assault of 2007 had been with an Êzîdî girl who was then killed – before. Generally, the attacks of 2007 are brought into connection with the murder of Du'a Khalil Aswad. Are you really sure that this was the background?

Yes, this was a man from a neighbouring Muslim village who fell in love with an Êzîdî girl from Tîl Êzêr, who was then killed by her family.[27]

What is your official organisational position on these questions? Do you intervene when you become aware that an Êzîdî girl falls in love with a Muslim and is thinking about marrying him?

When we become aware of such a thing, we try to convince the girl not to marry the Muslim. This is contrary to our culture and religion, and it is not a good thing to go against their rules. Even though the YJŞ is protected by its own armed force, we must also respect the Êzîdî culture and religion.

Isn't this contrary to the spirit of the political movement you belong to?

No, because we don't kill these girls but only give them advice and try to convince them by arguments. This is a crucial difference.

What are your wishes for the future of Sinjar and for the future of Êzîdî society? How do you want your future life to look like?

We want to be a self-administered province within Iraq where women and men can live together as equals and in which our

Êzîdî culture is protected. The political and social rights of women must be protected, including the right of all women to defend themselves.

Lamiya Aji Bashar (Lamîa Hacî Beşar)
Human rights activist, born in Koço in 1998; kidnapped by IS in 2014; wounded by a landmine during her escape in April 2016; won the 2016 Sakharov Prize together with Nadia Murad
20 February 2019

You came from north Iraq to Baden-Württemberg with a special contingent of 1,000 particularly vulnerable women and girls and you were awarded the 2016 Sakharov Prize of the EU Parliament together with Nadia Murad. What did it mean to you to win that prize? How has it changed your life?

For me, the prize represented a big support and encouragement. It showed me that my people and I are not alone, but that there are thousands of people who have sympathy for the suffering of the Êzîdî. We could see that many decisions were taken to enhance the protection of the Êzîdî and other Iraqi minorities. We owe this to the support by the EU and the international community. There have also been some personal changes for me. Now I often have to participate in international meetings and events, but I still try to lead a normal life. I attend language and integration courses and spend a lot of time with the rest of my family. In this way, we can support each other in healing our wounds, even though these cannot really be healed.

How did you feel when you had to tell your story in public over and over again? I have always admired the way you did this, but I suppose that it is difficult for you to talk about all the things that happened to you in IS captivity.

My real motivation was the screaming, helpless voices of the women and children I continue to hear. It is certainly not easy for a young girl to talk about these cruel, personal stories. But whenever I thought about this deeply, my motivation grew even stronger because the world needs to become aware of this to make sure that this can never happen again, neither to the Êzîdî nor to any other people in the world.

The women who, like you, came to Germany with the special contingent were actually supposed to be accepted for only two years and to be sent back to Iraq after that. But very few of them have returned. Why is that?

You are right, the plan for the special contingent was different from what then happened. The women were offered a two-year special status and then that status was extended to three years. But now we also have the option for everyone of us who wants to stay in Germany to do so. Only a few persons or families who came with the contingent have returned. And given the circumstances under which the Êzîdî have to live in Iraq, it is unrealistic to expect anyone to want to return, isn't it? The Êzîdî in Iraq have been living as refugees in tents for four and a half years, and a return to their home region is still impossible because many villages are still mined and there is still great political insecurity.

How are these women doing now in Germany? Do you know anything about the other women?

They are doing great, I would say – they are doing very well. In the schools, the children are very well integrated. The women are trying to find their way; some of them are enrolled in language courses or doing an apprenticeship. And they are also well integrated in the Êzîdî society in Germany. We want all women and children with the same fate as ours to be taken abroad. Abroad, their chances of survival are much better than in Iraq.

Mirza Dinnayi
Representative of the aid organisation Air Bridge Iraq and adviser of the Êzîdî Friendship Group in the EU parliament
4 March 2019

We have known each other for many years and you accompanied my wife Mary and me to the Bava Şêx and to Laliş long before the genocide of 2014. Back then, practically no one in the world even knew about the existence of the Êzîdî. This situation radically changed in 2014. At that time, even US media called me to ask who the Êzîdî are. What does it mean for you that the world has come to know the Êzîdî only because of the genocide by IS? What does it do to a group when it is identified only with its suffering, but not with the cultural and religious wealth that is also present?

On the one hand, it is unfortunate that such small groups are ignored by the world to a degree that they become known only through their suffering. Because of the way the media presented us, we always ended up with having to talk about the victimhood of our people and not being allowed to talk about the other aspects of our humanitarian ethics and our cultural wealth. But on the other hand, we are also glad that we are getting the solidarity of so many people, that we don't need to fear being all alone in this world, and that people are interested in us even though we don't play any role in the cosmetic competition that dominates politics, business and security. For a people like my own, which has survived 72 genocides and which has always been alone, it is extremely important to feel this solidarity.

In August 2014, you flew to the mountain under IS siege with helicopters of the Iraqi army, bringing water and food and flying people out from there. In the process, you got wounded in a helicopter crash in which your Arab-Muslim pilot was killed. How did all of this come about?

I signed up as a volunteer with the Iraqi aviation to accompany a team that wanted to fly to Sinjar. The pilot was an acquaintance of mine and during that operation, we became real friends and also built friendships with other pilots. It was important to me to be really close to the population. I wanted to make the best use of all my abilities to stem this catastrophe. I didn't only want to bring food and water to the mountains, but I also wanted to transmit the cruel images of the victims to the rest of the world. I invited journalists, politicians, and other people to go to the mountains themselves to get a true picture of what was happening. Once, I smuggled Michel Reimon,[28] an EU MP from Austria who I got to know through you, to the mountains. Actually, it was not permitted to take such high-ranking foreign politicians with us. Had the Iraqi or the Kurdish government learned that we did this, they would have punished both the pilot and myself. The pilots and the airport security service thought that Mr Reimon was a journalist – and because of that, he was sometimes treated with a lot of hostility. One of the guys said to me, 'Mirza, you are taking these journalists to the mountains every day and then they write stories and do nothing, and they never show us their documentaries.' We agreed that I would prepare Mr Reimon's video for the Iraqi Ministry of Defence. Actually, the only video material of the ministry, the one that they always show, comes from that very film.

And what happened when you had that accident?

At first, the day of the crash was just like any other day. We had made a trip to the mountains with the helicopter. During the second trip, we crashed. The reason was that we had overloaded the helicopter. We were supposed to take up to 25 persons with us. But we generally took up to 45 people in because we simply had too many people on the mountain and far too few helicopters. I survived the crash with a broken leg and few broken ribs. The pilot I had befriended was killed and a woman and two children also died. I was lying beneath the bodies of all the other people because I had been seated when we started. During the minutes when we were jammed within the crashed machine, I was lying under all the other people in the helicopter. I could neither see nor breathe. Mentally, I went through all the phases of my own death. My childhood and my whole life went by before my eyes like a video tape. I was asking myself, 'Is this the end of my life? Is IS right in destroying my people? Is God on their side or on ours? What wrong have we done?' Then I remembered that my parents had died just a few months ago, and I said to myself, 'Thanks be to God that they don't have to see my death.' It was the birthday of my own son and I hadn't had the time to congratulate him because I went to my mission each day at 5 a.m. Iraqi time, three o'clock German time. At that moment, my most fervent wish was, 'Please, don't let me die today. My son grew up like a German, he will not want to celebrate any of his birthdays anymore for the rest of his life if I die on this very day.' In this last second, I gave up; I accepted my death and got ready to leave my body. But all of a sudden, I saw a flashlight and fresh air flowed through to my lungs. I began to hope again. As I breathed a second time, my breath became stronger. And I realised that we were being saved. I was the last to leave the rubble of the helicopter. This experience gave me courage and taught me that our life has a higher destination and that I have to fight even harder for the victims and for justice. I spent three months in a wheelchair until my wounds had healed. But only 15 days after the accident, I was in Geneva and delivered the first Êzîdî speech before the UN Human Rights Commission. Since that day, I haven't had a single break, because the catastrophe is even worse than all of us think.

Do you know what became of the people who you evacuated with your helicopter trips? Where are they now?

Sometimes, I meet some of the people we saved, in Europe or in Iraq. Some of them went back to the mountains, whereas others emigrated all the way to the US. It was very many people. Sometimes they approach me and tell me, 'You took my hand and allowed me to climb into the helicopter', even though I can hardly recognise them.

During the last few years, you were also active for the special contingent of the 1,000 women and girls from northern Iraq who were accommodated in Baden-Württemberg, and you have tried, together with the Êzîdî Friendship Group in the EU parliament, to initiate similar programmes in Austria and other states of the EU. Even though there have been a number of meetings with high-ranking politicians in Austria, in the end this project failed. Can you tell us how this looked like from your personal perspective?

Unfortunately, we were unsuccessful, despite all our activities: the meetings on various levels ranging from the Federal Chancellor of the time, Kern, to NGOs, church representatives, and politicians of the federal states Upper Austria and Vienna, and the ardent commitment of the Êzîdî Friendship Group, and particularly Josef Weidenholzer.[29] We were always told, 'Yes, you are right, one must do something for these victims.' But without any results.

As a commuter between Iraq, Germany and Brussels, you were able to observe the European policy with regard to the Êzîdî in Iraq from close up. How do you see the role of Europe, the EU and the individual member states? What was done and what should be done?

So far, the EU parliament has passed three important resolutions that were pushed by the Êzîdî Friendship Group. These resolutions, concerning the recognition of the genocide, the mass graves, and the situation of the Iraqi minorities, were very important. But there is no united EU diplomacy or policy. We still need to be active in this realm in order to push this even further. We all hope that the Êzîdî Friendship Group will continue to exist after the EU elections, when Josef Weidenholzer will no longer be a member of the EU parliament, and that the EU will intensify its commitment to the reconstruction of Sinjar. This reconstruction is impossible to realise with Iraqi means alone, and most of the people who were expelled in 2014 continue to live as refugees in tent camps in Kurdistan. Moreover, we need support in the identification of the victims in the mass graves and in the legal accounting of the crimes. The survivors have the right to see legal trials of both the Iraqi and the European perpetrators who committed a genocide against the Êzîdî under the umbrella of IS. Here, Europe also has a responsibility, and it must live up to it.

Notes

PART I   HISTORY OF SINJAR AND THE GENOCIDE

2 Sinjar in ancient times

1. Dohuk is the capital of the Dahuk Governorate in the Autonomous Region of Kurdistan in Iraq.
2. Kitchen, 2012: 239.
3. Penn, 2015: 113.
4. Naval Intelligence Division, 2014: 80.

3 From the Islamic conquest to the periphery of the Ottoman Empire

1. The Turkish name for the city Diyarbakır (Kurdish: Amed) stems from this Arabic provincial name.
2. The Shammar are a big Arab tribal federation which hails from the north of today's Saudi Arabia and from the neighbouring areas of Iraq and Jordan. From 1835 to 1921, their area of origin around the Jebel Shammar with the city of Hā'il formed the autonomous empire of the ar-Raschīd before this entity was conquered by the dynasty of the Saud. The first Shammar came to Iraq already in the seventeenth century. Today, they are a large tribe with two main sub-groups, which has more than 1.5 million Sunni and Shiite Muslim members in Iraq alone.
3. Sheikh Sharaf ad-Din (Kurdish: Şêx Şerfedîn), born in 1215, fought in alliance with the Seljuks against the Mongols and after his death became an important saint of the Êzîdî. His mausoleum, built around 1274, was heavily contested in 2014.
4. The Safavids started out as members of a Shiite Sufi order and founded the League of the Kızılbaş ('Redheads'), who were probably also the predecessors of the Anatolian Alevi. After the Safavids took power in Iran, this group, which deviated from the orthodox Shia and was thus heterodox, became part of the orthodox Twelver Shia, while those Kızılbaş who stayed in the Ottoman Empire became Alevi.
5. The Mamelukes were military slaves of East European, Central Asian, or Caucasian origin and achieved great political importance already under the Abbasids. In Egypt, they were at first able to govern as independent rulers (the Bahri and Burji Mamelukes) and later ruled under Ottoman suzerainty. In India, the Sultanate of Delhi was founded as a Mameluke

sultanate and in Iraq, Georgian Mamelukes under an Ottoman from Georgia, Pasha Hassan (1704–1723), were able to secure power for themselves under Ottoman suzerainty. After Hassan's death, the appointment of the originally envisioned pasha foundered on the resistance of the Georgian Mamelukes, who by then already numbered 2,000 men. Suleyman Abu Layla expelled the pasha chosen by the sultan from Baghdad and became the first Mameluke pasha of Iraq, even though his rule continued to be under the suzerainty of the Ottoman sultan.

6. Paşalık was the early name of the Ottoman provinces, which were then transformed into so-called Wilayats in the course of the unification and centralisation of the empire through the Tanzimat reforms from 1861 to 1866.
7. The originally Christian al-Jalili family, which then converted to Sunni Islam, ruled Mosul from 1726 and 1834. Its rule was concentrated on the rich trading city of Mosul and was weaker in the periphery of the Paşalık. With the centralisation of the Ottoman Empire, Mosul came under the direct rule of the empire again, but the al-Jalili family continued to be politically and economically influential.
8. Fuccaro, 1999: 32.

4 The religion of the Êzîdî

1. Guest, 2010: 34.
2. Cf. Hutter, 2003.
3. Kreyenbroek, 2016: 32–33.
4. Tagay and Ortaç, 2016: 57–58.
5. Schmidinger, 2019: 10–11.
6. Islam considers Jews, Christians and Sabians as 'people of the book', which gave them a specific protected status that was denied to polytheistic religions.
7. Bittner, 1913.
8. See www.youtube.com/watch?v=gldTJ89CVOw (accessed 24 February 2019).
9. Ibid.
10. Açıkyıldız, 2010: 141.
11. Tagay and Ortaç, 2016: 79.

5 Social order and religious office-holders of the Êzîdî

1. In most Sufi communities, 'Murîd' is the designation for a believer or a successor of a Sufi Sheikh, in particular the student of a Sheikh or Pîr who, by virtue of this role, becomes the spiritual leader (muršid) of the murīd. Both this conceptualisation and the tripartition of society

probably stem from Sufism, which was introduced among the Êzîdî by Sheikh 'Adī.

2. Dulz, 2001: 39.

6 The tribal society in Sinjar

1. Fuccaro, 1994: 62.
2. Ibid: 65.
3. Ibid: 66.

7 Sinjar in the late Ottoman Empire

1. Guest, 2010: 63.
2. Taylor, 2005: 33.
3. Fuccaro, 1999: 32.
4. Quoted after Guest, 2010: 75.
5. Kurdish: *Mihemed Paşay Rewanduz* or *Mîrê korâ* (blind prince).
6. McDowall, 2007: 42.
7. The Tur Abdin is a mountain massif surrounding the city of Midyat to the east of Mardin which is the traditional home of very many Christian monasteries and churches as well as of an Aramaic-speaking population, but where there were also Êzîdî villages until the massacres of Bedirxan Beg. Some of these villages continued to exist well into the 1980s. In the course of the military battles between the Turkish army and the PKK, almost all of the remaining Êzîdî fled to Germany. Today, most of the Êzîdî villages of the region are completely desolate.
8. Açıkyıldız, 2010: 52.
9. Allison, 2001: 87–88.
10. Unfortunately, there has been no research on the question which concrete personal connections between Êzîdî from Sinjar and Armenians from Mardin made this escape possible. The mutual relationships between these persecuted minorities were certainly the basis that made it possible for the Armenians to escape and survive.
11. See www.ezidipress.com/blog/hemoye-shero-der-mann-der-20-000-christen-vor-dem-voelkermord-rettete (accessed 2 April 2019).
12. The highest official of an Ottoman district, appointed by the central government. In today's Turkey, this office still exists under the name Kaymakam, a word that was borrowed from Arabic.
13. 'Assyrian Christians' is the label of the Aramaic-speaking Christians who belong to the Assyrian Church of the East and used to live primarily in the region around Hakkari and Urmiya before they were deported and murdered together with the Armenian population in 1915. In the European literature, this group is frequently referred to as 'Nestorians', but the members of the church itself reject this name.

14. Guest, 2010: 179.

8 The British occupation and protectorate

1. After the failed coup of 2016, Erdoğan pointed to the 'national pact' of 1920 which had also raised claims to Mosul and Aleppo. In military terms, Turkey has already been present in the environment of Mosul and in the north of the Kurdistan Region of Iraq for quite a while, but this was with the tacit approval of the Kurdish regional government.
2. Fuccaro, 1999: 90.
3. In Arabic, Hākim has a broad range of meanings which reach from judge and governor to leader.
4. Guest, 2010: 183.
5. Fuccaro, 1999: 99f.
6. Guest, 2010: 183.
7. Fuccaro, 1999: 133.
8. Cf. Pedersen, 2010.
9. Fuccaro, 1999: 133.

9 The Êzîdî in Iraq

1. During the massacre of Simele in August 1933, 63 Assyrian villages were attacked by the Iraqi army and up to 3,000 Assyrians were killed. After this, many survivors fled to French-governed Syria and settled on the river Harbur, from where they were expelled in 2015 by the attacks of IS.
2. Dulz, 2001: 57.
3. Açıkyıldız, 2010: 33.
4. Dinnayi, 2004: 200.
5. Spät, 1985: 81f.

10 Resentments against the Êzîdî

1. Cf. Allison, 2001: 37.

11 Ethno-confessional groups in the Sinjar region

1. Fuccaro, 1999: 192.
2. From 1708 to 1972, Mardin was the seat of an eparchy of the Armenian-Catholic Church, which up to 1954 also included Iraq. Even today, there is a very small Armenian-Catholic parish in Mardin with a church, but without a resident priest. It is the only Armenian-Catholic community in Turkish Kurdistan.
3. Sayighian El-Baghdadi, 1944: 48.

4. Interview with Seta Ohanian, historian at the Armenian Academy of Science, 14 October 2018.
5. Interview with a Syrian-Orthodox man from Sinjar who now lives in a Christian village in the province Dohuk, 20 September 2017.
6. Wahhabism is a strict Sunni doctrine which goes back to Muhammad ibn 'Abd al-Wahhābs (1702–1792). It is still the state religion of Saudi Arabia and has had a considerable influence on extremist Sunni currents.
7. *Ziyaret* means 'visit' in Iranian languages. Referring to a place, it means a place that is visited. In the context of Sinjar and many other religious groups in the Middle East, it refers to sacred places, especially holy tombs, that are visited by believers.
8. Ghulāt cults were currents of Shiite Islam which had a particular veneration for Ali and Hussein and even regarded them as the incarnation of God. For 'Abdallāh ibn Saba', one of the most important founders of this current, Ali was God.
9. Fuccaro, 1999: 53.
10. Ibid.
11. Jabar, 2002: 131.

12 Sinjar under the rule of the Ba'th Party

1. Dulz, 2001: 54.
2. Fischer-Tahir, 2003: 152ff.
3. Dulz, 2001: 55.
4. Dinnayi, 2004: 202.
5. Dulz, 2001: 73.
6. The conflict between the parties that went down into history as 'fratricide' (Kurdish: Birakujî) led to a split of the autonomous Kurdistan Region of Iraq into two parts which, though it was partially overcome in 2003, is still clearly palpable today. Thus, there are still two different security forces of the PDK and the PUK which wear different uniforms and are each under a different command.

13 After the fall of Saddam Hussein: between Baghdad and Erbil

1. Cerha, 2009: 21.
2. Schmidinger, 2015: 47.
3. Interview with a member of the Babawat from Sinjar who now lives in Dohuk, September 2017.
4. Interview with an Êzîdî from Xanasor, September 2017.
5. Iraqi-Kurdistan is based on a rent economy which enables the ruling PDK to secure the loyalty of different groups of the population through the distribution of the oil rent.

14 The massacre of 14 August 2007: the 73rd firman?

1. Omarkhali, 2017: 108, 221, 241, 314.
2. Ibid.: 120.
3. Ibid.: 119.
4. See www.independent.co.uk/news/world/middle-east/the-death-sentence-that-drags-dua-back-into-a-bloody-feud-1956187.html (accessed 2 April 2019).
5. Felter and Fishman, 2007: 4.
6. Interview with Akhin Intiqam (Axîn Intiqam), commander of the Women's Unit of Sinjar (Yekinêyen Jinên Şengalê, YJŞ), 14 January 2019.

15 Encircled by jihadists

1. Bakhdida is also called Qaraqosh or, in Arabic, al-Hamdaniya. The educational institution established as an autonomous university in 2014 (which was immediately forced to move to a container campus near Erbil after the attack of IS) was named 'University al-Hamdaniya'.
2. Schmidinger, 2015: 59–60.
3. In Iraq, the label 'Turkmens' refers both to Turkish-speaking descendants of urban Ottoman upper classes and nomadic Turk-speaking tribes. The Iraqi Turkmens speak a variety of Turkish similar to the one of the Turkish in Turkey and must not be confused with the inhabitants of the Republic of Turkmenistan.
4. See www.nbcnews.com/id/17883992/ns/world_news-mideast_n_africa/t/tal-afar-bomb-toll-hits-deadliest-iraq-war (accessed 3 April 2019).
5. See www.bbc.com/news/world-middle-east-28103124 (accessed 2 April 2019).

16 The IS genocide in August 2014

1. Schmidinger, 2018a: 91–92.
2. Kartal, 2016: 59.
3. Kingery, 2018: 22.
4. See https://reliefweb.int/sites/reliefweb.int/files/resources/21st%20Mar_UNITAD%20Statement_Conclusion%20of%20First%20Kojo%20Exhumation_ENG.pdf (accessed 9 November 2021).
5. See www.ezidipress.com/blog/irak-ueber-70-opfer-in-sieben-weiteren-massengraebern-entdeckt/?fbclid=IwAR2WsfsBbDu3IJG2p7t9Ctggyk8RL9kueCVBSHnjkBnRjfvwiuOK4PiHBVE (accessed 9 April 2019).
6. Among the politicians I contacted, only two Austrian EU deputies were interested in the topic, namely the Green MEP Michel Reimon, and the Social-Democrat and vice president of the S&D caucus in the EU par-

liament, Josef Weidenholzer. The latter even contacted me himself in reaction to my Facebook postings. I got Reimon into contact with my friend Mirza Dinnayi, who then, on 10 August, brought him to the Sinjar Mountains in a helicopter of the Iraqi army. His video and his reports contributed to conveying the urgency of the problem to a broader public. Weidenholzer joined me on my visits to the camps of the expelled and survivors in January 2015 and on my visit to Sinjar in June 2016.

7. In the Second World War, *Voice of America* broadcast propaganda against the Nazis and during the Cold War, it supplied dissidents in the states of the Warsaw Pact with the US view of the world. Cf. Shand, 2018: 16.

8. Ibid.

9. Ibid.: 145.

10. Mikhail, 2018: 61.

11. Kingery, 2018: 29.

12. Mikhail, 2018: 63.

13. Mato, 2016: 59.

14. See www.al-monitor.com/pulse/originals/2019/03/iraq-yazidi-sinjar-museum-genocide.html (9 April 2019).

15. Fuccaro, 1997: 570.

16. Shand, 2018: 49.

17 Genocide

1. *Dabiq*, Issue 4, 1435 (2014): 14.

2. Ortaç, 2016: 22.

18 The reintroduction of slavery and sexual violence

1. *Dabiq*, Issue 4, 1435 (2014): 14–15.

2. Ibid.: 15.

3. Ibid.: 16.

4. Fast breaking: under normal circumstances, a very rich evening meal after sunset during the fasting month Ramadan.

5. Breakfast before sunrise during Ramadan.

6. Small former settlement in Sinjar near Til Êzêr, where a large mass grave of victims of IS was found in November 2017.

7. Al-Ba'j is a Sunni-Arab village south of Sinjar many of whose inhabitants participated in the activities of IS.

8. Jabhat al-Nusra is a jihadist militia in Syria which used to be member of al-Qaida until 2016. In theory, Jabhat al-Nusra, which has been ruling Idlib since the summer of 2017, and IS have been enemies since the split of IS from al-Qaida in 2016, but the ideological differences between the two groups are only marginal. As this testimony proves, captured Êzîdî women were traded between the two jihadist groups.

9. Many of the names used by individual jihadists point to their origin. In this case, the person is probably a man from Dagestan, a Russian constituent republic east of Chechnya between the Caucasus and the Caspian Sea.

10. For Jabhat al-Nusra, the Êzîdî girls and women were more like an article of trade. Even though the fighters of Jabhat al-Nusra also practised rape in ample abandon, the organisation as such first and foremost attempted to resell the women it had bought or captured during battles; the primary goal was financial gain.

11. Shand, 2018: 7.

12. Ferman, 2016: 118.

13. Even though in my own field research I was told of prices of $5,000 and more as the ransom for a young woman, this lower sum still represented a very big profit for both the sellers and the middlemen.

14. See www.middleeastmonitor.com/20160603-un-daesh-earned-45m-in-ransoms-from-yazidis-in-2014 (accessed 6 April 2019).

15. See www.thestar.com/news/canada/2015/08/15/jewish-schindler-rescues-iraqi-girls-from-slavery.html (accessed 6 April 2019).

16. See www.ezidipress.com/blog/gesetzentwurf-iraks-praesident-fordert-umfassende-unterstuetzung-fuer-befreite-ezidische-frauen (accessed 4 April 2019).

17. See www.baden-wuerttemberg.de/de/service/presse/pressemitteilung/pid/institut-fuer-psychotherapie-in-dohuk-startet-studienbetrieb-1 (accessed 4 April 2019).

19 Struggle for liberation

1. Schmidinger, 2016: 41.

2. See www.ezidipress.com/blog/qasim-shesho-eziden-muessen-mit-schweren-waffen-ausgeruestet-werden (accessed 4 April 2019).

3. See the interview with Haydar Shesho on 2 June 2016 in Part III of this book.

4. See www.gppi.net/2017/08/04/iraq-after-isil-rabia (accessed 15 April 2019).

5. See www.independent.co.uk/news/world/middle-east/isis-latest-kurdish-forces-break-the-siege-of-mount-sinjar-9934934.html (accessed 19 April 2019).

6. See www.gov.uk/government/publications/british-forces-air-strikes-in-iraq-monthly-list/raf-air-strikes-in-iraq-december-2014#december-19 (accessed 19 April 2019).

7. See www.bundestag.de/dokumente/textarchiv/2014/kw36_de_sonder sitzung-296154 (accessed 19 April 2019).

8. Schmidinger, 2016: 40.

9. See www.n-tv.de/politik/Kurden-halten-deutschen-Jesiden-Chef-fest-article 14868481.html (accessed 19 April 2019).

10. Schmidinger, 2017: 259.

11. See www.nytimes.com/2015/11/14/world/middleeast/sinjar-iraq-islamic-state.html (accessed 6 April 2019).

12. It appears that the government in Baghdad was afraid that the Kurdish forces Peshmerga and the YBŞ could militarily entrench themselves in regions the central government was not willing to cede to them. It is ironic that the Êzîdî in the south then asked for help from the very government that was actively impeding their liberation.

13. See www.theguardian.com/world/2017/jan/12/charity-yazidi-survivors-isis-sexual-slavery-shut-down-kurdish-authorities-yazda-women-children (accessed 6 April 2019).

14. Schmidinger, 2017: 260.

15. See https://anfdeutsch.com/kurdistan/pdk-kraefte-eroeffnen-feuer-auf-demonstrierende-150 (accessed 5 April 2019).

16. In May 2017, I did a series of interviews in Xanke/Xanik, one of the largest camps of Êzîdî internally displaced people (IDP) from Sinjar, and also witnessed one of the speeches by PDK functionaries mentioned in the text.

17. See www.hrw.org/news/2017/12/27/iraq-yezidi-fighters-allegedly-execute-civilians (accessed 5 April 2019).

18. Schmidinger, 2018b: 299.

19. Interview with Qasim Shesho on 19 October 2018 in Part III of this book.

20. See https://anfdeutsch.com/kurdistan/was-sagt-Sengal-zum-rueckzug-der-guerilla-3458 (accessed 8 April 2019).

21. See www.sn.at/politik/weltpolitik/erdogan-eroeffnet-tuerkische-offensive-in-sinjar-im-nordirak-25868431 (accessed 8 April 2019).

22. See https://anfdeutsch.com/kurdistan/autonomierat-Sengal-uebernimmt-kontrolle-ueber-siba-Sex-xidir-7338 (accessed 8 April 2019).

23. Schmidinger, 2018b: 301.

24. Report containing a motion for a non-legislative resolution on the draft Council decision on the conclusion of a Partnership and Cooperation Agreement between the European Union and its Member States, of the one part, and the Republic of Iraq, of the other part (10209/1/2012 – C8-0038/2018 – 2010/0310M(NLE)).

20 The life of the displaced

1. See https://kurdistantribune.com/conditions-yezidi-refugee-camps-turkey (accessed 9 April 2019).

2. Ibid.

3. Schmidinger, 2016: 35.

4. See www.hdp.org.tr/en/statements/the-relocation-of-yazidis-in-fidanlik-camp-diyarbakir/9718 (accessed 4 April 2019).
5. Dulz, 2016: 144.
6. See www.brha-duhok.org/wp-content/uploads/Report%20of%202016.pdf (accessed 4 April 2019).
7. Interview with a refugee in the Xanke camp, 30 May 2017.
8. See http://iraqdtm.iom.int/ReturneeLocationAssessment.aspx (accessed 4 April 2019).
9. Interview with an expelled woman in the Xanke camp, 29 May 2017.
10. Interview with a refugee in the Xanke camp, 30 May 2017.
11. Cf. McGee, 2018.

22 Marginalised and instrumentalised

1. Schneckener, König and Wienand, 2018: 235.
2. See www.usip.org/publications/2021/06/unemployment-replaces-isis-top-security-concern-minorities-iraq (accessed 3 July 2021)
3. See https://parliament.iq/wp-content/uploads/2021/03/4621_2.pdf?__cf_chl_jschl_tk__=c84fbf991b1a11de719a78fe41e5835ba5200a30-1625295314-0-ARWTGqeuiIryYicBKJ7JDge9hajgUili6JZQ9zgoouJJbdh BmhlYqPYooYyt6bIzcN5uvNLAWpRRbvyImvD9dxigraAfexwX3zf hiOBNpnmU-oDB689ZZA-AoANtxqv6lqjs68xKkzIQMtroo6rQw8DX qMjg3xTumWgixY5iqLISVclVmooO8JbFOj-2Ru-L5mDonWZaNcr gLWOuDntvS5iN95poBauGcpssg_rzecZN6DpTQe5spJLUt489iamS DAXyTSpzokuCgveLIXoUoBTDySvt9XeLmmafSGJWL-uLsKoEwqL_ t2gPdjnzfhfzWSoj4SmJ-sWSWsCqR4a61WoBcSb2_hEJZ7mlnZa boutFtWf1_PIKT2_-AWs38_zfLIMuXNqHKUoqp4gaQXJo8pA9H GEkn_6PCBIffNIoBqYT5ECK8GX5_3B4ZOdI2r4_ug (accessed 3 July 2021).

1. Fighters, in circles close to the PKK also often used in the sense of 'comrades'.
2. West-Kurdistan, meaning Syrian Kurdistan.
3. Northern Kurdistan, meaning Turkish Kurdistan.
4. The attacks on two villages in Sinjar on 14 August 2017, described in Chapter 14 of this book, in which almost 800 people were killed.
5. Êzîdî village in the proximity of Duhok.
6. An originally Christian place west of Duhok which today is a suburb of the city on the road to the west. In 1933, it was the site of one of the worst massacres in Iraq against the Assyrian Christians.
7. The DShK 1938, a heavy Soviet/Russian machine gun, is called 'Doshka' in Iraq.

8. Khalaf Bahri is a traditional religious Sheikh of the Êzîdî who was politically close to the YPG, or rather, the YBŞ, and frequently presided over funeral ceremonies for fallen fighters of the YBŞ, but who enjoyed a high reputation in the region far beyond this particular group.

9. Sheikh Ismail is one of the traditional religious leaders of Şerfedîn.

10. Abu Mahdi al-Muhandis was the head of the Kata'ib Hezbollah, one of the most important Shiite militia within the People's Mobilisation Units. The Kata'ib Hezbollah closely works with Iran and supports the Syrian regime in the Syrian civil war. As the leader of the Kata'ib Hezbollah, Abu Mahdi al-Muhandis became the most important conduct between the People's Mobilisation Units and Iran; he also became the deputy president of all People's Mobilisation Units.

11. Mîr Tehsîn Seîd Beg was the traditional political leader of the Êzîdî from 1944 until his death in 2019 and was considered to be close to the PDK.

12. Nêçîrvan Barzanî is the nephew of Masoud Barzani (Mesûd Barzanî) and has been the Prime Minister of the Autonomous Region of Kurdistan in Iraq from 2006 to 2009 and then from 2012 on.

13. Bashiqa and Bahzani are Arabic-speaking Êzîdî villages in the Nineveh Governorate.

14. Mesrûr Barzanî is the son of Masoud Barzani and President of the Security Council of the Kurdistan Region of Iraq and, in this function, responsible for the security forces of the PDK.

15. Kurdish security police.

16. International donor conference for the reconstruction of Iraq, which pledged support to the tune of billions in February 2018.

17. An important Êzîdî saint who is buried in Şerfedînand, and whose tomb is located in the centre of the most important Êzîdî sanctuary in Sinjar.

18. Meaning, in this context, the city of Sinjar.

19. Important large Arab tribe living in the environment of Sinjar.

20. Riham and Farida preferred not to tell me their surnames.

21. The district of Sinjar is divided into two sub-districts: Şingal and Sinunê. The mayor of Sinunê is responsible for the whole sub-district, which encompasses the northern side of the mountain range. The 13 Kurdish schools mentioned in the text are those run by the Autonomous Council of Sinjar, the administrative institution established in 2015 with the support of the YBŞ. The Arab schools in the eastern part of the area are under the control of the Iraqi Ministry of Education.

22. Tevgera Azadiya Demokrat Êzîdiyan, Free Democratic Êzîdî Movement.

23. As mentioned in an earlier note, 'Doshka' means the DShK 1938, a heavy Soviet machine gun.

24. In Kurdish, Serok means leader; Apo is both the familiar form for Abdullah and the appellation for 'uncle'. Here, Serok Apo refers to Abdullah Öcalan, the political leader of the Kurdish Workers' Party

PKK. In the movements close to the PKK, Serok Apo is a widely used term for Öcalan.

25. Until 2016, Jabhat al-Nusra was the branch organisation of al-Qaida in Syria. Today, it acts under the name Hayat Tahrir ash-Sham and has at least officially ceased to be a member of al-Qaida.

26. Peshmerga units of the Kurdish National Council in Syria (ENKS) dominated by Sunni Kurds. The ENKS competes with the Kurdish administration in Syria and is supported by the Iraqi PDK. Until October 2017, Masoud Barzani's Roj Peshmerga were deployed at the border between Sinjar and Rojava/Syria to impede the cooperation between the YBŞ in Sinjar and the YPG/YPJ in Rojava. In March 2017, this led to armed clashes between the YBŞ and the Roj Peshmerga near Xanasor.

27. Because the question of who was behind the attack was never solved and because, in contrast to other jihadist attacks in Iraq, no claim of responsibility was ever made, it is impossible to tell whether this was the real background of the attack of Tîl Êzêr on 14 August 2007. Many other Êzîdî in Sinjar don't see it that way and some of my Êzîdî friends from the region have explicitly disputed this interpretation. But the commander interviewed here, Axîn Intiqam, insisted on this version of the story even after I asked her about it for a second time.

28. Michel Reimon was a member of the EU Parliament for the Greens from 2014 to 2019. Before that, he worked as a journalist and from 2010 to 2014, he was a state parliament member of the Austrian state Burgenland.

29. Austrian member of the EU Parliament (SPÖ) and deputy caucus president of the S&D (Socialists and Democrats) group in the EUP who made his first trip to Iraq in January 2015 together with the author of the present book. Since then, he has become a spokesperson for the Êzîdî; he was a central figure in the founding of the Êzîdî Friendship Group (EFG).

Bibliography

Açıkyıldız, Birgül. 2010. *The Yezidis: The History of a Community, Culture and Religion.* London: I. B. Tauris.

Allison, Christine. 2001. *The Yezidi Oral Tradition in Iraqi Kurdistan.* Abingdon: Routledge.

Bittner, Maximilian. 1913. *Die heiligen Bücher der Jesiden oder Teufelsanbeter.* Vienna: Denkschriften der Kaiserlichen Akademie der Wissenschaften in Wien.

Cerha, Birgit. 2009. *Kirkuk: Test für Iraks Stabilität.* Vienna: Institut für Kurdologie.

Dinnayi, Mirza. 2004. Die Verfolgung der 'Teufelsanbeter': Yezidi zwischen ba'thistischer Repression und sunnitischem Islamismus. In Mary Kreutzer and Thomas Schmidinger (eds), *Irak: Von der Repulik der Angst zur bürgerlichen Demokratie?*, 197–204. Freiburg im Breisgau: ça ira Verlag.

Dulz, Irene. 2001. *Die Yeziden im Irak: Zwischen 'Modelldorf' und Flucht.* Münster: LIT Verlag.

Dulz, Irene. 2016. The Displacement of the Yezidis after the Rise of ISIS in Northern Iraq. *Kurdish Studies* 4(2): 131–147.

Felter, Joseph and Brian Fishman. 2007. *Al-Qa'ida's Foreign Fighters in Iraq.* West Point, NY: Combating Terrorism Center.

Ferman, Leyla. 2016. Vergewaltigung von Frauen in Konflikten: Das Beispiel der Ezidinnen aus Shingal. In Gesellschaft Ezidischer AkademikerInnen (eds), *Im Transformationsprozess: Die Eziden und das Ezidentum gestern, heute, morgen; Beiträge der zweiten internationalen GEA-Konferenz vom 04. bis 05.10.2014 in Bielefeld,* 111–126. Berlin: Verlag für Wissenschaft und Bildung.

Fischer-Tahir, Andrea. 2003. *'Wir gaben viele Märtyrer': Widerstand und kollektive Iden-titätsbildung in Irakisch-Kurdistan.* Münster: Unrast Verlag.

Fuccaro, Nelida. 1994. Aspects of the Social and Political History of the Yazidi Enclave of Jabal Sinjar (Iraq) under the British Mandate, 1919–1932. Durhamtheses, Durham University. Retrieved from http://etheses.dur.ac.uk/5832.

Fuccaro, Nelida, 1997. Ethnicity, State Formation, and Conscription in Postcolonial Iraq: The Case of the Yazidi Kurds of Jabal Sinjar. *International Journal of Middle East Studies* 29(4): 559–580.

Fuccaro, Nelida. 1999. *The Other Kurds: Yazidis in Colonial Iraq.* London: I. B. Tauris.

Guest, John S. 2010. *Survival among the Kurds: A History of the Yezidis.* Abingdon: Routledge.

Hutter, Manfred. 2003. Zoroastrismus. In Johann Figl (ed.), *Handbuch Religionswis-senschaft*, 348–394. Göttingen: Vandenhoeck & Ruprecht.

Jabar, Faleh A. 2002. *Ayatollahs, Sufis and Ideologues: State, Religion and Social Movements in Iraq*. London: Saqi.

Kartal, Celalettin. 2016. *Deutsche Yeziden: Geschichte – Gegenwart – Prognosen*. Marburg: Tectum.

Kingery, Paul. 2018. *Kocho: ISIS Massacre in a Yezidi Village*. Self-published at Amazon.

Kitchen, Robert A. 2012. Babai the Great. In Augustine Casiday (ed.), *The Orthodox Christian World*, 237–243. Abingdon: Routledge.

Kreyenbroek, Philip G. 2016. Die Eziden, die Ahl-e Haqq und die Religion des Zarathustra. In Gesellschaft Ezidischer AkademikerInnen (eds), *Im Transformationsprozess: Die Eziden und das Ezidentum gestern, heute, morgen: Beiträge der zweiten internationalen GEA-Konferenz vom 04. bis 05.10.2014 in Bielefeld*, 27–33. Berlin: Verlag für Wissenschaft und Bildung.

Mato, Naif J. 2016. The Massacre of Koço. In Katharina Brizić et al. (eds), *Wiener Jahrbuch für Kurdische Studien*, Vol. 4: *Şingal 2014: Der Angriff des 'Islamischen Staates', der Genozid an den Êzîdî und die Folgen*, 57–59. Vienna: Caesarpress.

McDowall, David. 2007. *A Modern History of the Kurds*. London: I. B. Tauris.

McGee, Thomas. 2018. Saving the Survivors: Yezidi Women, Islamic State and the Ger-man Admissions Programme. *Kurdish Studies* 6(1): 85–109.

Mikhail, Dunya. 2018. *The Beekeeper of Sinjar*. London: Serpent's Tail.

Naval Intelligence Division. 2014. *Iraq and the Persian Gulf*. Abingdon: Routledge.

Omarkhali, Khanna. 2017. *The Yezidi Religious Textual Tradition: From Oral to Written; Categories, Transmission, Scripturalisation and Canonisation of the Yezidi Oral Religious Texts*. Wiesbaden: Harrassowitz.

Ortaç, Serhat. 2016. Der Angriff auf die Ezîdî in Şingal im Lichte der Genozidkonvention. In Katharina Brizić et al. (eds), *Wiener Jahrbuch für Kurdische Studien*, Vol. 4: *Şingal 2014: Der Angriff des 'Islamischen Staates', der Genozid an den Êzîdî und die Folgen*, 9–32. Vienna: Caesarpress.

Pedersen, Susan. 2010. Getting Out of Iraq – in 1932: The League of Nations and the Road to Normative Statehood. *American Historical Review* 115(4): 975–1000.

Penn, Michael Philip. 2015. *When Christians First Met Muslims: A Sourcebook of the Earliest Syriac Writings on Islam*. Oakland, CA: University of California Press.

Sayighian al-Baghdadi, Nerses. 1944. *The History of the Armenian Catholics in Iraq*. Beirut: Katholisches Pressehaus.

Schmidinger, Thomas. 2015. *Jihadismus: Ideologie, Prävention und Deradikalisierung*. Vienna: Mandelbaum Verlag.

Schmidinger, Thomas. 2016. Şingal nach dem Genozid: Die politische und militärische Entwicklung in der Region seit 2014. In Katharina Brizić et al. (eds), *Wiener Jahrbuch für Kurdische Studien*, Vol. 4: *Şingal 2014: Der Angriff des 'Islamischen Staates', der Genozid an den Êzîdî und die Folgen*, 33–55. Vienna: Caesarpress.

Schmidinger, Thomas. 2017. Şingal: Vom Genozid zum Bürgerkrieg? In Katharina Brizić et al. (eds), *Wiener Jahrbuch für Kurdische Studien*, Vol. 5: *Sprache – Migration – Zusammenhalt: Kurdisch und seine Diaspora*, 258–263. Vienna: Praesens.

Schmidinger, Thomas. 2018a. *Rojava: Revolution, War, and the Future of the Syrian Kurds*. London: Pluto Press.

Schmidinger, Thomas. 2018b. Şingal: Rückkehr unter irakische Kontrolle und politische Marginalisierung. In Zeynep Arslan et al. (eds), *Wiener Jahrbuch für Kurdische Studien*, Vol. 6: *Dersim 1938: Genozid, Vertreibung und die Folgen: Achtzig Jahre danach*, 299–302. Vienna: Praesens.

Schmidinger, Thomas. 2019. *The Battle for the Mountain of the Kurds: Self-Determination and Ethnic Cleansing in the Afrin Region of Rojava*. Oakland, CA: PM Books.

Schneckener, Ulrich, Christoph König and Sandra Wienand. 2018. *Der lange Schatten der Miliz: Zur Persistenz von Gewalt in Kolumbien und Kurdistan-Irak*. Frankfurt: Campus Verlag.

Shand, Susan. 2018. *Sinjar: 14 Days that saved the Yazidis from Islamic State*. Lanham, MD: Lyons Press.

Spät, Eszter. 1985. *The Yezidis*. London: Saqi.

Tagay, Şefik and Serhat Ortaç. 2016. *Die Eziden und das Ezidentum: Geschichte und Gegenwart einer vom Untergang bedrohten Religion*. Hamburg: Landeszentrale für politische Bildung.

Taylor, Gordon. 2005. *Fever and Thirst: An American Doctor among the Tribes of Kurdistan, 1835–1844*. Chicago, IL: Academic Chicago Publishers.

Index

Thanks to our Patreon subscriber:

Ciaran Kane

Who has shown generosity and
comradeship in support of our publishing.

Check out the other perks you get by subscribing
to our Patreon – visit patreon.com/plutopress.

Subscriptions start from £3 a month.